CAMBRIDGE TEXTS IN THE
HISTORY OF POLITICAL THOUGHT

━━

PETER KROPOTKIN
The Conquest of Bread and Other Writings

彼得·克鲁泡特金
PETER KROPOTKIN

"面包的征服"
及其他著作
The Conquest of Bread
and Other Writings

EDITED BY

MARSHALL SHATZ

University of Massachusetts at Boston

中国政法大学出版社

剑桥政治思想史原著系列

丛书编辑

Raymond Geuss
剑桥大学社会科学与政治科学高级讲师

Quentin Skinner
剑桥大学政治科学教授

在政治理论领域，"剑桥政治思想史原著系列"作为主要的学生教科丛书，如今已牢固确立了其地位。本丛书旨在使学生能够获得从古希腊到20世纪初期西方政治思想史方面所有最为重要的原著。它囊括了所有著名的经典原著，但与此同时，它又扩展了传统的评价尺度，以便能够纳入范围广泛、不那么出名的作品。而在此之前，这些作品中有许多从未有过现代英文版本可资利用。只要可能，所选原著都会以完整而不删节的形式出版，其中的译作则是专门为本丛书的目的而安排。每一本书都有一个评论性的导言，加上历史年表、生平梗概、进一步阅读指南，以及必要的词汇表和原文注解。本丛书的最终目的是，为西方政治思想的整个发展脉络提供一个清晰的轮廓。

本丛书已出版著作的书目，请查阅书末。

CAMBRIDGE TEXTS IN THE
HISTORY OF POLITICAL THOUGHT

Series editors

RAYMOND GEUSS

Lecturer in Social and Political Sciences, University of Cambridge

QUENTIN SKINNER

Professor of Political Science in the University of Cambridge

Cambridge Texts in the History of Political Thought is now firmly established as the major student textbook series in political theory. It aims to make available to students all the most important texts in the history of western political thought, from ancient Greece to the early twentieth century. All the familiar classic texts will be included, but the series does at the same time seek to enlarge the conventional canon by incorporating an extensive range of less well-known works, many of them never before available in a modern English edition. Wherever possible, texts are published in complete and unabridged form, and translations are specially commissioned for the series. Each volume contains a critical introduction together with chronologies, biographical sketches, a guide to further reading and any necessary glossaries and textual apparatus. When completed, the series will aim to offer an outline of the entire evolution of western political thought.

For a list of titles published in the series, please see end of book.

Contents

Contents

Introduction

The intellectual commerce between Russia and the West in the nineteenth century for the most part flowed in an easterly direction. Russian Marxism, for example, was only one of a long series of political, social and philosophical systems imported from Western Europe and adapted to Russian circumstances, often undergoing considerable alteration in the process. One notable exception, which helped to redress Russia's intellectual balance of trade, so to speak, was anarchism. Anarchism had Western roots, to be sure, specifically in the thought of William Godwin and Pierre-Joseph Proudhon, but for over half a century it derived much of its vitality, both as a social theory and as a revolutionary movement, from the efforts of two Russians, Michael Bakunin and Peter Kropotkin. (Meanwhile, yet another Russian, Leo Tolstoy, would create a distinctive variety of religious anarchism.)

Both Bakunin and Kropotkin, however, spent long years as émigrés in the West, and it was in Western Europe that they formulated their anarchist ideology. The interaction of Russian and Western elements was particularly complex in the case of Kropotkin, for unlike Bakunin he actively participated in the Russian revolutionary movement before he emigrated, spent even longer in the West, and then returned to Russia in his final years. Kropotkin's anarchism therefore was the product of a lifetime of interplay between his Russian and Western experiences.

Like many another nineteenth-century Russian revolutionary, including Bakunin, Kropotkin was born into the landowning Russian nobility. Kropotkin's origins, however, were more aristocratic than most. His family traced its ancestry back to the rulers of Smolensk, one of the independent principalities of medieval Russia. Thus he was born Prince Peter Alekseevich Kropotkin, in Moscow, on 27 November 1842 (according to the old Russian calendar, which was twelve days behind the Western calendar). His father, an army officer, owned some 1,200 'souls', or male serfs, the customary measure of wealth in pre-emancipation Russia. Kropotkin spent his early years in the tranquil quarter of Moscow where many of the old noble families maintained houses, with summers on one of the family's country estates. For all its material privileges, Kropotkin's childhood was no idyll: his mother died when he was three, leaving him to the care of his father, a narrow-minded martinet, and his stepmother, whom he detested. Like many other lonely children of the nobility, he found warmth and affection among the family's numerous house-serfs. Judging by the account in his autobiography, *Memoirs of a Revolutionist*, these childhood experiences were one of the sources of his abiding dedication to the 'people' of Russia. Kropotkin's closest friend was his older brother Alexander, who shared many of his interests and ideas but from whom he was separated in his early teens when they were sent to different schools. Their correspondence is a rich biographical source for Kropotkin's early years, supplementing the memoirs he penned many years later. Alexander's temperament was not as firm as his brother's, however, and in 1886, while exiled in Siberia for a political offence, he committed suicide.

Though Kropotkin later repudiated the privileges of his youth, they did provide him with an excellent education. He was first tutored at home by French, German and Russian teachers, then attended a Moscow gymnasium for two years. In 1857 he entered the Corps of Pages in St Petersburg, an elite military school, attached to the imperial court, whose top pupils served as pages to the tsar and his family. To supplement the school's sometimes meagre intellectual diet, Kropotkin devoured whatever books he could get his hands on. His correspondence with his brother Alexander, who was attending a military school in Moscow, is filled with references to an astonishing number of readings in philosophy, literature, and especially history, as well as a variety of other subjects – and this at a time when Kropotkin was still in his teens. As his later writings would attest, he possessed the most well-developed and wide-ranging intellect ever to place itself in the service of anarchism.

In 1861 Kropotkin, as the top student in his class, became the personal page of Emperor Alexander II. He entered the life of the court at a crucial moment in Russian history. This was precisely the year when the emancipation of the serfs was announced and other major reforms were being introduced in an effort to modernize the Russian economy and Russian society. Already a critic of Russia's autocratic form of government, Kropotkin was torn between welcoming the reforms and questioning the system that was implementing them. At the same time, he was experiencing a personal crisis: his intellectual interests were pulling him towards the university and further education, while his military schooling – and his father – were pushing him into a career as an army officer. His response to these conflicts upon graduating from the Corps of Pages in 1862 took family and friends alike by surprise. Although he could have had his pick of the most illustrious Guards regiments in the Russian army, he chose instead to join an obscure Cossack regiment in Eastern Siberia. He hoped that remote Siberia, far from the stifling bureaucratic atmosphere of the capital, would offer greater opportunity to participate in contemporary reform efforts, and at the same time he succeeded in postponing any final decision about his future career. In a letter to his brother the year before he graduated, he had expressed the sentiments with which he now set off for his Siberian service: a readiness for hard work and a desire to be useful to society. Unlike many another critic of the Russian autocracy, including Michael Bakunin, Kropotkin came to Siberia as a free man in service to the tsar, not a political exile. Ironically, his experiences there helped to turn him into an active opponent of the tsarist government.

Upon arriving in Siberia, Kropotkin was appointed aide-de-camp to the liberal chief of staff of the Eastern Siberian Military District. The military here performed many of the functions of a civil administration, and Kropotkin was soon immersed in administrative reform projects. He became secretary to two commissions, one to study the prison and exile system, the other to plan a system of municipal self-government. Despite the expenditure of a great deal of time and energy, the recommendations of these commissions were never implemented. They were thwarted by official corruption, the inertia of the bureaucracy in Petersburg, and the growing reaction that was overtaking the imperial government, especially in the wake of the Polish insurrection of 1863.

Frustrated and disillusioned by his administrative experiences, Kropotkin turned to a very different field, geographical exploration. Large parts of Siberia's vast expanses were still uncharted, and Kropotkin led several important geographical and geological expeditions in Eastern Siberia and the Chinese possession of Manchuria. The journeys were not only personally rewarding but scientifically significant: Kropotkin began to formulate a geological theory that contradicted the accepted wisdom concerning the formation of the Siberian landscape. His scientific work confirmed a commitment to the natural sciences and to scientific values that would remain with him for the rest of his life.

In 1867, after five years in Siberia, Kropotkin resigned from military service and returned to St Petersburg. His desire to be useful to society had not abated, but he no longer regarded service in the state administration as the way to satisfy that desire (although he continued to hold down a minor and undemanding government post in St Petersburg). He had continued to read widely in Siberia, and among other things had sampled the writings of the French anarchist Pierre-Joseph Proudhon, which could only have confirmed him in his conclusion. Reviewing his Siberian experiences in his memoirs, he declared that by the time they ended 'I was prepared to become an anarchist'.

Kropotkin's return to St Petersburg marked the beginning of a new phase of his life that would last into the 1880s: the career of a revolutionary activist. Several years of intellectual and moral preparation were required before he took this fateful step, however. First, he achieved his long-sought goal of entering St Petersburg University, where he studied mathematics. Meanwhile, he continued his work for the Russian Geographical Society and seemed destined for a brilliant scientific career. The moment of decision came in 1871: while on a geographical expedition in Finland, he received a telegram offering him the post of secretary of the Geographical Society – and declined it. The passage in his memoirs in which he recounts this episode is worth quoting because it provides considerable insight into his character and his motivations at this turning-point in his life. He greatly valued the intellectual rewards of scientific discovery, he explains.

> But what right had I to these highest joys, when all around me was nothing but misery and struggle for a mouldy bit of bread; when whatsoever I should spend to enable me to live in that world of higher emotions must needs be taken from the very mouths of those who grew the wheat and had not bread enough for their children?

Such sentiments were not unique to Kropotkin at this time. A familiar figure in Russia in these years was the so-called 'repentant nobleman', a conscience-stricken member of the upper classes who renounced his privileges and sought to repay his 'debt' to the toilers at whose expense they had been purchased. In Kropotkin's case, the privilege he felt most keenly was not material luxury (on which he never placed much value) but his cultural and intellectual development; it was this form of 'exploitation' of the people that Kropotkin now renounced as an inadmissible self-indulgence. For many individuals moved by such considerations, the logical next step was to join the revolutionary movement, which had already begun to gather force in Russia. Before Kropotkin did so, he completed his political education with a trip to Western Europe.

Early in 1872, he travelled to Switzerland, a centre of émigré Russian radical activity as well as of the International Working Men's Association (commonly referred to as the First International). In Zurich and Geneva he familiarized himself with the deepening split between the Marxist and Bakuninist wings of the International which, at the Hague Congress in September of that year, would finally shatter the organization. Most important, he spent a week among the watchmakers of the Jura Mountain region. Their Jura Federation, part of the International, was a stronghold of Bakuninism, and they impressed him deeply with their independence and egalitarianism. This reinforced his growing anti-state sentiments, and in his memoirs he declares bluntly that now 'I was an anarchist'. After a short trip to Belgium, he returned to Russia determined to act upon his convictions. To his lasting regret, however, he failed to meet Bakunin, who was living out the last years of his life in Switzerland. The two great leaders of anarchism passed like ships in the night.

Kropotkin now joined the Chaikovsky Circle in St Petersburg. This was one of the first underground organizations generated by the Populist movement which dominated Russian radical thought and activity in the 1860s and 1870s. Populism drew its inspiration from the Russian peasant commune (the *obshchina*), which practised a form of collective landholding and land distribution as well as internal self-government. Populism's ultimate aim was to achieve a socialist society in Russia by building on the commune's traditions of autonomy and egalitarianism (as the Populist intellectuals interpreted them), thereby avoiding the Western path to socialism through painful industrialization and proletarianization. The Chaikovsky Circle, named after one of its founders, Nicholas Chaikovsky, was dedicated to the dissemination of socialist ideas. At first it confined itself to spreading prohibited literature among the students, but soon it began to extend its educational activities directly to the industrial workers of the capital. Members of the circle organized clandestine workers' meetings, where they gave lectures that combined basic education with socialist themes. Kropotkin was particularly active in this effort, and he proved to be an able teacher. Since many of the industrial workers in St Petersburg were recently arrived peasants who retained close ties to their villages, the Chaikovsky Circle hoped they would serve as a transmission belt to carry the socialist message back to a larger audience in the countryside.

Other than its commitment to socialism and to the peasants, Russian Populism had neither a programme nor a doctrine, much less a central organization. There was considerable disagreement among Populists over such issues as whether the state should play a role in social and economic transformation and whether to concentrate on long-term education of the peasants or on attempts to incite them to insurrection. In the course of his work in the Chaikovsky Circle, Kropotkin drafted a programme for discussion among his colleagues, giving it the earnest title 'Must We Occupy Ourselves with an Examination of the Ideal of a Future System?' It was not accepted by the circle as a whole, but it provides a good summary of Kropotkin's own views at this point in the evolution of his ideas. Two elements in this lengthy essay are of particular note. First, he adopted a firmly anti-state position, citing Proudhon's critique of the state and calling for the replacement of

government by voluntary federations of self-governing communes
and worker associations. Secondly, while acknowledging the value
of enlightening the workers and peasants, he adopted the Bakuninist
position that a mass insurrection was necessary to achieve meaning-
ful social change, even if, in Kropotkin's words, it required 'rivers
of blood'. Thus Proudhon and Bakunin, the Jura watchmakers and
the Russian peasants, all made their contributions to Kropotkin's
outlook as it had taken shape by 1873. In essential respects, he
would adhere to this outlook with remarkable consistency right up
to his death fifty years later.

Kropotkin's underground activities came to an abrupt halt early
in 1874, when the police broke up the Chaikovsky Circle. Kropotkin
was arrested and incarcerated in the Peter-Paul Fortress, where
political prisoners were kept. When he fell dangerously ill, his
influential relatives were able to pull strings and have him transferred to a prison hospital on the outskirts of the city (it still
counted for something to be a prince in Imperial Russia, even if
he was also a revolutionary). There, the restoration of his health
and a lax prison administration enabled him to make a daring
escape. In Kropotkin's incomparable account in his memoirs, the
meticulously organized plot had all the ingredients of a spy-thriller:
safe houses, a coded message hidden in a watch, a heart-stopping
getaway through the streets of the capital. Forced to leave not only
St Petersburg but Russia itself, Kropotkin sought refuge in Great
Britain and within a few weeks landed in Hull. He now began
four decades as an émigré in Western Europe – not until 1917
could he return to Russia – but he was not yet ready to give up
the revolutionary activities his arrest in Russia had interrupted.

After a brief stay in England, Kropotkin moved to Switzerland.
There he joined the Jura Federation and, as he describes in the
chapter of his memoirs included in this volume, he devoted himself
to the cause of anarchism both as an organizer and as a journalist.
In 1879, he and his associates founded an anarchist newspaper
called *Le Révolté*, which Kropotkin not only edited but at first
largely wrote. Later transferred to France, under the name *La
Révolte* and finally *Les Temps Nouveaux*, it was for many years one
of the most important anarchist publications in Europe. Meanwhile,
he attended to his personal life as well: in 1878 he married

Sofia Ananeva-Rabinovich. Active in radical circles herself, she was prepared to share the difficult life of an anarchist, and the marriage endured until Kropotkin's death in 1921.

Kropotkin's stay in Switzerland soon came to an end, however. In 1881, a Populist revolutionary organization assassinated Alexander II of Russia. Although he had serious misgivings about the value of such acts of terrorism, Kropotkin felt compelled to defend the perpetrators of the assassination, and for his pains he was expelled from Switzerland. He tried to resume his activities in France, but in 1882, as part of a crackdown on anarchist organizations, Kropotkin was arrested. He was tried on the rather bizarre charge of belonging to the International – an organization which years earlier had been declared illegal in France but which no longer in fact existed – and was sentenced to five years' imprisonment, to be served at the central prison in Clairvaux. He was released after three years, thanks in part to an international lobbying campaign by influential admirers, and in the spring of 1886 he returned once again to London. England would now remain his home until the Russian Revolution. The move effectively brought an end to his career as a revolutionary activist. His health was increasingly fragile, and he was cut off from the main centres of the anarchist movement, particularly the French-speaking areas of Europe where he felt most at home. As a result, although he maintained contact with anarchists everywhere and gave them whatever support and encouragement he could, he now became primarily a theorist and expounder of anarchist principles – the full-bearded patriarch and world-famous spokesman of anarchism.

Both the quantity and the range of Kropotkin's writings after 1886 are extraordinary, an output facilitated by his ability to write fluently in both French and English. He continued to write extensively for the anarchist press, including the newspaper *Le Révolté* and its successors *La Révolte* and *Les Temps Nouveaux*, and the English paper *Freedom*, which he helped to found in 1886. In Britain he contributed articles on a variety of subjects to a number of publications, including the scientific journal *Nature*, the magazine *Nineteenth Century*, and several editions of the *Encyclopaedia Britannica*. He published at least ten major books, some of which originated as series of articles, as well as numerous pamphlets and shorter works. The subjects of his books often went well beyond anarchism. *The Great French Revolution*, for example, was a lengthy work that focused on the movement of the masses rather than the leaders in the revolution, and *Mutual Aid*, one of his best-known books, traced the importance of social co-operation rather than competition as a factor in evolution.

While his health held up he was an indefatigable lecturer as well as writer. In 1897–98 he made an extensive lecture tour of the United States and Canada, and in 1901 he made a second American tour. The first trip to America resulted in the publication of his most famous work, *Memoirs of a Revolutionist*. Written in English, it was first serialized in *The Atlantic Monthly* in 1897–98 and then published in book form in 1899; it has remained a classic ever since. Except for his strictly scientific articles, his publications were not scholarly works in the accepted sense of the word. Although they drew on Kropotkin's considerable erudition, his aim was to disseminate useful knowledge to a broad educated public, though always from an anarchist point of view. In this he amply succeeded, acquiring what was probably the largest international audience of any Russian radical of his day. The *Encyclopaedia Britannica* article on anarchism, included in this volume, is an excellent example of the kind of learned popularization at which he excelled.

Within this enormous literary legacy, *The Conquest of Bread* stands out as Kropotkin's most detailed description of the anarchist society he envisioned. *The Conquest of Bread* originated as a series of articles in the 1880s in *Le Révolté* and *La Révolte*, and was published in book form in 1892. It appeared in English translation in 1906 and then in an editorially improved version in 1913. In its general features it embodies the defining characteristic of anarchism itself (or 'anarchy', as Kropotkin terms it, the word anarchism not yet having come into universal use): immediate abolition of the state and its replacement by a decentralized network of small, self-sufficient communities linked by voluntary agreement. What set anarchism sharply apart both from liberalism and from other forms of socialism was its rejection of the very principle of the state, which anarchism viewed as nothing but an instrument of coercion and subjugation. Thus Kropotkin rejects all forms of government, whether representative or authoritarian, from parliamentary democracy to the Marxist 'dictatorship of the proletariat'.

The Conquest of Bread, however, also reflects the more specific form of anarchism which Kropotkin espoused, called anarchist communism. It represented an extension or further development of anarchist collectivism, which had been advocated by Michael Bakunin and his adherents in the First International. Under anarchist collectivism, the means of production were to be socialized, but remuneration and thus consumption were to be based on the amount of labour an individual performed. In other words, a wage system of some sort was to be retained, although a far more equitable one than what prevailed under capitalism. Anarchist communism called for the socialization not only of production but of the distribution of goods: the community would supply the subsistence requirements of each individual member free of charge, and the criterion 'to each according to his labour' would be superseded by the criterion 'to each according to his needs'. Kropotkin did not originate the concept of anarchist communism but became one of its foremost exponents, and in *The Conquest of Bread* he provides a rationale for it. Although not all anarchists accepted it, it formed the dominant credo of the international anarchist movement, at least until the rise of revolutionary syndicalism at the turn of the century. To Kropotkin, the source of poverty in the modern world was not lack of production but inequitable distribution, which could be rectified only in a society reorganized on anarchist principles. In *The Conquest of Bread*, Kropotkin makes clear his belief that an anarchist society, applying modern technology to industrial and agricultural production, could without difficulty supply the needs of all its members. He developed this idea further in *Fields, Factories and Workshops* of 1899, which forms a kind of sequel to *The Conquest of Bread*.

According to Kropotkin, the anarchist-communist society can be achieved only by means of a social revolution carried out by the people themselves. This, too, was one of the defining characteristics of anarchism. In sharp contrast to the Marxists, or 'the German state socialists', as Kropotkin calls them, anarchists rejected any kind of transitional government or temporary seizure of power by a revolutionary party, convinced that such a step would inevitably perpetuate the existence of a state. Therefore he devotes considerable attention to the revolutionary expropriation of property, the method by which the people themselves would carry out the economic and social transformation. What is conspicuously lacking in *The Conquest of Bread*, however, is any discussion of the degree to which a mass social revolution might require violence in order to succeed. This was an issue that bedevilled the anarchist movement as a whole, and Kropotkin's own position over the years displayed a certain degree of ambivalence and inconsistency. The issue became particularly pressing in the 1880s and 1890s, when anarchists began to practise 'propaganda by deed', that is, acts of terror (as distinct from 'propaganda by word'). As the militant stance he adopted in the Chaikovsky Circle indicates, Kropotkin did not shrink from the idea of revolutionary violence, and he often expressed sympathy for the perpetrators of 'propaganda by deed' or at least refrained from criticizing them publicly. On the whole, however, he came to regard individual acts of terrorism and assassination as useless and demoralizing, and approved only of those deeds that were aimed at arousing the people themselves to collective forms of revolt. Once he settled in England, of course, and devoted himself to anarchist theory rather than to underground activity, he did not have to confront this issue directly and tended to minimize it in his writings. He did truly believe, however, in 'the good sense and instinct for justice which animates the masses', as he puts it in *The Conquest of Bread*. Therefore, although he can fairly be accused of presenting social revolution in this work as an overly reasonable and good-natured affair, it is not unrepresentative of his thinking. On the whole, violence played a less important role as a stepping-stone to anarchism for Kropotkin than it did for some other anarchists.

In the broader context of Kropotkin's thought, two general themes that run throughout his writings formed the philosophical underpinnings of his anarchist ideology. One was the scientific. It is hardly surprising that science should occupy such a prominent place in Kropotkin's outlook. Not only had he been a practising scientist himself, but he came of age in the late 1850s and early 1860s, when scientific positivism dominated Russian radical thought. (Readers of Russian literature will recall two novels of the period that vividly illustrate this domination: in Turgenev's *Fathers and Sons* the hero, Bazarov, seeks truth in the dissection of frogs, while in Chernyshevsky's *What Is to Be Done?* the heroes are both medical students.) A number of Kropotkin's writings were devoted to demonstrating that anarchism was a scientific theory of society. In *Modern Science and Anarchism*, for example, he stated:

> Anarchism is a world-concept based upon a mechanical expla-
> nation of all phenomena, embracing the whole of nature – that
> is, including in it the life of human societies and their economic,
> political, and moral problems. Its method of investigation is that
> of the exact natural sciences . . . Its aim is to construct a synthetic
> philosophy comprehending in one generalization all the phenom-
> ena of nature – and therefore also the life of societies.

Kropotkin's anarchism, of course, shared with Marxism the claim to be scientifically based – both ideologies descended from the Enlightenment's confidence that reason and the growth of human knowledge would resolve the problems of human society. Marx's 'science', however, derived ultimately from the metaphysics of Hegel and German philosophy, while Kropotkin sought his grounding in the biological and physical sciences. At the heart of Kropotkin's 'scientific anarchism' was his interpretation of Darwin's theory of evolution. In *Mutual Aid* he argued that social solidarity and co-operation within species, not struggle and competition, were the dominant factors in the evolution both of animals and of humans. This led him to an investigation of the natural, utilitarian origins of morality. In several works, including the book *Ethics*, which he left unfinished at his death, he contended that ethical principles originate not in religious precepts but in man's instinctive tendency to act in such a way as to promote the preservation of the species. Anarchism, by promoting mutual co-operation and opposing the divisive influences of the state, is thus the social philosophy that most fully expresses the ethical needs of man as revealed by modern science.

It might well be asked, if anarchist principles were those that conformed most closely to the innate needs of human existence, why had they not yet triumphed? What accounted for the persistent strength of the 'unnatural' behaviour that brought harm to the species? Even in his historical works, such as *The Great French Revolution* or his account of the development of the modern state in *Mutual Aid*, Kropotkin fails to explain adequately why the forces of communalism and social solidarity so often gave way to the forces of oppression, self-interest, and exploitation. Kropotkin believed that there were natural laws of the moral and social order, that those laws could be revealed by scientific investigation, and that people would instinctively act in accordance with them once a revolution removed the artificial restraints on their behaviour. Nature, reason, and morality necessarily moved in the same direction and would ultimately converge. It was an outlook deeply rooted in the assumptions of the eighteenth and nineteenth centuries; from a twentieth-century point of view it can only be described as distinctly pre-Freudian.

Alongside science, there is a second element that lies at the foundations of Kropotkin's anarchism, and that is the humanistic. What Kropotkin experienced among the Russian peasants, the Swiss watchmakers, and his own comrades in the revolutionary movement was a moral community whose members instinctively recognized each other's fundamental human worth and dignity. Similarly, in the anarchist society, where the coercive institutions of state, church and capitalism had been done away with, the people's innate sense of social justice and sympathy would spontaneously emerge, and all would at last find freedom, equality and fulfilment as human beings. Kropotkin's own commitment to anarchism is the best evidence for the profoundly humanistic roots of his anarchism. What is most striking, and most moving, in his autobiography is its account of the growth of his moral consciousness. There was nothing scientific or, indeed, 'natural' about the transformation of this Russian aristocrat, serf owner and *page de chambre* to the tsar into the sworn enemy of an unjust social order. It was the result of a prolonged and hard-won intellectual and moral struggle. In one of his most widely circulated and widely translated pamphlets, 'An Appeal to the Young', he urged the same whole-hearted moral commitment and spirit of self-sacrifice on all educated youth.

Thus two distinct and, in philosophical terms, not wholly compatible, currents flowed through the large body of Kropotkin's writings, and through his long life as well. Whether he fully reconciled them is debatable. It appears, however, that both were equally important to him in sustaining his dedication to the anarchist cause and his confidence that it would prevail.

From 1914 onward, that confidence was subjected to a series of cruel tests. When the First World War broke out Kropotkin, to the consternation of many of his fellow anarchists, vigorously supported the Allies against the Central Powers. In numerous statements and in a series of articles published in a Moscow newspaper between 1914 and 1917, he denounced German militarism and expansionism and warned of the dire consequences for Russia of a German victory. In many respects, Kropotkin's position was a reprise of Bakunin's staunchly pro-French stance in the Franco-Prussian War of 1870–71, a precedent which Kropotkin cited. Anarchists had always regarded France as the homeland of revolution, and the fact that Germany was the stronghold of their Social Democratic opponents reinforced their tendency to identify Imperial Germany with authoritarianism and state centralization. In addition, Kropotkin's long sojourn in the democratic countries of the West had given him a considerable respect for the freedom they allowed even to their critics. Although he did not exaggerate the virtues of the Allies, he maintained that their victory offered better prospects for an eventual social revolution than a German victory. A bitter split now took place in the international anarchist movement, just as it did within the socialist Second International, and Kropotkin found himself under attack from some of his closest colleagues. To many anarchists Kropotkin's position constituted an unacceptable violation of their fundamental anti-militarist and anti-state principles, and they held both sides in the war to be equally reprehensible. To Kropotkin and his adherents, their opponents' stand seemed dangerously unrealistic in its refusal to draw vital distinctions. Kropotkin never wavered in his view, and he always remained convinced that the defeat of Imperial Germany had averted the threat of a Europe-wide despotism.

These disputes could be forgotten for the moment when the Russian Revolution broke out in 1917. Kropotkin had long been cut off from direct involvement in Russian affairs, but in the early years of the twentieth century he had begun to re-establish links to his homeland. A Russian press and then the first Russian-language anarchist newspaper, called *Bread and Freedom*, both located in Switzerland, enabled some of his writings to begin reaching Russia. Meanwhile, several anarchist groups arose within the Russian Empire, although their proclivity for terrorism created a certain gulf between Kropotkin and this new generation of Russian anarchists. Finally, the revolution of 1905 drew him into a period of intense engagement in Russian developments, and in 1909 he

published *The Terror in Russia*, a book exposing the tsarist
repressions that followed the revolution. When word came of the
overthrow of the tsar in February, 1917, Kropotkin immediately
started to plan his return to Russia. On 30 May (according to the
old Russian calendar, which was still in use) he was greeted by a
large crowd upon his arrival in Petrograd, as the overly Germanic-
sounding St Petersburg had been renamed – forty-one years after
he had left it.

A few months later, in October, the Bolsheviks seized power
and began to consolidate their rule. Shortly thereafter the country
was plunged into civil war, and persecution of non-Bolshevik parties
intensified. The anarchists, with their inclination to violent forms
of opposition, were a particular object of the Soviet government's
attention, and repressions against them began in the spring of
1918. Kropotkin himself was left unmolested, however, and the
government even helped to provide for his subsistence. He was a
venerated revolutionary icon, after all, and Lenin seems to have
had genuine respect for him; old and frail as he was, moreover,
he constituted no political threat. After stays in Petrograd and
Moscow, Kropotkin and his wife in June of 1918 settled in the
village of Dmitrov, some forty miles north of Moscow, in a small
house with a vegetable garden – a not insignificant benefit in those
hungry times in Russia. There he lent his support to the local
co-operative, worked on his book *Ethics*, which was published after
his death, and relied upon correspondence and visitors to keep
him abreast of current developments.

Given his circumstances, it was difficult for him to compose any
sustained analysis of the Russian Revolution. His views found
expression in letters, a few brief public pronouncements, some
unfinished essays. But the fragmentary nature of his comments
may also have reflected the genuine dilemma he faced. On the
one hand, the Bolsheviks seemed intent on confirming all the
anxious warnings about Marxist 'state communism' that anarchists
had voiced since Bakunin's day. Kropotkin saw the Bolsheviks as
a new edition of the Jacobins in the French Revolution. He was
willing to recognize their commitment to socialism, but he could
not accept their centralizing, authoritarian methods. On the other
hand, like the non-Bolshevik left as a whole, he could see no
alternative to the Bolsheviks except reaction, which would close

the door to the very possibility of socialism. He therefore sought to draw a line between the sweeping revolutionary transformation Russia was undergoing, which he defended, and the Bolsheviks' political dictatorship and use of terror, which he indignantly denounced. In his open letter to the workers of the West, reprinted in this volume, he vigorously rejected armed intervention by the Western powers in Russia's civil war while distinguishing between the creative force of the revolution, for which he urged Western support, and the authoritarian proclivities of the Bolsheviks, which were retarding that creativity. He bombarded Soviet government agencies and Lenin personally with letters, and in the spring of 1919, although he rarely left Dmitrov, he journeyed to the Kremlin for a personal meeting with Lenin. There he made an effort to expound the principles of non-authoritarian social organization to the Bolshevik leader (to little evident effect). Subsequently, in the two brief letters to Lenin contained in this volume, he complained of the high-handedness of the government's officials, and, even more fearlessly, denounced the government's brutality.

Kropotkin's reaction to events in Russia was complicated by the fact that he viewed the Russian Revolution, as he had viewed the First World War, from the perspective of one who had lived in the West for four decades. The impact of his Western experience revealed itself most tellingly early in 1919, when the Soviet government made Kropotkin a proposal, apparently authorized by Lenin himself, to publish a Russian edition of four of his major works. Kropotkin refused the offer on the grounds that his acceptance would constitute moral approval of the government's publishing monopoly and hence of its stifling of free thought. He then cited an episode from his life in the West to demonstrate the importance of freedom of expression for Russia: when Swiss printing firms refused to print his anarchist newspaper *Le Révolté* for fear of losing government contracts, the anarchists had taken up a subscription among the workers, purchased their own printing equipment, and thus kept the voice of anarchism alive. That kind of collective self-organization and self-expression might have been possible in Switzerland, but by the time of Kropotkin's death it was no longer an option in Soviet Russia. In a personal memorandum penned just a few weeks before he died, he asked the age-old Russian question 'what is to be done?' and found a kind of solace in viewing the revolution as a natural phenomenon, a force of nature which even the government itself was powerless to control.

Peter Kropotkin died on 8 February 1921. His funeral in Moscow, which the government permitted an anarchist committee to organize, brought some 20,000 mourners into the streets in a procession accompanied by anarchist banners and slogans. It was to be the last public display of anarchist sentiment. Just a month later, the sailors of the Kronstadt naval base outside of Petrograd revolted against Bolshevik rule. The bloody suppression of Kronstadt, where anarchism had a small following, gave the government a pretext for eliminating the last remaining anarchist groups and organizations. The anarchist movement in Russia, which Kropotkin's writings and personal example had done so much to inspire, now came to an end.

Principal events in Kropotkin's life

Events occurring within Russia before 1918 are dated in the Old Style, that is, according to the Julian calendar then in use, which in the nineteenth century was twelve days and in the twentieth century thirteen days behind the Western calendar. Events occurring outside Russia, and from 1918 within Russia as well, are dated in the New Style, that is, according to the Western calendar.

1842	27 November: born in Moscow.
1853–5	Attends First Moscow Gymnasium.
1857	Enters Corps of Pages in St Petersburg.
1861	19 February: emancipation of the Russian serfs. Becomes personal page of Alexander II.
1862	Graduates from Corps of Pages, joins Amur Cossack regiment in Eastern Siberia.
1862–7	Serves in administrative positions in Siberia, explores Manchuria and Eastern Siberia.
1863	Polish insurrection against Russian rule.
1867	Resigns from military service, returns to St Petersburg. Enrols in faculty of mathematics and physical sciences at St Petersburg University.
1867–71	Publishes geographical works, continues field research.
1870–1	Franco-Prussian War.
1871	18 March: Paris Commune begins. Declines position of secretary to Russian Geographical Society.

1872	February–May: travels to Switzerland and Belgium, becomes acquainted with International Working Men's Association and anarchists of Jura Federation. Joins Chaikovsky Circle in St Petersburg, conducts socialist propaganda among workers. September: Bakunin and followers expelled from International at Hague Congress.
1873	Drafts programme for Chaikovsky Circle, 'Must We Occupy Ourselves with an Examination of the Ideal of a Future System?'
1874	March: arrested and imprisoned in Peter-Paul Fortress.
1876	June: escapes from St Petersburg Military Hospital. Arrives in England, lives in Edinburgh and then London. 1 July: death of Michael Bakunin.
1877	Moves to Switzerland, joins Jura Federation.
1878	Visits anarchist organizations in Spain. 8 October: marries Sofia Ananeva-Rabinovich.
1879	Founds anarchist newspaper *Le Révolté* in Geneva.
1880	Publishes 'Appeal to the Young'.
1881	1 March: assassination of Alexander II. Expelled from Switzerland.
1882	December: arrested in France.
1883	January: tried in Lyons, sentenced to five years in prison.
1883–6	Imprisoned at Clairvaux.
1885	Publication of first anarchist book, *Words of a Rebel* (in French).
1886	January: released from Clairvaux prison, settles in England. Helps found anarchist newspaper *Freedom*. Suicide of brother Alexander.
1887	Birth of daughter, named Alexandra. Publishes *In Russian and French Prisons*.
1892	Publishes *The Conquest of Bread* (in French).
1897–8	Lectures in United States and Canada.
1898–9	Memoirs serialized in *Atlantic Monthly*.
1899	*Memoirs of a Revolutionist* published in book form.

	Publishes *Fields, Factories and Workshops*.
1901	Second visit to United States: lectures in Boston on Russian literature, and in other cities.
	Publishes *Modern Science and Anarchism* (in Russian).
1902	Publishes *Mutual Aid*.
1903	Participates in founding of Russian-language anarchist newspaper *Bread and Freedom*.
1905	Revolution in Russia.
	Publishes *Russian Literature* (later reissued as *Ideals and Realities in Russian Literature*).
1909	Publishes *The Great French Revolution*.
	Publishes *The Terror in Russia*.
1914	Takes pro-Allied position on First World War.
1917	23 February: revolution begins in Petrograd.
	2 March: abdication of Nicholas II.
	12 June: Kropotkin arrives in Petrograd.
	25 October: Bolshevik seizure of power.
1918	Settles in Dmitrov, near Moscow.
1919	May: meets with Lenin in Kremlin.
1921	8 February: dies in Dmitrov.
	13 February: buried at Novo-Devichy Monastery in Moscow.
	March: Kronstadt uprising; suppression of anarchists.
1922	Kropotkin's *Ethics* published.

Bibliographical note

All of Kropotkin's major writings, as well as an extensive literature about him, are available in English. The following bibliography lists only English-language works except for some especially important items in Russian.

Kropotkin's writings

Books

Several of Kropotkin's books have been reissued a number of times over the years. The following list gives the original date of publication, the first publication in English, and later editions where they are particularly notable.

The Conquest of Bread. In French: Paris, 1892. In English, London: Chapman and Hall, 1906; revised edition, 1913.
Dnevnik P. A. Kropotkina (The Diary of P. A. Kropotkin). Edited by A. A. Borovoi. Moscow-Petrograd: Gos. izdat., 1923. The diary Kropotkin kept in Siberia, 1862–7.
Ethics: Origin and Development. In Russian: Petrograd-Moscow, 1922. In English, New York: McVeagh, 1924.
Fields, Factories and Workshops. Boston: Houghton, Mifflin, 1899.
The Great French Revolution. London: Heinemann, 1909. Reissued, Montreal-New York: Black Rose Books, 1989.
In Russian and French Prisons. London: Ward and Downey, 1887.
Memoirs of a Revolutionist. Boston: Houghton, Mifflin, 1899. Of the numerous reprints of this book, two are particularly useful.

The edition by James Allen Rogers (Garden City, N.Y.: Anchor Books, 1962) is somewhat abridged but appends excerpts from the Russian version not contained in the English-language edition. The edition by Nicolas Walter (New York: Dover Publications, 1971) is particularly well annotated.

Modern Science and Anarchism. In Russian: London, 1901. In English, Philadelphia: Social Science Club, 1903.

Mutual Aid. London: Heinemann, 1902. The edition published by Extending Horizons Books (Boston, 1955) contains Thomas Huxley's 'The Struggle for Existence', to which *Mutual Aid* was a response.

Petr i Aleksandr Kropotkiny: Perepiska (Peter and Alexander Kropotkin: Correspondence). Vol. 1: 1857–62. Vol. 2: 1862–71. Moscow-Leningrad: Academia, 1932–3. The correspondence between Kropotkin and his brother.

Pis'ma o tekushchikh sobytiiakh (Letters on Current Events). Moscow: Zadruga, 1918. Ten articles by Kropotkin on the First World War, written between 1914 and 1917.

Russian Literature. New York: McClure, Phillips, 1905. Reissued as *Ideals and Realities in Russian Literature*, New York: Knopf, 1915.

The Terror in Russia: An Appeal to the British Nation. London: Methuen, 1909.

Words of a Rebel. In French: Paris, 1885. In English, Montreal and New York: Black Rose Books, 1992.

Anthologies

Baldwin, Roger N., ed. *Kropotkin's Revolutionary Pamphlets*. New York and London: Benjamin Blom, 1927. Reissued 1968. Contains 'An Appeal to the Young' and an abridged form of 'Modern Science and Anarchism', among other items.

Capouya, Emile and Keitha Tompkins, eds. *The Essential Kropotkin*. New York: Liveright, 1975. A collection of several of Kropotkin's short works and excerpts from his books.

Kropotkin, Peter. *Act for Yourselves. Articles from* Freedom, *1886–1907*. Edited by Nicolas Walter and Heiner Becker. London: Freedom Press, 1988.

Miller, Martin A., ed. *Selected Writings on Anarchism and Revolution: P. A. Kropotkin*. Cambridge, Mass., and London: MIT Press,

1970. Contains, among other things, 'Must We Occupy Ourselves with an Examination of the Ideal of a Future System?'
Read, Herbert, ed. *Kropotkin. Selections from His Writings.* London:
Freedom Press, 1942. A compilation of brief extracts from
various works.
In addition to his books, a number of Kropotkin's short works
were published separately. For a bibliography that includes his
articles, pamphlets, and published correspondence, see below, Caroline Cahm, *Kropotkin and the Rise of Revolutionary Anarchism*, pp.
353–7.

Works on Kropotkin

The following are works wholly or substantially about Kropotkin.

Biographies

Miller, Martin A. *Kropotkin.* Chicago and London: University of
Chicago Press, 1976. A thorough, scholarly biography, with
an excellent bibliography.
Pirumova, N. M. *Petr Alekseevich Kropotkin.* Moscow: Nauka, 1972.
A brief but useful Soviet biography.
Woodcock, George and Ivan Avakumovic. *The Anarchist Prince: A
Biographical Study of Peter Kropotkin.* London and New York:
T. V. Boardman, 1950. A comprehensive, readable biography,
but less scholarly and critical than Miller.

Other works

Avrich, Paul. *Anarchist Portraits.* Princeton: Princeton University
Press, 1988. Contains a detailed account of Kropotkin's visits
to America.
Cahm, Caroline. *Kropotkin and the Rise of Revolutionary Anarchism,
1872–1886.* Cambridge and New York: Cambridge University
Press, 1989. A detailed study of Kropotkin's years as a revol-
utionary activist, with an extensive bibliography.
Hulse, James W. *Revolutionists in London: A Study of Five Unorthodox
Socialists.* Oxford: Clarendon Press, 1970. Places Kropotkin in
the context of Victorian London.

Maksimov, G. P., ed. *P. A. Kropotkin i ego uchenie. Internatsional'nyi sbornik* (P. A. Kropotkin and His Teachings. An International Collection). Chicago: Federatsiia Russkikh A.-K. Grupp, 1931. An important collection of articles, memoirs, and some of Kropotkin's letters.

Osovsky, Stephen. *Peter Kropotkin*. Boston: Twayne, 1979. A survey of Kropotkin's ideas and their contemporary significance.

Pirumova, N. M., ed. 'P. A. Kropotkin'. *Voprosy filosofii* (Moscow), no. 11 (1991), pp. 38–71. Includes statements and letters of Kropotkin from 1918 to 1920, some previously unpublished.

Shub, David. 'Kropotkin and Lenin'. *The Russian Review*, 12 (October 1953), pp. 227–34. On the relations and contacts between them.

Todes, Daniel P. *Darwin without Malthus: The Struggle for Existence in Russian Evolutionary Thought*. New York and Oxford: Oxford University Press, 1989. Places Kropotkin's theory of mutual aid in the context of Russian Darwinism.

The anarchist background

Avrich, Paul. *The Russian Anarchists*. Princeton: Princeton University Press, 1967. The best history of Russian anarchism.

ed. *The Anarchists in the Russian Revolution*. Ithaca, N.Y.: Cornell University Press, 1973. A documentary collection.

Carlson, Andrew R. *Anarchism in Germany*. Vol. 1: *The Early Movement*. Metuchen, N.J.: Scarecrow Press, 1972. Informative on anarchists in Switzerland in Kropotkin's time.

Carter, April. *The Political Theory of Anarchism*. London: Routledge and Kegan Paul, 1971.

Cole, G. D. H. *A History of Socialist Thought*. Vol. 2: *Marxism and Anarchism, 1850–1890*. London: Macmillan, 1954.

Crowder, George. *Classical Anarchism: The Political Thought of Godwin, Proudhon, Bakunin, and Kropotkin*. Oxford: Clarendon Press, 1991. A serious philosophical analysis of anarchist ideology.

D'Agostino, Anthony. *Marxism and the Russian Anarchists*. San Francisco: Germinal Press, 1977.

Joll, James. *The Anarchists*. London: Eyre and Spottiswoode, 1964. A good survey of the anarchist movement.

Bibliographical note

Sonn, Richard D. *Anarchism*. New York: Twayne, 1992. A short
survey in the light of Soviet communism's collapse.

Stafford, David. *From Anarchism to Reformism*. Toronto and Buffalo:
University of Toronto Press. A study of Paul Brousse, with
considerable background on the Jura Federation.

Thomas, Paul. *Karl Marx and the Anarchists*. London and Boston:
Routledge and Kegan Paul, 1980.

Venturi, Franco. *Roots of Revolution*. New York: Knopf, 1960. The
most thorough history of Russian Populism.

Woodcock, George. *Anarchism: A History of Libertarian Ideas and
Movements*. Cleveland and New York: Meridian Books, 1962.
A comprehensive history of anarchism.

Biographical synopses

AMANA was a co-operative community established in Iowa in 1855.

BARRAL. See Kropotkin's note 1, p. 198.

COCHRANE, JOSEPHINE G., of Shelbyville, Illinois, was the inventor of the dishwasher.

DE PAEPE, CESAR, was a Belgian socialist who moved from anarchism to Marxism.

FABIANS. The Fabian Society, founded in London in 1884, was an organization of middle-class intellectuals dedicated to an evolutionary, democratic form of socialism.

GEORGE, HENRY, was an American economist and social reformer who advocated a single tax based on land rent. His best-known work was *Progress and Poverty*, published in 1880. His *Social Problems* was published in 1883.

GRONLUND, LAURENCE, born in Denmark, was an American lawyer and advocate of socialism in the late nineteenth century.

GUESDE, JULES, originally an anarchist, in the 1880s became the leader of the Marxist movement in France.

HALLETT. A Major Hallett of Brighton, England, greatly increased crop yields by developing new varieties of cereal grains.

HUXLEY, THOMAS HENRY, was an English biologist and proponent of Darwin's theory of evolution.

JACQUARD, JOSEPH-MARIE, was the inventor of the Jacquard loom, introduced in 1805, which used punched cards to automate the weaving of cloth.

JOULE, JAMES PRESCOTT, an English physicist, discovered the first law of thermodynamics.

LAPLACE, LAMARCK, and LAVOISIER. Pierre-Simon Laplace was a French mathematician and astronomer. Jean-Baptiste Lamarck was a pioneer French biologist whose theory of the inheritability of acquired characteristics was overturned by Darwin. Antoine-Laurent Lavoisier was the French pioneer of modern chemistry, guillotined during the French Revolution.

LA BRUYERE, JEAN DE, was a seventeenth-century moralist who penned satirical character sketches for the purpose of reforming manners.

LEVERDAYS, EMILE, was a nineteenth-century French political writer.

LIEBIG, JUSTUS, was the German pioneer of agricultural chemistry.

LITTRE, MAXIMILIEN-PAUL-EMILE, was a French philologist, author of an etymological dictionary of the French language.

LYELL, CHARLES, was the British pioneer of modern geology.

MAURY, MATTHEW FONTAINE, author of *Physical Geography of the Sea* (1855–6), was an American oceanographer who demonstrated the feasibility of a transatlantic cable.

MENDELEEFF. Dmitry Ivanovich Mendeleyev was the Russian chemist who devised the periodic table of the elements.

MICHELET, JULES, was one of the outstanding French historians of the nineteenth century, best known for his massive history of the French Revolution.

MIGNET, FRANÇOIS-AUGUSTE-MARIE, was an early nineteenth-century French historian, author of a history of the French Revolution.

MORRIS, WILLIAM, was an English designer and socialist. His *News from Nowhere* depicts a utopia very close to anarchism.

MOUCHOT, A., was a French physicist who devised a mechanism for the utilization of solar heat.

PHALANSTERIANS. The phalanstery was the name Charles Fourier (1772–1837), a French pioneer of socialism, gave to the model community he advocated. It included communal living arrangements for its members.

PLAYFAIR, LYON, was a British chemist and politician.

Biographical synopses

PONCE, M. See Kropotkin's note 1, p. 198.
PROUDHON, PIERRE-JOSEPH (1809–65), was one of the ideological founders of anarchism. He advocated a system called Mutualism, in which individual producers would exchange goods valued according to labour.
RUSKIN, JOHN, was a prominent English art critic of the late nineteenth century.
RODBERTUS, JOHANN KARL, was a conservative German economist whose ideas anticipated the concept of state socialism.
SEGUIN, MAYER and GROVE. Marc Séguin was a French engineer instrumental in the development of the steam locomotive. Julius Robert von Mayer was a German physicist who developed the mechanical theory of heat. William Robert Grove was a British physicist who also contributed to the development of modern forms of energy.
SISMONDI and SAY. Jean Charles Léonard Simonde de Sismondi was a Swiss economist of the early nineteenth century. Jean Baptiste Say was a French economist of the early nineteenth century.
STEPHENSON, GEORGE, was the English engineer who developed the railway locomotive.
WATRIN and THOMAS. Watrin was a supervisor murdered by workers in the 1880s. Clément Thomas was a general killed at the beginning of the Paris Commune of 1871.
WATT, JAMES, was the Scottish inventor of the steam engine.
YOUNG ICARIA. Icaria was the name of the settlement founded by the French socialist Etienne Cabet (1788–1856) at Nauvoo, Illinois, in 1849.

The Conquest of Bread

The Conquest of Bread is Kropotkin's most detailed exposition of anarchist communism. The central place it occupied in his thought is indicated by the number of times he reissued it over the years. It originated as a series of articles in anarchist newspapers in the 1880s and appeared in book form in French in 1892. Kropotkin published English editions in 1906 and 1913, and in 1919 he prepared a new Russian edition which was published in 1922.

The text reprinted here is that of the revised English edition of 1913, published in London.

3

Preface

One of the current objections to communism, and socialism altogether, is that the idea is so old, and yet it has never been realized. Schemes of ideal states haunted the thinkers of ancient Greece; later on, the early Christians joined in communist groups; centuries later, large communist brotherhoods came into existence during the reform movement. Then, the same ideals were revived during the great English and French Revolutions; and finally, quite lately, in 1848, a revolution, inspired to a great extent with socialist ideals, took place in France. 'And yet, you see,' we are told, 'how far away is still the realization of your schemes. Don't you think that there is some fundamental error in your understanding of human nature and its needs?'

At first sight this objection seems very serious. However, the moment we consider human history more attentively, it loses its strength. We see, first, that hundreds of millions of men have succeeded in maintaining amongst themselves, in their village communities, for many hundreds of years, one of the main elements of socialism – the common ownership of the chief instrument of production, the land, and the apportionment of the same according to the labour capacities of the different families; and we learn that if the communal possession of the land has been destroyed in Western Europe, it was not from within, but from without, by the governments which created a land monopoly in favour of the nobility and the middle classes. We learn, moreover, that the medieval cities succeeded in maintaining in their midst, for several centuries in succession, a certain socialized organization of production and

4

trade; that these centuries were periods of a rapid intellectual, industrial and artistic progress; while the decay of these communal institutions came mainly from the incapacity of men of combining the village with the city, the peasant with the citizen, so as jointly to oppose the growth of the military states, which destroyed the free cities.

The history of mankind, thus understood, does not offer, then, an argument against communism. It appears, on the contrary, as a succession of endeavours to realize some sort of communist organization, endeavours which were crowned here and there with a partial success of a certain duration; and all we are authorized to conclude is, that mankind has not yet found the proper form for combining, on communistic principles, agriculture with a suddenly developed industry and a rapidly growing international trade. The latter appears especially as a disturbing element, since it is no longer individuals only, or cities, that enrich themselves by distant commerce and export; but whole nations grow rich at the cost of those nations which lag behind in their industrial development.

These conditions, which began to appear by the end of the eighteenth century, took, however, their full development in the nineteenth century only, after the Napoleonic wars came to an end. And modern communism has to take them into account.

It is now known that the French Revolution, apart from its political significance, was an attempt made by the French people, in 1793 and 1794, in three different directions more or less akin to socialism. It was, first, *the equalization of fortunes*, by means of an income tax and succession duties, both heavily progressive, as also by a direct confiscation of the land in order to subdivide it, and by heavy war taxes levied upon the rich only. The second attempt was a sort of *municipal communism* as regards the consumption of some objects of first necessity, bought by the municipalities, and sold by them at cost price. And the third attempt was to introduce a wide *national system of rationally established prices of all commodities*, for which the real cost of production and moderate trade profits had to be taken into account. The Convention worked hard at this scheme, and had nearly completed its work, when reaction took the upper hand.

It was during this remarkable movement, which has never yet been properly studied, that modern socialism was born – Fourierism

5

with L'Ange, at Lyons, and authoritarian communism with Buonarroti, Babeuf, and their comrades. And it was immediately after the Great Revolution that the three great theoretical founders of modern socialism – Fourier, Saint Simon and Robert Owen, as well as Godwin (the no-state socialism) – came forward; while the secret communist societies, originated from those of Buonarroti and Babeuf, gave their stamp to militant, authoritarian communism for the next fifty years.

To be correct, then, we must say that modern socialism is not yet a hundred years old, and that, for the first half of these hundred years, two nations only, which stood at the head of the industrial movement, i.e., Britain and France, took part in its elaboration. Both – bleeding at that time from the terrible wounds inflicted upon them by fifteen years of Napoleonic wars, and both enveloped in the great European reaction that had come from the East.

In fact, it was only after the revolution of July, 1830, in France, and the reform movement of 1830–2 in this country, had begun to shake off that terrible reaction, that the discussion of socialism became possible for a few years before the revolution of 1848. And it was during those years that the aspirations of Fourier, Saint Simon, and Robert Owen, worked out by their followers, took a definite shape, and the different schools of socialism which exist nowadays were defined.

In Britain, Robert Owen and his followers worked out their schemes of communist villages, agricultural and industrial at the same time; immense co-operative associations were started for creating with their dividends more communist colonies; and the Great Consolidated Trades' Union was founded – the forerunner of both the Labour Parties of our days and the International Working Men's Association.

In France, the Fourierist Considérant issued his remarkable manifesto, which contains, beautifully developed, all the theoretical considerations upon the growth of capitalism, which are now described as 'scientific socialism'. Proudhon worked out his idea of anarchism and mutualism, without state interference. Louis Blanc published his *Organization of Labour*, which became later on the programme of Lassalle. Vidal in France and Lorenz Stein in Germany further developed, in two remarkable works, published in 1846 and 1847 respectively, the theoretical conceptions of Considérant;

and finally Vidal, and especially Pecqueur, developed in detail the system of collectivism, which the former wanted the National Assembly of 1848 to vote in the shape of laws.

However, there is one feature, common to all socialist schemes of that period, which must be noted. The three great founders of socialism who wrote at the dawn of the nineteenth century were so entranced by the wide horizons which it opened before them, that they looked upon it as a new revelation, and upon themselves as upon the founders of a new religion. Socialism had to be a religion, and they had to regulate its march, as the heads of a new church. Besides, writing during the period of reaction which had followed the French Revolution, and seeing more its failures than its successes, they did not trust the masses, and they did not appeal to them for bringing about the changes which they thought necessary. They put their faith, on the contrary, into some great ruler, some socialist Napoleon. He would understand the new revelation; he would be convinced of its desirability by the successful experiments of their phalansteries, or associations; and he would peacefully accomplish by his own authority the revolution which would bring well-being and happiness to mankind. A military genius, Napoleon, had just been ruling Europe, why should not a social genius come forward, carry Europe with him and translate the new Gospel into life? That faith was rooted very deep, and it stood for a long time in the way of socialism; its traces are even seen amongst us, down to the present day.

It was only during the years 1840–8, when the approach of the revolution was felt everywhere, and the proletarians were beginning to plant the banner of socialism on the barricades, that faith in the people began to enter once more the hearts of the social schemers: faith, on the one side, in republican democracy, and on the other side in *free* association, in the organizing powers of the working men themselves.

But then came the revolution of February, 1848, the middle-class Republic, and, with it, shattered hopes. Four months only after the proclamation of the Republic, the June insurrection of the Paris proletarians broke out, and it was crushed in blood. The wholesale shooting of the working men, the mass deportations to New Guinea, and finally the Napoleonian *coup d'état* followed. The socialists were prosecuted with fury, and the weeding out was so terrible and so

7

thorough that for the next twelve or fifteen years the very traces of socialism disappeared; its literature vanished so completely that even names, once so familiar before 1848, were entirely forgotten; ideas which were then current – the stock ideas of the socialists before 1848 – were so wiped out as to be taken, later on, by our generation, for new discoveries.

However, when a new revival began, about 1866, when communism and collectivism once more came forward, it appeared that the conception as to the means of their realization had undergone a deep change. The old faith in political democracy was dying out, and the first principles upon which the Paris working men agreed with the British trade-unionists and Owenites, when they met in 1862 and 1864, at London, was that 'the emancipation of the working men must be accomplished by the working men themselves'. Upon another point they also were agreed. It was that the labour unions themselves would have to get hold of the instruments of production, and organize production themselves. The French idea of the Fourierist and mutualist 'Association' thus joined hands with Robert Owen's idea of 'The Great Consolidated Trades' Union', which was extended now, so as to become an International Working Men's Association.

Again this new revival of socialism lasted but a few years. Soon came the war of 1870–1, the uprising of the Paris Commune – and again the free development of socialism was rendered impossible in France. But while Germany accepted now from the hands of its German teachers, Marx and Engels, the socialism of the French 'forty-eighters', that is, the socialism of Considérant and Louis Blanc, and the collectivism of Pecqueur, France made a further step forward.

In March, 1871, Paris had proclaimed that henceforward it would not wait for the retardatory portions of France: that it intended to start within its Commune its own social development.

The movement was too short-lived to give any positive result. It remained communalist only; it merely asserted the rights of the Commune to its full autonomy. But the working classes of the old International saw at once its historical significance. They understood that the free commune would be henceforth the medium in which the ideas of modern socialism may come to realization. The free agro-industrial communes, of which so much was spoken in England

8

and France before 1848, need not be small phalansteries, or small communities of 2,000 persons. They must be vast agglomerations, like Paris, or, still better, small territories. These communes would federate to constitute nations in some cases, even irrespectively of the present national frontiers (like the Cinque Ports or the Hansa). At the same time large labour associations would come into existence for the inter-communal service of the railways, the docks, and so on.

Such were the ideas which began vaguely to circulate after 1871 amongst the thinking working men, especially in the Latin countries. In some such organization, the details of which life itself would settle, the labour circles saw the medium through which socialist forms of life could find a much easier realization than through the seizure of all industrial property by the state, and the state organization of agriculture and industry.

These are the ideas to which I have endeavoured to give a more or less definite expression in this book.

Looking back now at the years that have passed since this book was written, I can say in full conscience that its leading ideas must have been correct. State socialism has certainly made considerable progress. State railways, state banking and state trade in spirits have been introduced here and there. But every step made in this direction, even though it resulted in the cheapening of a given commodity, was found to be a new obstacle in the struggle of the working men for their emancipation. So that we find growing amongst the working men, especially in Western Europe, the idea that even the working of such a vast national property as a railway network could be much better handled by a federated union of railway employees, than by a state organization.

On the other side, we see that countless attempts have been made all over Europe and America, the leading idea of which is, on the one side, to get into the hands of the working men themselves wide branches of production, and, on the other side, to always widen in the cities the circles of the functions which the city performs in the interest of its inhabitants. Trade unionism, with a growing tendency towards organizing the different trades internationally, and of being not only an instrument for the improvement of the conditions of labour, but also of becoming an organization which might, at a given moment, take into its hands the management

9

of production; co-operation, both for production and for distribution, both in industry and agriculture, and attempts at combining
both sorts of co-operation in experimental colonies; and finally, the
immensely varied field of the so-called municipal socialism – these
are the three directions in which the greatest amount of creative
power has been developed lately.

Of course, none of these may, in any degree, be taken as a
substitute for communism, or even for socialism, both of which
imply the common possession of the instruments of production.
But we certainly must look at all these attempts as upon *experiments* –
like those which Owen, Fourier and Saint Simon tried in their
colonies – experiments which prepare human thought to conceive
some of the practical forms in which a communist society might
find its expression. The synthesis of all these partial experiments
will have to be made some day by the constructive genius of some
one of the civilized nations. But samples of the bricks out of which
the great synthetic building will have to be built, and even samples
of some of its rooms, are being prepared by the immense effort
of the constructive genius of man.

Brighton
January, 1913.

CHAPTER I
Our riches

I

The human race has travelled a long way, since those remote ages when men fashioned their rude implements of flint and lived on the precarious spoils of hunting, leaving to their children for their only heritage a shelter beneath the rocks, some poor utensils – and Nature, vast, unknown and terrific, with whom they had to fight for their wretched existence.

During the long succession of agitated ages which have elapsed since, mankind has nevertheless amassed untold treasures. It has cleared the land, dried the marshes, hewn down forests, made roads, pierced mountains; it has been building, inventing, observing, reasoning; it has created a complex machinery, wrested her secrets from Nature, and finally it pressed steam and electricity into its service. And the result is, that now the child of the civilized man finds at his birth, ready for his use, an immense capital accumulated by those who have gone before him. And this capital enables man to acquire, merely by his own labour combined with the labour of others, riches surpassing the dreams of the fairy tales of the Thousand and One Nights.

The soil is cleared to a great extent, fit for the reception of the best seeds, ready to give a rich return for the skill and labour spent upon it – a return more than sufficient for all the wants of humanity. The methods of rational cultivation are known.

On the wide prairies of America each hundred men, with the aid of powerful machinery, can produce in a few months enough wheat to maintain ten thousand people for a whole year. And where man wishes to double his produce, to treble it, to multiply it a hundredfold, he *makes* the soil, gives to each plant the requisite care, and thus obtains enormous returns. While the hunter of old had to scour fifty or sixty square miles to find food for his family, the civilized man supports his household, with far less pains, and far more certainty, on a thousandth part of that space. Climate is no longer an obstacle. When the sun fails, man replaces it by artificial heat; and we see the coming of a time when artificial light also will be used to stimulate vegetation. Meanwhile, by the use of glass and hot-water pipes, man renders a given space ten and fifty times more productive than it was in its natural state.

The prodigies accomplished in industry are still more striking. With the co-operation of those intelligent beings, modern machines – themselves the fruit of three or four generations of inventors, mostly unknown – a hundred men manufacture now the stuff to provide ten thousand persons with clothing for two years. In well-managed coal-mines the labour of a hundred miners furnishes each year enough fuel to warm ten thousand families under an inclement sky. And we have lately witnessed the spectacle of wonderful cities springing up in a few months for international exhibitions, without interrupting in the slightest degree the regular work of the nations.

And if in manufactures as in agriculture, and as indeed through our whole social system, the labour, the discoveries and the inventions of our ancestors profit chiefly the few, it is none the less certain that mankind in general, aided by the creatures of steel and iron which it already possesses, could already procure an existence of wealth and ease for every one of its members.

Truly, we are rich – far richer than we think; rich in what we already possess, richer still in the possibilities of production of our actual mechanical outfit; richest of all in what we might win from our soil, from our manufactures, from our science, from our technical knowledge, were they but applied to bringing about the well-being of all.

II

In our civilized societies we are rich. Why then are the many poor? Why this painful drudgery for the masses? Why, even to the best-paid workman, this uncertainty for the morrow, in the midst of all the wealth inherited from the past, and in spite of the powerful means of production, which could ensure comfort to all, in return for a few hours of daily toil?

The socialists have said it and repeated it unwearyingly. Daily they reiterate it, demonstrating it by arguments taken from all the sciences. It is because all that is necessary for production – the land, the mines, the highways, machinery, food, shelter, education, knowledge – all have been seized by the few in the course of that long story of robbery, enforced migration and wars, of ignorance and oppression, which has been the life of the human race before it had learned to subdue the forces of Nature. It is because, taking advantage of alleged rights acquired in the past, these few appropriate today two-thirds of the products of human labour, and then squander them in the most stupid and shameful way. It is because, having reduced the masses to a point at which they have not the means of subsistence for a month, or even for a week in advance, the few can allow the many to work, only on the condition of themselves receiving the lion's share. It is because these few prevent the remainder of men from producing the things they need, and force them to produce, not the necessaries of life for all, but whatever offers the greatest profits to the monopolists. In this is the substance of all socialism.

Take, indeed, a civilized country. The forests which once covered it have been cleared, the marshes drained, the climate improved. It has been made habitable. The soil, which bore formerly only a coarse vegetation, is covered today with rich harvests. The rock walls in the valleys are laid out in terraces and covered with vines. The wild plants, which yielded nought but acrid berries, or uneatable roots, have been transformed by generations of culture into succulent vegetables or trees covered with delicious fruits. Thousands of highways and railroads furrow the earth, and pierce the mountains. The shriek of the engine is heard in the wild gorges of the Alps, the Caucasus and the Himalayas. The rivers have been made navigable; the coasts, carefully surveyed, are easy of access; artificial harbours, laboriously dug out and protected against the fury of the sea, afford shelter to the ships. Deep shafts have been sunk in the rocks; labyrinths of underground galleries have been dug out where coal may be raised or minerals extracted. At the crossings of the highways great cities have sprung up, and within their borders all the treasures of industry, science and art have been accumulated.

Whole generations, that lived and died in misery, oppressed and ill-treated by their masters, and worn out by toil, have handed on this immense inheritance to our century.

For thousands of years millions of men have laboured to clear the forests, to drain the marshes, and to open up highways by land and water. Every rood of soil we cultivate in Europe has been watered by the sweat of several races of men. Every acre has its story of enforced labour, of intolerable toil, of the people's sufferings. Every mile of railway, every yard of tunnel, has received its share of human blood.

The shafts of the mine still bear on their rocky walls the marks made by the pick of the workman who toiled to excavate them. The space between each prop in the underground galleries might be marked as a miner's grave; and who can tell what each of these graves has cost, in tears, in privations, in unspeakable wretchedness to the family who depended on the scanty wage of the worker cut off in his prime by fire-damp, rockfall, or flood?

The cities, bound together by railroads and waterways, are organisms which have lived through centuries. Dig beneath them and you find, one above another, the foundations of streets, of houses, of theatres, of public buildings. Search into their history and you will see how the civilization of the town, its industry, its special characteristics, have slowly grown and ripened through the co-operation of generations of its inhabitants before it could become what it is today. And even today, the value of each dwelling, factory and warehouse, which has been created by the accumulated labour of the millions of workers, now dead and buried, is only maintained by the very presence and labour of legions of the men who now inhabit that special corner of the globe. Each of the atoms composing what we call the Wealth of Nations owes its value to the fact that it is a part of the great whole. What would a London dockyard or a great Paris warehouse be if they were not situated in these great centres of international commerce? What would become of our mines, our factories, our workshops and our railways, without the immense quantities of merchandise transported every day by sea and land?

Millions of human beings have laboured to create this civilization on which we pride ourselves today. Other millions, scattered through the globe, labour to maintain it. Without them nothing would be left in fifty years but ruins.

There is not even a thought, or an invention, which is not common property, born of the past and the present. Thousands of inventors, known and unknown, who have died in poverty, have co-operated in the invention of each of these machines which embody the genius of man.

Thousands of writers, of poets, of scholars, have laboured to increase knowledge, to dissipate error, and to create that atmosphere of scientific thought, without which the marvels of our century could never have appeared. And these thousands of philosophers, of poets, of scholars, of inventors, have themselves been supported by the labour of past centuries. They have been upheld and nourished through life, both physically and mentally, by legions of workers and craftsmen of all sorts. They have drawn their motive force from the environment.

The genius of a Séguin, a Mayer, a Grove, has certainly done more to launch industry in new directions than all the capitalists in the world. But men of genius are themselves the children of industry as well as of science. Not until thousands of steam-engines had been working for years before all eyes, constantly transforming heat into dynamic force, and this force into sound, light and electricity, could the insight of genius proclaim the mechanical origin and the unity of the physical forces. And if we, children of the nineteenth century, have at last grasped this idea, if we know now how to apply it, it is again because daily experience has prepared the way. The thinkers of the eighteenth century saw and declared it, but the idea remained undeveloped, because the eighteenth century had not grown up like ours, side by side with the steam-engine. Imagine the decades that might have passed while we remained in ignorance of this law, which has revolutionized modern industry, had Watt not found at Soho skilled workmen to embody his ideas in metal, bringing all the parts of his engine to perfection, so that steam, pent in a complete mechanism, and rendered more docile than a horse, more manageable than water, became at last the very soul of modern industry.

Every machine has had the same history – a long record of sleepless nights and of poverty, of disillusions and of joys, of partial improvements discovered by several generations of nameless workers, who have added to the original invention these little nothings, without which the most fertile idea would remain fruitless. More than that: every new invention is a synthesis, the resultant of innumerable inventions which have preceded it in the vast field of mechanics and industry.

Science and industry, knowledge and application, discovery and practical realization leading to new discoveries, cunning of brain and of hand, toil of mind and muscle – all work together. Each discovery, each advance, each increase in the sum of human riches, owes its being to the physical and mental travail of the past and the present.

By what right then can anyone whatever appropriate the least morsel of this immense whole and say – This is mine, not yours?

III

It has come about, however, in the course of the ages traversed by the human race, that all that enables man to produce and to increase his power of production has been seized by the few. Some time, perhaps, we will relate how this came to pass. For the present let it suffice to state the fact and analyse its consequences.

Today the soil, which actually owes its value to the needs of an ever-increasing population, belongs to a minority who prevent the people from cultivating it – or do not allow them to cultivate it according to modern methods.

The mines, though they represent the labour of several generations, and derive their sole value from the requirements of the industry of a nation and the density of the population – the mines also belong to the few; and these few restrict the output of coal, or prevent it entirely, if they find more profitable investments for their capital. Machinery, too, has become the exclusive property of the few, and even when a machine incontestably represents the improvements added to the original rough invention by three or four generations of workers, it none the less belongs to a few owners. And if the descendants of the very inventor who constructed the first machine for lace-making, a century ago, were to present themselves today in a lace factory at Basle or Nottingham, and claim their rights, they would be told: 'Hands off! this machine is not yours,' and they would be shot down if they attempted to take possession of it.

The railways, which would be useless as so much old iron without the teeming population of Europe, its industry, its commerce and its marts, belong to a few shareholders, ignorant perhaps of the whereabouts of the lines of rails which yield them revenues greater than those of medieval kings. And if the children of those who perished by thousands while excavating the railway cuttings and tunnels were to assemble one day, crowding in their rags and hunger, to demand bread from the shareholders, they would be met with bayonets and grapeshot, to disperse them and safeguard 'vested interests'.

In virtue of this monstrous system, the son of the worker, on entering life, finds no field which he may till, no machine which he may tend, no mine in which he may dig, without accepting to leave a great part of what he will produce to a master. He must sell his labour for a scant and uncertain wage. His father and his grandfather have toiled to drain this field, to build this mill, to perfect this machine. They gave to the work the full measure of their strength, and what more could they give? But their heir comes into the world poorer than the lowest savage. If he obtains leave to till the fields, it is on condition of surrendering a quarter of the produce to his master, and another quarter to the government and the middlemen. And this tax, levied upon him by the state, the capitalist, the lord of the manor, and the middleman, is always increasing; it rarely leaves him the power to improve his system of culture. If he turns to industry, he is allowed to work – though not always even that – only on condition that he yield a half or two-thirds of the product to him whom the land recognizes as the owner of the machine.

We cry shame on the feudal baron who forbade the peasant to turn a clod of earth unless he surrendered to his lord a fourth of his crop. We called those the barbarous times. But if the forms have changed, the relations have remained the same, and the worker is forced, under the name of free contract, to accept feudal obligations. For, turn where he will, he can find no better conditions. Everything has become private property, and he must accept, or die of hunger.

The result of this state of things is that all our production tends in a wrong direction. Enterprise takes no thought for the needs of the community. Its only aim is to increase the gains of the speculator. Hence the constant fluctuations of trade, the periodical industrial crises, each of which throws scores of thousands of workers on the streets.

The working people cannot purchase with their wages the wealth which they have produced, and industry seeks foreign markets among the monied classes of other nations. In the East, in Africa, everywhere, in Egypt, Tonkin or the Congo, the European is thus bound to promote the growth of serfdom. And so he does. But soon he finds that everywhere there are similar competitors. All the nations evolve on the same lines, and wars, perpetual wars, break out for the right of precedence in the market. Wars for the possession of the East, wars for the empire of the sea, wars to impose duties on imports and to dictate conditions to neighbouring states; wars against those 'blacks' who revolt! The roar of the cannon never ceases in the world, whole races are massacred, the states of Europe spend a third of their budgets in armaments; and we know how heavily these taxes fall on the workers.

Education still remains the privilege of a small minority, for it is idle to talk of education when the workman's child is forced, at the age of 13, to go down into the mine or to help his father on the farm. It is idle to talk of studying to the worker, who comes home in the evening wearied by excessive toil, and its brutalizing atmosphere. Society is thus bound to remain divided into two hostile camps, and in such conditions freedom is a vain word. The radical begins by demanding a greater extension of political rights, but he soon sees that the breath of liberty leads to the uplifting of the proletariat, and then he turns round, changes his opinions, and reverts to repressive legislation and government by the sword.

A vast array of courts, judges, executioners, policemen and gaolers is needed to uphold these privileges; and this array gives rise in its turn to a whole system of espionage, of false witness, of spies, of threats and corruption.

The system under which we live checks in its turn the growth of the social sentiment. We all know that without uprightness, without self-respect, without sympathy and mutual aid, humankind must perish, as perish the few races of animals living by rapine, or the slave-keeping ants. But such ideas are not to the taste of the ruling classes, and they have elaborated a whole system of pseudo-science to teach the contrary.

Fine sermons have been preached on the text that those who have should share with those who have not, but he who would carry out this principle would be speedily informed that these beautiful sentiments are all very well in poetry, but not in practice. 'To lie is to degrade and besmirch oneself,' we say, and yet all civilized life becomes one huge lie. We accustom ourselves and our children to hypocrisy, to the practice of a double-faced morality. And since the brain is ill at ease among lies, we cheat ourselves with sophistry. Hypocrisy and sophistry become the second nature of the civilized man.

But a society cannot live thus; it must return to truth, or cease to exist.

Thus the consequences which spring from the original act of monopoly spread through the whole of social life. Under pain of death, human societies are forced to return to first principles: the means of production being the collective work of humanity, the product should be the collective property of the race. Individual appropriation is neither just nor serviceable. All belongs to all. All things are for all men, since all men have need of them, since all men have worked in the measure of their strength to produce them, and since it is not possible to evaluate everyone's part in the production of the world's wealth.

All things for all. Here is an immense stock of tools and implements; here are all those iron slaves which we call machines, which saw and plane, spin and weave for us, unmaking and remaking, working up raw matter to produce the marvels of our time. But nobody has the right to seize a single one of these machines and say: 'This is mine; if you want to use it you must pay me a tax on each of your products,' any more than the feudal lord of medieval times had the right to say to the peasant: 'This hill, this meadow belong to me, and you must pay me a tax on every sheaf of corn you reap, on every rick you build.'

All is for all! If the man and the woman bear their fair share of work, they have a right to their fair share of all that is produced by all, and that share is enough to secure them well-being. No more of such vague formulae as 'The right to work', or 'To each the whole result of his labour'. What we proclaim is *the Right to Well-Being: Well-Being for All!*

CHAPTER II
Well-being for all

I

Well-being for all is not a dream. It is possible, realizable, owing to all that our ancestors have done to increase our powers of production.

We know, indeed, that the producers, although they constitute hardly one-third of the inhabitants of civilized countries, even now produce such quantities of goods that a certain degree of comfort could be brought to every hearth. We know further that if all those who squander today the fruits of others' toil were forced to employ their leisure in useful work, our wealth would increase in proportion to the number of producers, and more. Finally, we know that contrary to the theory enunciated by Malthus – that oracle of middle-class economics – the productive powers of the human race increase at a much more rapid ratio than its powers of reproduction. The more thickly men are crowded on the soil, the more rapid is the growth of their wealth-creating power.

Thus, although the population of England has only increased from 1844 to 1890 by 62 per cent, its production has grown, even at the lowest estimate, at double that rate – to wit, by 130 per cent. In France, where the population has grown more slowly, the increase in production is nevertheless very rapid. Notwithstanding the crises through which agriculture is frequently passing, notwithstanding state interference, the blood-tax (conscription), and speculative commerce and finance, the production of wheat in France has increased fourfold, and industrial production more than tenfold, in the course of the last eighty years. In the United States the progress is still more striking. In spite of immigration, or rather precisely because of the influx of surplus European labour, the United States have multiplied their wealth tenfold.

However, these figures give but a very faint idea of what our wealth might become under better conditions. For alongside of the rapid development of our wealth-producing powers we have an overwhelming increase in the ranks of the idlers and middlemen. Instead of capital gradually concentrating itself in a few hands, so that it would only be necessary for the community to dispossess a few millionaires and enter upon its lawful heritage – instead of this socialist forecast proving true, the exact reverse is coming to pass: the swarm of parasites is ever increasing.

In France there are not ten actual producers to every thirty inhabitants. The whole agricultural wealth of the country is the work of less than 7 million men, and in the two great industries, mining and the textile trades, you will find that the workers number less than $2\frac{1}{2}$ million. But the exploiters of labour, how many are they? In the United Kingdom a little over 1 million workers – men, women and children – are employed in all the textile trades; less than 900,000 work the mines; much less than 2 million till the ground, and it appeared from the last industrial census that only a little over 4 million men, women and children were employed in all the industries.[a] So that the statisticians have to exaggerate all the figures in order to establish a maximum of 8 million producers to 45 million inhabitants. Strictly speaking, the creators of the goods exported from Britain to all the ends of the earth comprise only from 6 to 7 million workers. And what is the number of the shareholders and middlemen who levy the first fruits of labour from far and near, and heap up unearned gains by thrusting themselves between the producer and the consumer?

Nor is this all. The owners of capital constantly reduce the output by restraining production. We need not speak of the cartloads of oysters thrown into the sea to prevent a dainty, hitherto reserved for the rich, from becoming a food for the people. We need not

---

[a] 4,013,711 now employed in all the 53 branches of different industries, including the State Ordnance Works, and 241,530 workers engaged in the construction and maintenance of railways, their aggregate production reaching the value of £1,041,037,000, and the net output being £406,799,000.

speak of the thousand and one luxuries – stuffs, foods, etc., etc. – treated after the same fashion as the oysters. It is enough to remember the way in which the production of the most necessary things is limited. Legions of miners are ready and willing to dig out coal every day, and send it to those who are shivering with cold; but too often a third, or even one-half, of their number are forbidden to work more than three days a week, because, forsooth, the price of coal must be kept up! Thousands of weavers are forbidden to work the looms, although their wives and children go in rags, and although three-quarters of the population of Europe have no clothing worthy the name.

Hundreds of blast-furnaces, thousands of factories periodically stand idle, others only work half-time – and in every civilized nation there is a permanent population of about 2 million individuals who ask only for work, but to whom work is denied.

How gladly would these millions of men set to work to reclaim waste lands, or to transform ill-cultivated land into fertile fields, rich in harvests! A year of well-directed toil would suffice to multiply fivefold the produce of those millions of acres in this country which lie idle now as 'permanent pasture', or of those dry lands in the south of France which now yield only about 8 bushels of wheat per acre. But men, who would be happy to become hardy pioneers in so many branches of wealth-producing activity, must remain idle because the owners of the soil, the mines and the factories prefer to invest their capital – taken in the first place from the community – in Turkish or Egyptian bonds, or in Patagonian gold-mines, and so make Egyptian fellahs, Italian emigrants and Chinese coolies their wage-slaves.

This is the direct and deliberate limitation of production; but there is also a limitation indirect and not of set purpose, which consists in spending human toil on objects absolutely useless, or destined only to satisfy the dull vanity of the rich.

It is impossible to reckon in figures the extent to which wealth is restricted indirectly, the extent to which energy is squandered, while it might have served to produce, and above all to prepare the machinery necessary to production. It is enough to cite the immense sums spent by Europe in armaments, for the sole purpose of acquiring control of the markets, and so forcing her own goods on neighbouring territories, and making exploitation easier at home;

the millions paid every year to officials of all sorts, whose function it is to maintain the 'rights' of minorities – the right, that is, of a few rich men – to manipulate the economic activities of the nation; the millions spent on judges, prisons, policemen, and all the paraphernalia of so-called justice – spent to no purpose, because we know that every alleviation, however slight, of the wretchedness of our great cities is always followed by a considerable diminution of crime; lastly, the millions spent on propagating pernicious doctrines by means of the press, and news 'cooked' in the interest of this or that party, of this politician or of that group of speculators.

But over and above this we must take into account all the labour that goes to sheer waste – here, in keeping up the stables, the kennels and the retinue of the rich; there, in pandering to the caprices of society and the depraved tastes of the fashionable mob; there again, in forcing the consumer to buy what he does not need, or foisting an inferior article upon him by means of puffery, and in producing on the other hand wares which are absolutely injurious, but profitable to the manufacturer. What is squandered in this manner would be enough to double the production of useful things, or so to plenish our mills and factories with machinery that they would soon flood the shops with all that is now lacking to two-thirds of the nation. Under our present system a full quarter of the producers in every nation are forced to be idle for three or four months in the year, and the labour of another quarter, if not of the half, has no better results than the amusement of the rich or the exploitation of the public.

Thus, if we consider on the one hand the rapidity with which civilized nations augment their powers of production, and on the other hand the limits set to that production, be it directly or indirectly, by existing conditions, we cannot but conclude that an economic system a trifle more reasonable would permit them to heap up in a few years so many useful products that they would be constrained to say – 'Enough! We have enough coal and bread and raiment! Let us rest and consider how best to use our powers, how best to employ our leisure.'

No, plenty for all is not a dream – though it was a dream indeed in those days when man, for all his pains, could hardly win a few bushels of wheat from an acre of land, and had to fashion by hand all the implements he used in agriculture and industry. Now it is no longer a dream, because man has invented a motor which, with a little iron and a few sacks of coal, gives him the mastery of a creature strong and docile as a horse, and capable of setting the most complicated machinery in motion.

But, if plenty for all is to become a reality, this immense capital – cities, houses, pastures, arable lands, factories, highways, education – must cease to be regarded as private property, for the monopolist to dispose of at his pleasure.

This rich endowment, painfully won, builded, fashioned, or invented by our ancestors, must become common property, so that the collective interests of men may gain from it the greatest good for all.

There must be *expropriation*. The well-being of all – the end, expropriation – the means.

II

Expropriation, such then is the problem which history has put before the men of the twentieth century: the return to communism in all that ministers to the well-being of man.

But this problem cannot be solved by means of legislation. No one imagines that. The poor, as well as the rich, understand that neither the existing governments, nor any which might arise out of possible political changes, would be capable of finding such a solution. They feel the necessity of a social revolution; and both rich and poor recognize that this revolution is imminent, that it may break out in a few years.

A great change in thought has taken place during the last half of the nineteenth century; but suppressed, as it was, by the propertied classes, and denied its natural development, this new spirit must now break its bonds by violence and realize itself in a revolution.

Whence will the revolution come? How will it announce its coming? No one can answer these questions. The future is hidden. But those who watch and think do not misinterpret the signs: workers and exploiters, revolutionists and conservatives, thinkers and men of action, all feel that a revolution is at our doors.

Well, then – What are we going to do when the thunderbolt has fallen?

We have all been bent on studying the dramatic side of revolutions so much, and the practical work of revolutions so little, that we are apt to see only the stage effects, so to speak, of these great movements: the fight of the first days; the barricades. But this fight, this first skirmish, is soon ended, and it is only after the breakdown of the old system that the real work of revolution can be said to begin.

Effete and powerless, attacked on all sides, the old rulers are soon swept away by the breath of insurrection. In a few days the middle-class monarchy of 1848 was no more, and while Louis Philippe was making good his escape in a cab, Paris had already forgotten her 'citizen king'. The government of Thiers disappeared, on the 18th of March, 1871, in a few hours, leaving Paris mistress of her destinies. Yet 1848 and 1871 were only insurrections. Before a popular revolution the masters of 'the old order' disappear with a surprising rapidity. Its upholders fly the country, to plot in safety elsewhere and to devise measures for their return.

The former government having disappeared, the army, hesitating before the tide of popular opinion, no longer obeys its commanders, who have also prudently decamped. The troops stand by without interfering, or join the rebels. The police, standing at ease, are uncertain whether to belabour the crowd, or to cry: 'Long live the commune!' while some retire to their quarters 'to await the pleasure of the new government'. Wealthy citizens pack their trunks and betake themselves to places of safety. The people remain. This is how a revolution is ushered in.

In several large towns the commune is proclaimed. In the streets wander scores of thousands of men, and in the evening they crowd into improvised clubs, asking: 'What shall we do?' and ardently discuss public affairs. All take an interest in them; those who yesterday were quite indifferent are perhaps the most zealous. Everywhere there is plenty of goodwill and a keen desire to make victory certain. It is a time when acts of supreme devotion are occurring. The masses of the people are full of the desire of going forward.

All this is splendid, sublime; but still, it is not a revolution. Nay, it is only now that the work of the revolutionist begins.

Doubtless there will be acts of vengeance. The Watrins and the Thomases will pay the penalty of their unpopularity; but these are mere incidents of the struggle – not the revolution.

Socialist politicians, radicals, neglected geniuses of journalism, stump orators – both middle-class people and workmen – will hurry to the town hall, to the government offices, to take possession of the vacant seats. Some will decorate themselves with gold and silver lace to their hearts' content, admire themselves in ministerial mirrors, and study to give orders with an air of importance appropriate to their new position. How could they impress their comrades of the office or the workshop without having a red sash, an embroidered cap, and magisterial gestures! Others will bury themselves in official papers, trying, with the best of wills, to make head or tail of them. They will indite laws and issue high-flown worded decrees that nobody will take the trouble to carry out – because revolution has come.

To give themselves an authority which they have not they will seek the sanction of old forms of government. They will take the names of 'Provisional Government', 'Committee of Public Safety', 'Mayor', 'Governor of the Town Hall', 'Commissioner of Public Safety', and what not. Elected or acclaimed, they will assemble in boards or in communal councils, where men of ten or twenty different schools will come together, representing – not as many 'private chapels', as it is often said, but as many different conceptions regarding the scope, the bearing, and the goal of the revolution. Possibilists, collectivists, radicals, Jacobins, Blanquists, will be thrust together, and waste time in wordy warfare. Honest men will be huddled together with the ambitious ones, whose only dream is power and who spurn the crowd whence they are sprung. All coming together with diametrically opposed views, all forced to enter into ephemeral alliances, in order to create majorities that can but last a day. Wrangling, calling each other reactionaries, authoritarians, and rascals, incapable of coming to an understanding on any serious measure, dragged into discussions about trifles, producing nothing better than bombastic proclamations; all giving themselves an awful importance while the real strength of the movement is in the streets.

All this may please those who like the stage, but it is not revolution. Nothing has been accomplished as yet.

And meanwhile the people suffer. The factories are idle, the workshops closed; trade is at a standstill. The worker does not even earn the meagre wage which was his before. Food goes up in price. With that heroic devotion which has always characterized them, and which in great crises reaches the sublime, the people will wait patiently. 'We place these three months of want at the service of the Republic,' they said in 1848, while 'their representatives' and the gentlemen of the new government, down to the meanest Jack-in-office, received their salary regularly.

The people suffer. With the childlike faith, with the good humour of the masses who believe in their leaders, they think that 'yonder', in the House, in the town hall, in the Committee of Public Safety, their welfare is being considered. But 'yonder' they are discussing everything under the sun except the welfare of the people. In 1793, while famine ravaged France and crippled the Revolution; whilst the people were reduced to the depths of misery, although the Champs Elysées were lined with luxurious carriages where women displayed their jewels and splendour, Robespierre was urging the Jacobins to discuss his treatise on the English Constitution. While the worker was suffering in 1848 from the general stoppage of trade, the Provisional Government and the National Assembly were wrangling over military pensions and prison labour, without troubling how the people managed to live during the terrible crisis. And could one cast a reproach at the Paris Commune, which was born beneath the Prussian cannon, and lasted only seventy days, it would be for this same error – this failure to understand that the Revolution could not triumph unless those who fought on its side were fed: that on 15 pence a day a man cannot fight on the ramparts and at the same time support a family.

The people suffer and say: 'How is a way out of these difficulties to be found?'

III

It seems to us that there is only one answer to this question: we must recognize, and loudly proclaim, that everyone, whatever his grade in the old society, whether strong or weak, capable or incapable, has, before everything, *the right to live*, and that society is bound to share amongst all, without exception, the means of existence it has at its disposal. We must acknowledge this, and proclaim it aloud, and act upon it.

Affairs must be managed in such a way that from the first day of the revolution the worker shall know that a new era is opening before him; that henceforward none need crouch under the bridges, while palaces are hard by, none need fast in the midst of plenty, none need perish with cold near shops full of furs; that all is for all, in practice as well as in theory, and that at last, for the first time in history, a revolution has been accomplished which considers the *needs* of the people before schooling them in their *duties*.

This cannot be brought about by Acts of Parliament, but only by taking immediate and effective possession of all that is necessary to ensure the well-being of all; this is the only really scientific way of going to work, the only way which can be understood and desired by the mass of the people. We must take possession, in the name of the people, of the granaries, the shops full of clothing, and the dwelling-houses. Nothing must be wasted. We must organize without delay a way to feed the hungry, to satisfy all wants, to meet all needs, to produce not for the special benefit of this one or that one, but so as to ensure to society as a whole its life and further development.

Enough of ambiguous words like 'the right to work', with which the people were misled in 1848, and which are still resorted to with the hope of misleading them. Let us have the courage to recognize that *well-being for all*, henceforward possible, must be realized.

When the workers claimed the right to work in 1848, national and municipal workshops were organized, and workmen were sent to drudge there at the rate of 1*s*. 8*d*. a day! When they asked the 'Organization of Labour', the reply was: 'Patience, friends, the government will see to it; meantime here is your 1*s*. 8*d*. Rest now, brave toiler, after your lifelong struggle for food!' And in the meantime the cannons were overhauled, the reserves called out, and the workers themselves disorganized by the many methods well known to the middle classes, till one fine day, in June, 1848, four months after the overthrow of the previous government, they were told to go and colonize Africa, or be shot down.

Very different will be the result if the workers claim the *right to well-being*! In claiming that right they claim the right to take possession of the wealth of the community – to take houses to dwell in according to the needs of each family; to socialize the stores of food and learn the meaning of plenty, after having known famine too well. They proclaim their right to all social wealth –

fruit of the labour of past and present generations – and learn by its means to enjoy those higher pleasures of art and science which have too long been monopolized by the rich.

And while asserting their right to live in comfort, they assert, what is still more important, their right to decide for themselves what this comfort shall be, what must be produced to ensure it, and what discarded as no longer of value.

The 'right to well-being' means the possibility of living like human beings, and of bringing up children to be members of a society better than ours, whilst the 'right to work' only means the right to be always a wage-slave, a drudge, ruled over and exploited by the middle class of the future. The right to well-being is the social revolution, the right to work means nothing but the treadmill of commercialism. It is high time for the worker to assert his right to the common inheritance, and to enter into possession of it.

CHAPTER III

Anarchist communism

I

Every society, on abolishing private property will be forced, we maintain, to organize itself on the lines of communistic anarchy. Anarchy leads to communism, and communism to anarchy, both alike being expressions of the predominant tendency in modern societies, the pursuit of equality.

Time was when a peasant family could consider the corn it sowed and reaped, or the woollen garments woven in the cottage, as the products of its own soil. But even then this way of looking at things was not quite correct. There were the roads and the bridges made in common, the swamps drained by common toil, the communal pastures enclosed by hedges which were kept in repair by each and all. If the looms for weaving or the dyes for colouring fabrics were improved by somebody, all profited; and even in those days a peasant family could not live alone, but was dependent in a thousand ways on the village or the commune.

But nowadays, in the present state of industry, when everything is interdependent, when each branch of production is knit up with all the rest, the attempt to claim an individualist origin for the products of industry is absolutely untenable. The astonishing perfection attained by the textile or mining industries in civilized countries is due to the simultaneous development of a thousand other industries, great and small, to the extension of the railroad system, to inter-oceanic navigation, to the manual skill of thousands of workers, to a certain standard of culture reached by the working classes as a whole – to the labours, in short, of men in every corner of the globe.

The Italians who died of cholera while making the Suez Canal, or of anchylosis in the St Gothard Tunnel, and the Americans mowed down by shot and shell while fighting for the abolition of slavery, have helped to develop the cotton industry in France and England, as well as the work-girls who languish in the factories of Manchester and Rouen, and the inventor who (following the suggestion of some worker) succeeds in improving the looms.

How, then, shall we estimate the share of each in the riches which *all* contribute to amass?

Looking at production from this general, synthetic point of view, we cannot hold with the collectivists that payment proportionate to the hours of labour rendered by each would be an ideal arrangement, or even a step in the right direction.

Without discussing whether exchange value of goods is really measured in existing societies by the amount of work necessary to produce it – according to the teaching of Adam Smith and Ricardo, in whose footsteps Marx has followed – suffice it to say here, leaving ourselves free to return to the subject later, that the collectivist ideal appears to us untenable in a society which considers the instruments of labour as a common inheritance. Starting from this principle, such a society would find itself forced from the very outset to abandon all forms of wages.

The mitigated individualism of the collectivist system certainly could not maintain itself alongside a partial communism – the socialization of land and the instruments of production. A new form of property requires a new form of remuneration. A new method of production cannot exist side by side with the old forms of consumption, any more than it can adapt itself to the old forms of political organization.

The wage system arises out of the individual ownership of the land and the instruments of labour. It was the necessary condition for the development of capitalist production, and will perish with it, in spite of the attempt to disguise it as 'profit-sharing'. The common possession of the instruments of labour must necessarily bring with it the enjoyment in common of the fruits of common labour.

We hold further that communism is not only desirable, but that existing societies, founded on individualism, *are inevitably impelled in the direction of communism.* The development of individualism during the last three centuries is explained by the efforts of the individual to protect himself from the tryanny of capital and of the state. For a time he imagined, and those who expressed his thought for him declared, that he could free himself entirely from the state and from society. 'By means of money,' he said, 'I can buy all that I need.' But the individual was on a wrong track, and modern history has taught him to recognize that, without the help of all, he can do nothing, although his strongboxes are full of gold.

In fact, along with this current of individualism, we find in all modern history a tendency, on the one hand to retain all that remains of the partial communism of antiquity, and, on the other, to establish the communist principle in the thousand developments of modern life.

As soon as the communes of the tenth, eleventh and twelfth centuries had succeeded in emancipating themselves from their lords, ecclesiastical or lay, their communal labour and communal consumption began to extend and develop rapidly. The township – and not private persons – freighted ships and equipped expeditions, for the export of their manufacture, and the benefit arising from the foreign trade did not accrue to individuals, but was shared by all. At the outset, the townships also bought provisions for all their citizens. Traces of these institutions have lingered on into the nineteenth century, and the people piously cherish the memory of them in their legends.

All that has disappeared. But the rural township still struggles to preserve the last traces of this communism, and it succeeds – except when the state throws its heavy sword into the balance.

Meanwhile new organizations, based on the same principle – *to every man according to his needs* – spring up under a thousand different forms; for without a certain leaven of communism the present societies could not exist. In spite of the narrowly egoistic turn given to men's minds by the commercial system, the tendency towards communism is constantly appearing, and it influences our activities in a variety of ways.

The bridges, for the use of which a toll was levied in the old days, have become public property and are free to all; so are the high roads, except in the East, where a toll is still exacted from the traveller for every mile of his journey. Museums, free libraries, free schools, free meals for children; parks and gardens open to all; streets paved and lighted, free to all; water supplied to every house without measure or stint – all such arrangements are founded on the principle: 'Take what you need.'

The tramways and railways have already introduced monthly and annual season tickets, without limiting the number of journeys taken; and two nations, Hungary and Russia, have introduced on their railways the zone system, which permits the holder to travel five hundred or eight hundred miles for the same price. It is but a short step from that to a uniform charge, such as already prevails in the postal service. In all these innovations, and in a thousand others, the tendency is not to measure the individual consumption. One man wants to travel eight hundred miles, another five hundred. These are personal requirements. There is no sufficient reason why one should pay twice as much as the other because his need is twice as great. Such are the signs which appear even now in our individualist societies.

Moreover, there is a tendency, though still a feeble one, to consider the needs of the individual, irrespective of his past or possible services to the community. We are beginning to think of society as a whole, each part of which is so intimately bound up with the others that a service rendered to one is a service rendered to all.

When you go into a public library – not indeed the National Library of Paris, but, say, into the British Museum or the Berlin Library – the librarian does not ask what services you have rendered to society before giving you the book, or the fifty books, which you require; he even comes to your assistance if you do not know how to manage the catalogue. By means of uniform credentials – and very often a contribution of work is preferred – the scientific society opens its museums, its gardens, its library, its laboratories and its annual conversaziones to each of its members, whether he be a Darwin or a simple amateur.

At St Petersburg, if you are elaborating an invention, you go into a special laboratory, where you are given a place, a carpenter's bench, a turning lathe, all the necessary tools and scientific instruments, provided only you know how to use them; and you are allowed to work there as long as you please. There are the tools; interest others in your idea; join with fellow workers skilled in various crafts, or work alone if you prefer it. Invent a flying machine, or invent nothing – that is your own affair. You are pursuing an idea – that is enough.

In the same way, those who man the lifeboat do not ask credentials from the crew of a sinking ship; they launch their boat, risk their lives in the raging waves, and sometimes perish, all to save men whom they do not even know. And what need to know them? 'They are human beings, and they need our aid – that is enough, that establishes their right – To the rescue!'

Thus we find a tendency, eminently communistic, springing up on all sides, and in various guises, in the very heart of theoretically individualist societies.

Suppose that one of our great cities, so egotistic in ordinary times, were visited tomorrow by some calamity – a siege, for instance – that same selfish city would decide that the first needs to satisfy were those of the children and the aged. Without asking what services they had rendered, or were likely to render to society, it would first of all feed them. Then the combatants would be cared for, irrespective of the courage or the intelligence which each had displayed, and thousands of men and women would outvie each other in unselfish devotion to the wounded.

This tendency exists, and is felt as soon as the most pressing needs of each are satisfied, and in proportion as the productive power of the race increases. It becomes an active force every time a great idea comes to oust the mean preoccupations of everyday life.

How can we doubt, then, that when the instruments of production are placed at the service of all, when business is conducted on communist principles, when labour, having recovered its place of honour in society, produces much more than is necessary to all – how can we doubt that this force (already so powerful) will enlarge its sphere of action till it becomes the ruling principle of social life?

Following these indications, and considering further the practical side of expropriation, of which we shall speak in the following chapters, we are convinced that our first obligation, when the revolution shall have broken the power upholding the present system, will be to realize communism without delay.

But ours is neither the communism of Fourier and the phalansterians, nor of the German state socialists. It is anarchist communism, communism without government – the communism of the free. It is the synthesis of the two ideals pursued by humanity throughout the ages – economic and political liberty.

II

In taking 'anarchy' for our ideal of political organization we are only giving expression to another marked tendency of human progress. Whenever European societies have developed up to a certain point, they have shaken off the yoke of authority and substituted a system founded more or less on the principles of individual liberty. And history shows us that these periods of partial or general revolution, when the old governments were overthrown, were also periods of sudden progress in both the economic and the intellectual field. So it was after the enfranchisement of the communes, whose monuments, produced by the free labour of the guilds, have never been surpassed; so it was after the great peasant uprising which brought about the Reformation and imperilled the papacy; and so it was again with the society, free for a brief space, which was created on the other side of the Atlantic by the malcontents from the Old World.

And, if we observe the present development of civilized nations, we see, most unmistakably, a movement ever more and more marked tending to limit the sphere of action of the government, and to allow more and more liberty to the individual. This evolution is going on before our eyes, though cumbered by the ruins and rubbish of old institutions and old superstitions. Like all evolutions, it only awaits a revolution to overthrow the old obstacles which block the way, that it may find free scope in a regenerated society.

After having striven long in vain to solve the insoluble problem – the problem of constructing a government 'which will constrain the individual to obedience without itself ceasing to be the servant of society', men at last attempt to free themselves from every form of government and to satisfy their need for organization by free contracts between individuals and groups pursuing the same aim. The independence of each small territorial unit becomes a pressing need; mutual agreement replaces law in order to regulate individual interests in view of a common object – very often disregarding the frontiers of the present states.

All that was once looked on as a function of the government is today called in question. Things are arranged more easily and more satisfactorily without the intervention of the state. And in studying the progress made in this direction, we are led to conclude that the tendency of the human race is to reduce government interference to zero; in fact, to abolish the state, the personification of injustice, oppression and monopoly.

We can already catch glimpses of a world in which the bonds which bind the individual are no longer laws, but social habits – the result of the need felt by each one of us to seek the support, the co-operation, the sympathy of his neighbours.

Assuredly the idea of a society without a state will give rise to at least as many objections as the political economy of a society without private capital. We have all been brought up from our childhood to regard the state as a sort of providence; all our education, the Roman history we learned at school, the Byzantine code which we studied later under the name of Roman law, and the various sciences taught at the universities, accustom us to believe in government and in the virtues of the state providential.

To maintain this superstition whole systems of philosophy have been elaborated and taught; all politics are based on this principle; and each politician, whatever his colours, comes forward and says to the people, 'Give my party the power; we can and we will free you from the miseries which press so heavily upon you.'

From the cradle to the grave all our actions are guided by this principle. Open any book on sociology or jurisprudence, and you will find there the government, its organization, its acts, filling so large a place that we come to believe that there is nothing outside the government and the world of statesmen.

The press teaches us the same in every conceivable way. Whole columns are devoted to parliamentary debates and to political intrigues; while the vast everyday life of a nation appears only in the columns given to economic subjects, or in the pages devoted to reports of police and law cases. And when you read the newspapers, you hardly think of the incalculable number of beings – all humanity, so to say – who grow up and die, who know sorrow, who work and consume, think and create outside the few encumbering personages who have been so magnified that humanity is hidden by their shadows, enlarged by our ignorance.

And yet as soon as we pass from printed matter to life itself, as soon as we throw a glance at society, we are struck by the infinitesimal part played by the government. Balzac already remarked how millions of peasants spend the whole of their lives without knowing anything about the state, save the heavy taxes they are compelled to pay. Every day millions of transactions are made without government intervention, and the greatest of them – those of commerce and of the Exchange – are carried on in such a way that the government could not be appealed to if one of the contracting parties had the intention of not fulfilling his agreement. Should you speak to a man who understands commerce, he will tell you that the everyday business transacted by merchants would be absolutely impossible were it not based on mutual confidence. The habit of keeping his word, the desire not to lose his credit, amply suffice to maintain this relative honesty. The man who does not feel the slightest remorse when poisoning his customers with noxious drugs covered with pompous labels, thinks he is in honour bound to keep his engagements. But if this relative morality has developed under present conditions, when enrichment is the only incentive and the only aim, can we doubt its rapid progress when appropriation of the fruits of others' labour will no longer be the basis of society?

Another striking fact, which especially characterizes our generation, speaks still more in favour of our ideas. It is the continual extension of the field of enterprise due to private initiative, and the prodigious development of free organizations of all kinds. We shall discuss this more at length in the chapter devoted to *'Free Agreement'*. Suffice it to mention that the facts are so numerous and so customary that they are the essence of the second half of the nineteenth century, even though political and socialist writers ignore them, always preferring to talk to us about the functions of the government.

These organizations, free and infinitely varied, are so natural an outcome of our civilization; they expand so rapidly and federate with so much ease; they are so necessary a result of the continual growth of the needs of civilized man; and lastly, they so advantageously replace governmental interference, that we must recognize in them a factor of growing importance in the life of societies. If they do not yet spread over the whole of the manifestations of life, it is that they find an insurmountable obstacle in the poverty of the worker, in the divisions of present society, in the private appropriation of capital, and in the state. Abolish these obstacles, and you will see them covering the immense field of civilized man's activity.

The history of the last fifty years furnishes a living proof that representative government is impotent to discharge all the functions we have sought to assign to it. In days to come the nineteenth century will be quoted as having witnessed the failure of parliamentarianism.

This impotence is becoming so evident to all; the faults of parliamentarianism, and the inherent vices of the representative principle, are so self-evident that the few thinkers who have made a critical study of them (J. S. Mill, Leverdays) did but give literary form to the popular dissatisfaction. It is not difficult, indeed, to see the absurdity of naming a few men and saying to them, 'Make laws regulating all our spheres of activity, although not one of you knows anything about them!'

We are beginning to see that government by majorities means abandoning all the affairs of the country to the tide-waiters who make up the majorities in the House and in election committees; to those, in a word, who have no opinion of their own.

Mankind is seeking and already finding new issues. The International Postal Union, the railway unions, and the learned societies give us examples of solutions based on free agreement in place and stead of law.

Today, when groups scattered far and wide wish to organize themselves for some object or other, they no longer elect an international parliament of Jacks-of-all-trades. They proceed in a different way. Where it is not possible to meet directly or come to an agreement by correspondence, delegates versed in the question at issue are sent, and they are told: 'Endeavour to come to an agreement on such or such a question, and then return, not with a law in your pocket, but with a proposition of agreement which we may or may not accept.'

Such is the method of the great industrial companies, the learned societies and numerous associations of every description, which already cover Europe and the United States. And such will be the method of a free society. A society founded on serfdom is in

keeping with absolute monarchy; a society based on the wage system
and the exploitation of the masses by the capitalists finds its political
expression in parliamentarianism. But a free society, regaining possession of the common inheritance, must seek, in free groups and
free federations of groups, a new organization, in harmony with
the new economic phase of history.

Every economic phase has a political phase corresponding to it,
and it would be impossible to touch private property unless a new
mode of political life be found at the same time.

CHAPTER IV

Expropriation

I

It is told of Rothschild that, seeing his fortune threatened by the revolution of 1848, he hit upon the following stratagem: 'I am quite willing to admit', said he, 'that my fortune has been accumulated at the expense of others; but if it were divided tomorrow among the millions of Europe, the share of each would only amount to four shillings. Very well, then, I undertake to render to each his four shillings if he asks me for it.'

Having given due publicity to his promise, our millionaire proceeded as usual to stroll quietly through the streets of Frankfort. Three or four passers-by asked for their four shillings, which he disbursed with a sardonic smile. His stratagem succeeded, and the family of the millionaire is still in possession of its wealth.

It is in much the same fashion that the shrewd heads among the middle classes reason when they say, 'Ah, expropriation! I know what that means. You take all the overcoats and lay them in a heap, and everyone is free to help himself and fight for the best.'

But such jests are irrelevant as well as flippant. What we want is not a redistribution of overcoats, although it must be said that even in such a case, the shivering folk would see advantage in it. Nor do we want to divide up the wealth of the Rothschilds. What we do want is so to arrange things that every human being born into the world shall be ensured the opportunity, in the first instance of learning some useful occupation, and of becoming skilled in it; and next, that he shall be free to work at his trade without asking leave of master or owner, and without handing over to landlord or capitalist the lion's share of what he produces. As to the wealth held by the Rothschilds or the Vanderbilts, it will serve us to organize our system of communal production.

The day when the labourer may till the ground without paying away half of what he produces, the day when the machines necessary to prepare the soil for rich harvests are at the free disposal of the cultivators, the day when the worker in the factory produces for the community and not the monopolist – that day will see the workers clothed and fed, and there will be no more Rothschilds or other exploiters.

No one will then have to sell his working power for a wage that only represents a fraction of what he produces.

'So far so good', say our critics, 'but you will have Rothschilds coming in from outside. How are you to prevent a person from amassing millions in China, and then settling amongst you? How are you going to prevent such a one from surrounding himself with lackeys and wage-slaves – from exploiting them and enriching himself at their expense?

'You cannot bring about a revolution all over the world at the same time. Well, then – are you going to establish custom-houses on your frontiers to search all who enter your country and confiscate the money they bring with them? – Anarchist policemen firing on travellers would be a fine spectacle!'

But at the root of this argument there is a great error. Those who propound it have never paused to inquire whence come the fortunes of the rich. A little thought would, however, suffice to show them that these fortunes have their beginnings in the poverty of the poor. When there are no longer any destitute, there will no longer be any rich to exploit them.

Let us glance for a moment at the Middle Ages, when great fortunes began to spring up.

A feudal baron seizes on a fertile valley. But as long as the fertile valley is empty of folk our baron is not rich. His land brings him in nothing; he might as well possess a property in the moon.

What does our baron do to enrich himself? He looks out for peasants – for poor peasants!

If every peasant-farmer had a piece of land, free from rent and taxes, if he had in addition the tools and the stock necessary for farm labour – Who would plough the lands of the baron? Everyone would look after his own. But there are thousands of destitute persons ruined by wars, or drought, or pestilence. They have neither horse nor plough. (Iron was very costly in the Middle Ages, and a draught-horse still more so.)

All these destitute creatures are trying to better their condition. One day they see on the road at the confines of our baron's estate a notice-board indicating by certain signs adapted to their comprehension that the labourer who is willing to settle on this estate will receive the tools and materials to build his cottage and sow his fields, and a portion of land rent free for a certain number of years. The number of years is represented by so many crosses on the signboard, and the peasant understands the meaning of these crosses.

So the poor wretches come to settle on the baron's lands. They make roads, drain the marshes, build villages. In nine or ten years the baron begins to tax them. Five years later he increases the rent. Then he doubles it, and the peasant accepts these new conditions because he cannot find better ones elsewhere. Little by little, with the aid of laws made by the barons, the poverty of the peasant becomes the source of the landlord's wealth. And it is not only the lord of the manor who preys upon him. A whole host of usurers swoop down upon the villages, multiplying as the wretchedness of the peasants increases. That is how these things happened in the Middle Ages. And today is it not still the same thing? If there were free lands which the peasant could cultivate if he pleased, would he pay £50 to some 'shabble of a duke'[b] for condescending to sell him a scrap? Would he burden himself with a lease which absorbed a third of the produce? Would he – on the *métayer* system – consent to give the half of his harvest to the landowner?

But he has nothing. So he will accept any conditions, if only he can keep body and soul together, while he tills the soil and enriches the landlord.

So in the nineteenth century, just as in the Middle Ages, the poverty of the peasant is a source of wealth to the landed proprietor.

---

[b] 'Shabble of a duke' is an expression coined by Carlyle; it is a somewhat free rendering of Kropotkin's 'Monsieur le Vicomte', but I think it expresses his meaning. – *Trans.*

II

The landlord owes his riches to the poverty of the peasants, and the wealth of the capitalist comes from the same source.

Take the case of a citizen of the middle class, who somehow or other finds himself in possession of £20,000. He could, of course, spend his money at the rate of £2,000 a year, a mere bagatelle in these days of fantastic, senseless luxury. But then he would have nothing left at the end of ten years. So, being a 'practical person', he prefers to keep his fortune intact, and win for himself a snug little annual income as well.

This is very easy in our society, for the good reason that the towns and villages swarm with workers who have not the wherewithal to live for a month, or even a fortnight. So our worthy citizen starts a factory. The banks hasten to lend him another £20,000, especially if he has a reputation for 'business ability'; and with this round sum he can command the labour of five hundred hands.

If all the men and women in the countryside had their daily bread assured, and their daily needs already satisfied, who would work for our capitalist at a wage of half a crown a day, while the commodities one produces in a day sell in the market for a crown or more?

Unhappily – we know it all too well – the poor quarters of our towns and the neighbouring villages are full of needy wretches, whose children clamour for bread. So, before the factory is well finished, the workers hasten to offer themselves. Where a hundred are required three hundred besiege the doors, and from the time his mill is started, the owner, if he only has average business capacities, will clear £40 a year out of each mill-hand he employs.

He is thus able to lay by a snug little fortune; and if he chooses a lucrative trade, and has 'business talents', he will soon increase his income by doubling the number of the men he exploits.

So he becomes a personage of importance. He can afford to give dinners to other personages – to the local magnates, the civic, legal and political dignitaries. With his money he can 'marry money'; by and by he may pick and choose places for his children, and later on perhaps get something good from the government – a contract for the army or for the police. His gold breeds gold; till at last a war, or even a rumour of war, or a speculation on the Stock Exchange, gives him his great opportunity.

Expropriation

Nine-tenths of the great fortunes made in the United States are (as Henry George has shown in his *Social Problems*) the result of knavery on a large scale, assisted by the state. In Europe, nine-tenths of the fortunes made in our monarchies and republics have the same origin. There are not two ways of becoming a millionaire.

This is the secret of wealth: find the starving and destitute, pay them half a crown, and make them produce five shillings' worth in the day, amass a fortune by these means, and then increase it by some lucky speculation, made with the help of the state.

Need we go on to speak of small fortunes attributed by the economists to forethought and frugality, when we know that mere saving in itself brings in nothing, so long as the pence saved are not used to exploit the famishing?

Take a shoemaker, for instance. Grant that his work is well paid, that he has plenty of custom, and that by dint of strict frugality he contrives to lay by from eighteen pence to two shillings a day, perhaps two pounds a month.

Grant that our shoemaker is never ill, that he does not half starve himself, in spite of his passion for economy; that he does not marry or that he has no children; that he does not die of consumption; suppose anything and everything you please!

Well, at the age of 50 he will not have scraped together £800; and he will not have enough to live on during his old age, when he is past work. Assuredly this is not how fortunes are made. But suppose our shoemaker, as soon as he has laid by a few pence, thriftily conveys them to the savings bank, and that the savings bank lends them to the capitalist who is just about to 'employ labour', i.e., to exploit the poor. Then our shoemaker takes an apprentice, the child of some poor wretch, who will think himself lucky if in five years' time his son has learned the trade and is able to earn his living.

Meanwhile our shoemaker does not lose by him, and if trade is brisk he soon takes a second, and then a third apprentice. By and by he will take two or three working men – poor wretches, thankful to receive half a crown a day for work that is worth five shillings, and if our shoemaker is 'in luck', that is to say, if he is keen enough and mean enough, his working men and apprentices will bring him in nearly one pound a day, over and above the product of his own toil. He can then enlarge his business. He will gradually

45

become rich, and no longer have any need to stint himself in the necessaries of life. He will leave a snug little fortune to his son.

That is what people call 'being economical and having frugal, temperate habits'. At bottom it is nothing more nor less than grinding the face of the poor.

Commerce seems an exception to this rule. 'Such a man', we are told, 'buys tea in China, brings it to France, and realizes a profit of 30 per cent on his original outlay. He has exploited nobody.'

Nevertheless, the case is quite similar. If our merchant had carried his bales on his back, well and good! In early medieval times that was exactly how foreign trade was conducted, and so no one reached such giddy heights of fortune as in our days. Very few and very hardly earned were the gold coins which the medieval merchant gained from a long and dangerous voyage. It was less the love of money than the thirst of travel and adventure that inspired his undertakings.

Nowadays the method is simpler. A merchant who has some capital need not stir from his desk to become wealthy. He telegraphs to an agent telling him to buy a hundred tons of tea; he freights a ship, and in a few weeks, in three months if it is a sailing ship, the vessel brings him his cargo. He does not even take the risks of the voyage, for his tea and his vessel are insured, and if he has expended four thousand pounds he will receive more than five or six thousand; that is to say, if he has not attempted to speculate in some novel commodities, in which case he runs a chance of either doubling his fortune or losing it altogether.

Now, how could he find men willing to cross the sea, to travel to China and back, to endure hardship and slavish toil and to risk their lives for a miserable pittance? How could he find dock labourers willing to load and unload his ships for 'starvation wages'? How? Because they are needy and starving. Go to the seaports, visit the cook-shops and taverns on the quays, and look at these men who have come to hire themselves, crowding round the dock gates, which they besiege from early dawn, hoping to be allowed to work on the vessels. Look at these sailors, happy to be hired for a long voyage, after weeks and months of waiting. All their lives long they have gone to the sea in ships, and they will sail in others still, until they have perished in the waves.

Enter their homes, look at their wives and children in rags, living one knows not how till the father's return, and you will have the answer to the question.

Multiply examples, choose them where you will, consider the origin of all fortunes, large or small, whether arising out of commerce, finance, manufactures or the land. Everywhere you will find that the wealth of the wealthy springs from the poverty of the poor. This is why an anarchist society need not fear the advent of a Rothschild who would settle in its midst. If every member of the community knows that after a few hours of productive toil he will have a right to all the pleasures that civilization procures, and to those deeper sources of enjoyment which art and science offer to all who seek them, he will not sell his strength for a starvation wage. No one will volunteer to work for the enrichment of your Rothschild. His golden guineas will be only so many pieces of metal – useful for various purposes, but incapable of breeding more.

In answering the above objection we have at the same time indicated the scope of expropriation. It must apply to everything that enables any man – be he financier, mill-owner, or landlord – to appropriate the product of others' toil. Our formula is simple and comprehensive.

We do not want to rob anyone of his coat, but we wish to give to the workers all those things the lack of which makes them fall an easy prey to the exploiter, and we will do our utmost that none shall lack aught, that not a single man shall be forced to sell the strength of his right arm to obtain a bare subsistence for himself and his babes. This is what we mean when we talk of expropriation; this will be our duty during the revolution, for whose coming we look, not two hundred years hence, but soon, very soon.

III

The ideas of anarchism in general and of expropriation in particular find much more sympathy than we are apt to imagine among men of independent character, and those for whom idleness is not the supreme ideal. 'Still', our friends often warn us, 'take care you do not go too far! Humanity cannot be changed in a day, so do not be in too great a hurry with your schemes of expropriation and anarchy, or you will be in danger of achieving no permanent result.'

Now, what we fear with regard to expropriation is exactly the contrary. We are afraid of not going far enough, of carrying out expropriation on too small a scale to be lasting. We would not have the revolutionary impulse arrested in mid-career, to exhaust itself in half measures, which would content no one, and while producing a tremendous confusion in society, and stopping its customary activities, would have no vital power – would merely spread general discontent and inevitably prepare the way for the triumph of reaction.

There are, in fact, in a modern state established relations which it is practically impossible to modify if one attacks them only in detail. There are wheels within wheels in our economic organization – the machinery is so complex and interdependent that no one part can be modified without disturbing the whole. This becomes clear as soon as an attempt is made to expropriate anything.

Let us suppose that in a certain country a limited form of expropriation is effected. For example, that, as it has been suggested more than once, only the property of the great landlords is socialized, whilst the factories are left untouched; or that, in a certain city, house property is taken over by the commune, but everything else is left to private ownership; or that, in some manufacturing centre, the factories are communalized, but the land is not interfered with.

The same result would follow in each case – a terrible shattering of the industrial system, without the means of reorganizing it on new lines. Industry and finance would be at a deadlock, yet a return to the first principles of justice would not have been achieved, and society would find itself powerless to construct a harmonious whole.

If agriculture were freed from great landowners, while industry still remained the bond-slave of the capitalist, the merchant and the banker, nothing would be accomplished. The peasant suffers today not only in having to pay rent to the landlord; he is oppressed on all hands by existing conditions. He is exploited by the tradesman, who makes him pay half a crown for a spade which, measured by the labour spent on it, is not worth more than sixpence. He is taxed by the state, which cannot do without its formidable hierarchy of officials, and finds it necessary to maintain an expensive army, because the traders of all nations are perpetually fighting for the markets, and any day a little quarrel arising from the exploitation of some part of Asia or Africa may result in war.

Then again the peasant suffers from the depopulation of country places: the young people are attracted to the large manufacturing towns by the bait of high wages paid temporarily by the producers of articles of luxury, or by the attractions of a more stirring life. The artificial protection of industry, the industrial exploitation of foreign countries, the prevalence of stock-jobbing, the difficulty of improving the soil and the machinery of production – all these agencies combine nowadays to work against agriculture, which is burdened not only by rent, but by the whole complex of conditions in a society based on exploitation. Thus, even if the expropriation of land were accomplished, and everyone were free to till the soil and cultivate it to the best advantage, without paying rent, agriculture, even though it should enjoy – which can by no means be taken for granted – a momentary prosperity, would soon fall back into the slough in which it finds itself today. The whole thing would have to be begun over again, with increased difficulties.

The same holds true of industry. Take the converse case: instead of turning the agricultural labourers into peasant-proprietors, make over the factories to those who work in them. Abolish the master-manufacturers, but leave the landlord his land, the banker his money, the merchant his Exchange; maintain the swarm of idlers who live on the toil of the workmen, the thousand and one middlemen, the state with its numberless officials – and industry would come to a standstill. Finding no purchasers in the mass of peasants who would remain poor; not possessing the raw material, and unable to export their produce, partly on account of the stoppage of trade, and still more so because industries spread all over the world, the manufacturers would feel unable to struggle, and thousands of workers would be thrown upon the streets. These starving crowds would be ready and willing to submit to the first schemer who came to exploit them; they would even consent to return to the old slavery, under promise of guaranteed work.

Or, finally, suppose you oust the landowners, and hand over the mills and factories to the worker, without interfering with the swarm of middlemen who drain the product of our manufacturers, and speculate in corn and flour, meat and groceries, in our great centres of commerce. Then, as soon as the exchange of produce is slackened; as soon as the great cities are left without bread, while the great manufacturing centres find no buyers for the articles of luxury they produce, the counter-revolution is bound to take place, and it would come, treading upon the slain, sweeping the towns and villages with shot and shell; indulging in orgies of proscriptions and deportations, such as were seen in France in 1815, 1848 and 1871.

All is interdependent in a civilized society; it is impossible to reform any one thing without altering the whole. Therefore, on the day a nation will strike at private property, under any one of its forms, territorial or industrial, it will be obliged to attack them all. The very success of the revolution will impose it.

Besides, even if it were desired, it would be impossible to confine the change to a partial expropriation. Once the principle of the 'divine right of property' is shaken, no amount of theorizing will prevent its overthrow, here by the slaves of the field, there by the slaves of the machine.

If a great town, Paris for example, were to confine itself to taking possession of the dwelling-houses or the factories, it would be forced also to deny the right of the bankers to levy upon the commune a tax amounting to £2,000,000, in the form of interest for former loans. The great city would be obliged to put itself in touch with the rural districts, and its influence would inevitably urge the peasants to free themselves from the landowner. It would be necessary to communalize the railways, that the citizens might get food and work, and lastly, to prevent the waste of supplies; and to guard against the trusts of corn-speculators, like those to whom the Paris Commune of 1793 fell a prey, it would have to place in the hands of the city the work of stocking its warehouses with commodities, and apportioning the produce.

Some socialists still seek, however, to establish a distinction. 'Of course', they say, 'the soil, the mines, the mills and manufactures must be expropriated, these are the instruments of production, and it is right we should consider them public property. But articles of consumption – food, clothes and dwellings – should remain private property.'

Popular common sense has got the better of this subtle distinction. We are not savages who can live in the woods, without other shelter than the branches. The civilized man needs a roof, a room, a hearth and a bed. It is true that the bed, the room and the house is a home of idleness for the non-producer. But for the worker, a room, properly heated and lighted, is as much an instrument of production as the tool or the machine. It is the place where the nerves and sinews gather strength for the work of the morrow. The rest of the workman is the daily repairing of the machine.

The same argument applies even more obviously to food. The so-called economists, who make the just-mentioned distinction, would hardly deny that the coal burnt in a machine is as necessary to production as the raw material itself. How then can food, without which the human machine could do no work, be excluded from the list of things indispensable to the producer? Can this be a relic of religious metaphysics? The rich man's feast is indeed a matter of luxury, but the food of the worker is just as much a part of production as the fuel burnt by the steam-engine.

The same with clothing. We are not New Guinea savages. And if the dainty gowns of our ladies must rank as objects of luxury, there is nevertheless a certain quantity of linen, cotton and woollen stuff which is a necessity of life to the producer. The shirt and trousers in which he goes to his work, the jacket he slips on after the day's toil is over, are as necessary to him as the hammer to the anvil.

Whether we like it or not, this is what the people mean by a revolution. As soon as they have made a clean sweep of the government, they will seek first of all to ensure to themselves decent dwellings and sufficient food and clothes – free of capitalist rent.

And the people will be right. The methods of the people will be much more in accordance with science than those of the economists who draw so many distinctions between instruments of production and articles of consumption. The people understand that this is just the point where the revolution ought to begin; and they will lay the foundations of the only economic science worthy the name – a science which might be called: 'The Study of the Needs of Humanity, and of the Economic Means to Satisfy Them.'

CHAPTER V

Food

I

If the coming revolution is to be a social revolution, it will be distinguished from all former uprisings not only by its aim, but also by its methods. To attain a new end, new means are required.

The three great popular movements which we have seen in France during the last hundred years differ from each other in many ways, but they have one common feature.

In each case the people strove to overturn the old regime, and spent their heart's blood for the cause. Then, after having borne the brunt of the battle, they sank again into obscurity. A government, composed of men more or less honest, was formed and undertook to organize a new regime: the Republic in 1793, Labour in 1848, the Free Commune in 1871. Imbued with Jacobin ideas, the government occupied itself first of all with political questions, such as the reorganization of the machinery of government, the purifying of the administration, the separation of church and state, civic liberty, and such matters. It is true the workmen's clubs kept an eye on the members of the new government, and often imposed their ideas on them. But even in these clubs, whether the leaders belonged to the middle or to the working classes, it was always middle-class ideas which prevailed. They discussed various political questions at great length, but forgot to discuss the question of bread.

Great ideas sprang up at such times, ideas that have moved the world; words were spoken which still stir our hearts, at the interval of more than a century. But the people were starving in the slums.

From the very commencement of the Revolution industry inevitably came to a stop – the circulation of produce was checked, and capital concealed itself. The master – the employer – had nothing to fear at such times, he battened on his dividends, if indeed he did not speculate on the wretchedness around; but the wage-earner was reduced to live from hand to mouth. Want knocked at the door.

Famine was abroad in the land – such famine as had hardly been seen under the old regime.

'The Girondists are starving us!' was the cry in the workmen's quarters in 1793, and thereupon the Girondists were guillotined, and full powers were given to 'the Mountain' and to the Commune. The Commune indeed concerned itself with the question of bread, and made heroic efforts to feed Paris. At Lyons, Fouché and Collot d'Herbois established city granaries, but the sums spent on filling them were woefully insufficient. The town councils made great efforts to procure corn; the bakers who hoarded flour were hanged – and still the people lacked bread.

Then they turned on the royalist conspirators and laid the blame at their door. They guillotined a dozen or fifteen a day – servants and duchesses alike, especially servants, for the duchesses had gone to Koblenz. But if they had guillotined a hundred dukes and viscounts every day, it would have been equally hopeless.

The want only grew. For the wage-earner cannot live without his wage, and the wage was not forthcoming. What difference could a thousand corpses more or less make to him?

Then the people began to grow weary. 'So much for your vaunted Revolution! You are more wretched than ever before,' whispered the reactionary in the ears of the worker. And little by little the rich took courage, emerged from their hiding-places, and flaunted their luxury in the face of the starving multitude. They dressed up like scented fops and said to the workers: 'Come, enough of this foolery! What have you gained by your Revolution?'

And, sick at heart, his patience at an end, the revolutionary had at last to admit to himself that the cause was lost once more. He retreated into his hovel and awaited the worst.

Then reaction proudly asserted itself, and accomplished a counter-revolutionary stroke. The Revolution dead, nothing remained but to trample its corpse under foot.

The White Terror began. Blood flowed like water, the guillotine was never idle, the prisons were crowded, while the pageant of rank and fashion resumed its old course, and went on as merrily as before.

This picture is typical of all our revolutions. In 1848 the workers of Paris placed 'three months of starvation' at the service of the Republic, and then, having reached the limit of their powers, they made, in June, one last desperate effort – an effort which was drowned in blood. In 1871 the Commune perished for lack of combatants. It had taken measures for the separation of church and state, but it neglected, alas, until too late, to take measures for providing the people with bread. And so it came to pass in Paris that *élégantes* and fine gentlemen could spurn the confederates, and bid them go sell their lives for a miserable pittance, and leave their 'betters' to feast at their ease in fashionable restaurants.

At last the Commune saw its mistake, and opened communal kitchens. But it was too late. Its days were already numbered, and the troops of Versailles were on the ramparts.

'Bread, it is bread that the revolution needs!'

Let others spend their time in issuing pompous proclamations, in decorating themselves lavishly with official gold lace, and in talking about political liberty! . . .

Be it ours to see, from the first day of the revolution to the last, in all the provinces fighting for freedom, that there is not a single man who lacks bread, not a single woman compelled to stand with the wearied crowd outside the bakehouse-door, that haply a coarse loaf may be thrown to her in charity, not a single child pining for want of food.

It has always been the middle-class idea to harangue about 'great principles' – great lies rather!

The idea of the people will be to provide bread for all. And while middle-class citizens, and workmen infested with middle-class ideas admire their own rhetoric in the 'talking shops', and 'practical people' are engaged in endless discussions on forms of government, we, the 'utopian dreamers' – we shall have to consider the question of daily bread.

We have the temerity to declare that all have a right to bread, that there is bread enough for all, and that with this watchword of *Bread for All* the revolution will triumph.

II

That we are utopians is well known. So utopian are we that we go the length of believing that the revolution can and ought to assure shelter, food, and clothes to all – an idea extremely displeasing to middle-class citizens, whatever their party colour, for they are quite alive to the fact that it is not easy to keep the upper hand of a people whose hunger is satisfied.

All the same, we maintain our contention: bread must be found for the people of the revolution, and the question of bread must take precedence of all other questions. If it is settled in the interests of the people, the revolution will be on the right road; for in solving the question of bread we must accept the principle of equality, which will force itself upon us to the exclusion of every other solution.

It is certain that the coming revolution – like in that respect to the revolution of 1848 – will burst upon us in the middle of a great industrial crisis. Things have been seething for half a century now, and can only go from bad to worse. Everything tends that way – new nations entering the lists of international trade and fighting for possession of the world's markets, wars, taxes ever increasing. National debts, the insecurity of the morrow, and huge colonial undertakings in every corner of the globe.

There are millions of unemployed workers in Europe at this moment. It will be still worse when revolution has burst upon us and spread like fire laid to a train of gunpowder. The number of the out-of-works will be doubled as soon as barricades are erected in Europe and the United States. What is to be done to provide these multitudes with bread?

We do not know whether the folk who call themselves 'practical people' have ever asked themselves this question in all its nakedness. But we do know that they wish to maintain the wage system, and we must therefore expect to have 'national workshops' and 'public works' vaunted as a means of giving food to the unemployed.

Because national workshops were opened in 1789 and 1793; because the same means were resorted to in 1848; because Napoleon III succeeded in contenting the Parisian proletariat for eighteen years by giving them public works – which cost Paris today its debt of £80,000,000, and its municipal tax of three or four pounds a head;' because this excellent method of 'taming the beast' was customary in Rome, and even in Egypt four thousand years ago; and lastly, because despots, kings and emperors have always employed the ruse of throwing a scrap of food to the people to gain time to snatch up the whip – it is natural that 'practical' men should extol this method of perpetuating the wage system. What need to rack our brains when we have the time-honoured method of the Pharaohs at our disposal?

Yet should the revolution be so misguided as to start on this path, it would be lost.

In 1848, when the national workshops were opened on 27 February, the unemployed of Paris numbered only 8,000; a fortnight later they had already increased to 49,000. They would soon have been 100,000, without counting those who crowded in from the provinces.

Yet at that time trade and manufacturers in France employed half as many hands as today. And we know that in time of revolution exchange and industry suffer most from the general upheaval. We have only to think, indeed, of the number of workmen whose labour depends directly or indirectly upon export trade, or of the number of hands employed in producing luxuries, whose consumers are the middle-class minority.

A revolution in Europe means, then, the unavoidable stoppage of at least half the factories and workshops. It means millions of workers and their families thrown on the streets. And our 'practical men' would seek to avert this truly terrible situation by means of national relief works; that is to say, by means of new industries created on the spot to give work to the unemployed!

It is evident, as Proudhon had already pointed out more than fifty years ago, that the smallest attack upon property will bring in its train the complete disorganization of the system based upon private enterprise and wage labour. Society itself will be forced to take production in hand, in its entirety, and to reorganize it to meet the needs of the whole people. But this cannot be accomplished in a day, or even in a month; it must take a certain time to reorganize the system of production, and during this time millions of men

' The municipal debt of Paris amounted in 1904 to 2,266,579,100 francs, and the charges for it were 121,000,000 francs.

will be deprived of the means of subsistence. What then is to be done?

There is only one really *practical* solution of the problem – boldly to face the great task which awaits us, and instead of trying to patch up a situation which we ourselves have made untenable, to proceed to reorganize production on a new basis.

Thus the really practical course of action, in our view, would be that the people should take immediate possession of all the food of the insurgent communes, keeping strict account of it all, that none might be wasted, and that by the aid of these accumulated resources everyone might be able to tide over the crisis. During that time an agreement would have to be made with the factory workers, the necessary raw material given them, and the means of subsistence assured to them, while they worked to supply the needs of the agricultural population. For we must not forget that while France weaves silks and satins to deck the wives of German financiers, the Empress of Russia, and the Queen of the Sandwich Islands, and while Paris fashions wonderful trinkets and playthings for rich folk all the world over, two-thirds of the French peasantry have not proper lamps to give them light, or the implements necessary for modern agriculture. Lastly, unproductive land, of which there is plenty, would have to be turned to the best advantage, poor soils enriched, and rich soils, which yet, under the present system, do not yield a quarter, no, nor a tenth of what they might produce, would be submitted to intensive culture, and tilled with as much care as a market garden or a flower plot. It is impossible to imagine any other practical solution of the problem; and, whether we like it or not, sheer force of circumstances will bring it to pass.

III

The most prominent characteristic of our present capitalism is *the wage system*, which in brief amounts to this:

A man, or a group of men, possessing the necessary capital, starts some industrial enterprise; he undertakes to supply the factory or workshops with raw material, to organize production, to pay the employees a fixed wage, and lastly, to pocket the surplus value or profits, under pretext of recouping himself for managing the concern, for running the risks it may involve, and for the fluctuations of price in the market value of the wares.

To preserve this system, those who now monopolize capital would be ready to make certain concessions; to share, for example, a part of the profits with the workers, or rather to establish a 'sliding scale', which would oblige them to raise wages when prices were high; in brief, they would consent to certain sacrifices on condition that they were still allowed to direct industry and to take its first fruits.

Collectivism, as we know, does not abolish the wage system, though it introduces considerable modifications into the existing order of things. It only substitutes the state, that is to say, some form of representative government, national or local, for the individual employer of labour. Under collectivism it is the representatives of the nation, or of the commune, and their deputies and officials who are to have the control of industry. It is they who reserve to themselves the right of employing the surplus of production – in the interests of all. Moreover, collectivism draws a very subtle but very far-reaching distinction between the work of the labourer and of the man who has learned a craft. Unskilled labour in the eyes of the collectivist is *simple* labour, while the work of the craftsman, the mechanic, the engineer, the man of science, etc., is what Marx calls *complex* labour, and is entitled to a higher wage. But labourers and craftsmen, weavers and men of science, are all wage-servants of the state – 'all officials', as was said lately, to gild the pill.

Well, then, the coming revolution could render no greater service to humanity than by making the wage system, in all its forms, an impossibility, and by rendering communism, which is the negation of wage-slavery, the only possible solution.

For even admitting that the collectivist modification of the present system is possible, if introduced gradually during a period of prosperity and peace – though for my part I question its practicability even under such conditions – it would become impossible in a period of revolution, when the need of feeding hungry millions would spring up with the first call to arms. A political revolution can be accomplished without shaking the foundations of industry, but a revolution where the people lay hands upon property will inevitably paralyse exchange and production. The millions of public money flowing into the Treasury would not suffice for paying wages to the millions of out-of-works.

This point cannot be too much insisted upon; the reorganization of industry on a new basis (and we shall presently show how tremendous this problem is) cannot be accomplished in a few days; nor, on the other hand, will the people submit to be half starved for years in order to oblige the theorists who uphold the wage system. To tide over the period of stress they will demand what they have always demanded in such cases – communization of supplies – the giving of rations.

It will be in vain to preach patience. The people will be patient no longer, and if food is not forthcoming they will plunder the bakeries.

Then, if the people are not strong enough to carry all before them, they will be shot down, to give collectivism a fair field for experiment. To this end '*order*' must be maintained at any price – order, discipline, obedience! And as the capitalists will soon realize that when the people are shot down by those who call themselves revolutionists, the revolution itself will become hateful in the eyes of the masses, they will certainly lend their support to the champions of *order* – even though they are collectivists. In such a line of conduct, the capitalists will see a means of hereafter crushing the collectivists in their turn. And if 'order is established' in this fashion, the consequences are easy to foresee. Not content with shooting down the 'marauders', the faction of 'order' will search out the 'ringleaders of the mob'. They will set up again the law courts and reinstate the hangman. The most ardent revolutionists will be sent to the scaffold. It will be 1793 over again.

Do not let us forget how reaction triumphed in the last century. First the 'Hébertists' and 'the madmen' were guillotined – those whom Mignet, with the memory of the struggle fresh upon him, still called 'anarchists'. The Dantonists soon followed them; and when the party of Robespierre had guillotined these revolutionaries, they in their turn had to mount the scaffold; whereupon the people, sick of bloodshed, and seeing the Revolution lost, threw up the sponge, and let the reactionaries do their worst.

If 'order is restored', we say, the Social Democrats will hang the anarchists; the Fabians will hang the Social Democrats, and will in their turn be hanged by the reactionaries; and the revolution will come to an end.

But everything confirms us in the belief that the energy of the people will carry them far enough, and that, when the revolution takes place, the idea of anarchist communism will have gained ground. It is not an artificial idea. The people themselves have breathed it in our ear, and the number of communists is ever increasing, as the impossibility of any other solution becomes more and more evident.

And if the impetus of the people is strong enough, affairs will take a very different turn. Instead of plundering the bakers' shops one day, and starving the next, the people of the insurgent cities will take possession of the warehouses, the cattle markets – in fact of all the provision stores and of all the food to be had. The well-intentioned citizens, men and women both, will form themselves into bands of volunteers and address themselves to the task of making a rough general inventory of the contents of each shop and warehouse.

If such a revolution breaks out in France, namely, in Paris, then in twenty-four hours the commune will know what Paris has not found out yet, in spite of its statistical committees, and what it never did find out during the siege of 1871 – the quantity of provisions it contains. In forty-eight hours millions of copies will be printed of the tables giving a sufficiently exact account of the available food, the places where it is stored, and the means of distribution.

In every block of houses, in every street, in every town ward, groups of volunteers will have been organized, and these commissariat volunteers will find it easy to work in unison and keep in touch with each other. If only the Jacobin bayonets do not get in the way; if only the self-styled 'scientific' theorists do not thrust themselves in to darken counsel! Or rather let them expound their muddle-headed theories as much as they like, provided they have no authority, no power! And that admirable spirit of organization inherent in the people, above all in every social grade of the French nation, but which they have so seldom been allowed to exercise, will initiate, even in so huge a city as Paris, and in the midst of a revolution, an immense guild of free workers, ready to furnish to each and all the necessary food.

Give the people a free hand, and in ten days the food service will be conducted with admirable regularity. Only those who have never seen the people hard at work, only those who have passed their lives buried among documents, can doubt it. Speak of the organizing genius of the 'Great Misunderstood', the people, to those who have seen it in Paris in the days of the barricades, or in London during the great dockers' strike, when half a million of starving folk had to be fed, and they will tell you how superior it is to the official ineptness of Bumbledom.

And even supposing we had to endure a certain amount of discomfort and confusion for a fortnight or a month, surely that would not matter very much. For the mass of the people it would still be an improvement on their former condition; and, besides, in times of revolution one can dine contentedly enough on a bit of bread and cheese while eagerly discussing events.

In any case, a system which springs up spontaneously, under stress of immediate need, will be infinitely preferable to anything invented between four walls by hidebound theorists sitting on any number of committees.

IV

The people of the great towns will be driven by force of circumstances to take possession of all the provisions, beginning with the barest necessaries, and gradually extending communism to other things, in order to satisfy the needs of all the citizens. The sooner it is done the better; the sooner it is done the less misery there will be and the less strife.

But upon what basis must society be organized in order that all may have their due share of food produce? This is the question that meets us at the outset.

We answer that there are no two ways of it. There is only one way in which communism can be established equitably, only one way which satisfies our instincts of justice and is at the same time practical; namely, the system already adopted by the agrarian communes of Europe.

Take for example a peasant commune, no matter where, even in France, where the Jacobins have done their best to destroy all communal usage. If the commune possesses woods and copses, then, so long as there is plenty of wood for all, everyone can take as much as he wants, without other let or hindrance than the public opinion of his neighbours. As to the timber-trees, which are always scarce, they have to be carefully apportioned.

The same with the communal pasture-land; while there is enough and to spare, no limit is put to what the cattle of each homestead may consume, nor to the number of beasts grazing upon the pastures. Grazing grounds are not divided, nor is fodder doled out, unless there is scarcity. All the Swiss communes, and scores of thousands in France and Germany, wherever there is communal pasture land, practise this system.

And in the countries of Eastern Europe, where there are great forests and no scarcity of land, you find the peasants felling the trees as they need them, and cultivating as much of the soil as they require, without any thought of limiting each man's share of timber or of land. But the timber will be allowanced, and the land parcelled out, to each household according to its needs, as soon as either becomes scarce, as is already the case in Russia.

In a word, the system is this: no stint or limit to what the community possesses in abundance, but equal sharing and dividing of those commodities which are scarce or apt to run short. Of the 350 millions who inhabit Europe, 200 millions still follow this system of natural communism.

It is a fact worth remarking that the same system prevails in the great towns in the distribution of one commodity at least, which is found in abundance, the water supplied to each house.

As long as there is no fear of the supply running short, no water company thinks of checking the consumption of water in each house. Take what you please! But during the great droughts, if there is any fear of the supply failing, the water companies know that all they have to do is to make known the fact, by means of a short advertisement in the papers, and the citizens will reduce their consumption of water and not let it run to waste.

But if water were actually scarce, what would be done? Recourse would be had to a system of rations. Such a measure is so natural, so inherent in common sense, that Paris twice asked to be put on rations during the two sieges which it underwent in 1871.

Is it necessary to go into details, to prepare tables, showing how the distribution of rations may work, to prove that it is just and

equitable, infinitely more just and equitable than the existing state
of things? All these tables and details will not serve to convince
those of the middle classes, nor, alas, those of the workers tainted
with middle-class prejudices, who regard the people as a mob of
savages ready to fall upon and devour each other, as soon as the
government ceases to direct affairs. But those only who have never
seen the people resolve and act on their own initiative could doubt
for a moment that if the masses were masters of the situation,
they would distribute rations to each and all in strictest accordance
with justice and equity.

If you were to give utterance, in any gathering of people, to the
opinion that delicacies – game and such-like – should be reserved
for the fastidious palates of aristocratic idlers, and black bread
given to the sick in the hospitals, you would be hissed. But say at
the same gathering, preach at the street corners and in the market-
places, that the most tempting delicacies ought to be kept for the
sick and feeble – especially for the sick. Say that if there are only
five brace of partridge in the entire city, and only one case of
sherry, they should go to sick people and convalescents. Say that
after the sick come the children. For them the milk of the cows
and goats should be reserved if there is not enough for all. To
the children and the aged the last piece of meat, and to the strong
man dry bread, if the community be reduced to that extremity.

Say, in a word, that if this or that article of consumption runs
short, and has to be doled out, to those who have most need most
should be given. Say that and see if you do not meet with universal
agreement.

The man who is full-fed does not understand this, but the
people do understand, and have always understood it; and even
the child of luxury, if he is thrown on the street and comes into
contact with the masses, even he will learn to understand.

The theorists – for whom the soldier's uniform and the barrack
mess-table are civilization's last word – would like no doubt to
start a regime of National Kitchens and 'Spartan Broth'. They
would point out the advantages thereby gained, the economy in
fuel and food, if such huge kitchens were established, where everyone could come for their rations of soup and bread and vegetables.

We do not question these advantages. We are well aware that
important economies have already been achieved in this direction –

as, for instance, when the handmill, or quern, and the baker's oven attached to each house were abandoned. We can see perfectly well that it would be more economical to cook broth for a hundred families at once, instead of lighting a hundred separate fires. We know, besides, that there are a thousand ways of preparing potatoes, but that cooked in one huge pot for a hundred families they would be just as good.

We know, in fact, that variety in cooking being a matter of the seasoning introduced by each cook or housewife, the cooking together of a hundredweight of potatoes would not prevent each cook or housewife from dressing and serving them in any way she pleased. And we know that stock made from meat can be converted into a hundred different soups to suit a hundred different tastes.

But though we are quite aware of all these facts, we still maintain that no one has a right to force the housewife to take her potatoes from the communal kitchen ready cooked if she prefers to cook them herself in her own pot on her own fire. And, above all, we should wish each one to be free to take his meals with his family, or with his friends, or even in a restaurant, if it seemed good to him.

Naturally, large public kitchens will spring up to take the place of the restaurants, where people are poisoned nowadays. Already the Parisian housewife gets the stock for her soup from the butcher, and transforms it into whatever soup she likes, and London house-keepers know that they can have a joint roasted, or an apple or rhubarb tart baked at the baker's for a trifling sum, thus economizing time and fuel. And when the communal kitchen – the common bakehouse of the future – is established, and people can get their food cooked without the risk of being cheated or poisoned, the custom will no doubt become general of going to the communal kitchen for the fundamental parts of the meal, leaving the last touches to be added as individual taste shall suggest.

But to make a hard and fast rule of this, to make a duty of taking home our food ready cooked, that would be as repugnant to our modern minds as the ideas of the convent or the barrack – morbid ideas born in brains warped by tyranny or superstition.

'Who will have a right to the food of the commune?' will assuredly be the first question which we shall have to ask ourselves. Every township will answer for itself, and we are convinced that the answers will all be dictated by the sentiment of justice. Until labour is reorganized, as long as the disturbed period lasts, and while it is impossible to distinguish between inveterate idlers and genuine workers thrown out of work, the available food ought to be shared by all without exception. Those who have been enemies to the new order will hasten of their own accord to rid the commune of their presence. But it seems to us that the masses of the people, which have always been magnanimous, and have nothing of vindictiveness in their disposition, will be ready to share their bread with all who remain with them, conquered and conquerors alike. It will be no loss to the revolution to be inspired by such an idea, and, when work is set agoing again, the antagonists of yesterday will stand side by side in the same workshops. A society where work is free will have nothing to fear from idlers.

'But provisions will run short in a month!' our critics at once exclaim.

'So much the better,' say we. It will prove that for the first time on record the people have had enough to eat. As to the question of obtaining fresh supplies, we shall discuss the means in our next chapter.

V

By what means could a city in a state of revolution be supplied with food? We shall answer this question, but it is obvious that the means resorted to will depend on the character of the revolution in the provinces, and in neighbouring countries. If the entire nation, or, better still, if all Europe should accomplish the social revolution simultaneously, and start with thoroughgoing communism, our procedure would be simplified; but if only a few communities in Europe make the attempt, other means will have to be chosen. The circumstances will dictate the measures.

We are thus led, before we proceed further, to glance at the state of Europe, and, without pretending to prophesy, we may try to foresee what course the revolution will take, or at least what will be its essential features.

Certainly it would be very desirable that all Europe should rise at once, that expropriation should be general, and that communistic principles should inspire all and sundry. Such a universal rising would do much to simplify the task of our century.

But all the signs lead us to believe that it will not take place. That the revolution will embrace Europe we do not doubt. If one of the four great continental capitals – Paris, Vienna, Brussels or Berlin – rises in revolution and overturns its government, it is almost certain that the three others will follow its example within a few weeks' time. It is, moreover, highly probable that the Peninsulas and even London and St Petersburg would not be long in following suit. But whether the revolution would everywhere exhibit the same characteristics is highly doubtful.

It is more than probable that expropriation will be everywhere carried into effect on a larger scale, and that this policy carried out by any one of the great nations of Europe will influence all the rest; yet the beginnings of the revolution will exhibit great local differences, and its course will vary in different countries. In 1789–93, the French peasantry took four years to finally rid themselves of the redemption of feudal rights, and the bourgeois to overthrow royalty. Let us keep that in mind, and therefore be prepared to see the revolution develop itself somewhat gradually. Let us not be disheartened if here and there its steps should move less rapidly. Whether it would take an avowedly socialist character in all European nations, at any rate at the beginning, is doubtful. Germany, be it remembered, is still realizing its dream of a united empire. Its advanced parties see visions of a Jacobin republic like that of 1848, and of the organization of labour according to Louis Blanc; while the French people, on the other hand, want above all things a free commune, whether it be a communist commune or not.

There is every reason to believe that, when the coming revolution takes place, Germany will go further than France went in 1793. The eighteenth-century Revolution in France was an advance on the English Revolution of the seventeenth, abolishing as it did at one stroke the power of the throne and the landed aristocracy, whose influence still survives in England. But, if Germany goes further and does greater things than France did in 1793, there can be no doubt that the ideas which will foster the birth of her revolution will be those of 1848; while the ideas which will inspire

66

the revolution in Russia will probably be a combination of those of 1789 with those of 1848.

Without, however, attaching to these forecasts a greater importance than they merit, we may safely conclude this much: the revolution will take a different character in each of the different European nations; the point attained in the socialization of wealth will not be everywhere the same.

Will it therefore be necessary, as is sometimes suggested, that the nations in the vanguard of the movement should adapt their pace to those who lag behind? Must we wait till the communist revolution is ripe in all civilized countries? Clearly not! Even if it were a thing to be desired, it is not possible. History does not wait for the laggards.

Besides, we do not believe that in any one country the revolution will be accomplished at a stroke, in the twinkling of an eye, as some socialists dream.[d] It is highly probable that if one of the five or six large towns of France – Paris, Lyons, Marseilles, Lille, Saint-Etienne, Bordeaux – were to proclaim the commune, the others would follow its example, and that many smaller towns would do the same. Probably also various mining districts and industrial centres would hasten to rid themselves of 'owners' and 'masters', and form themselves into free groups.

But many country places have not advanced to that point. Side by side with the revolutionized communes such places would remain in an expectant attitude, and would go on living on the individualist system. Undisturbed by visits of the bailiff or the tax-collector, the peasants would not be hostile to the revolutionaries, and thus, while profiting by the new state of affairs, they would defer the settlement of accounts with the local exploiters. But with that practical enthusiasm which always characterizes agrarian uprisings (witness the passionate toil of 1792) they would throw themselves into the task of

---

[d] No fallacy more harmful has ever been spread than the fallacy of a 'one-day revolution', which is propagated in superficial socialist pamphlets speaking of the revolution of the 18th of March at Berlin, supposed (which is absolutely wrong) to have given Prussia its representative government. We saw well the harm made by such fallacies in Russia in 1905–07. The truth is that up to 1871 Prussia, like Russia of the present day, had a scrap of paper which could be described as a 'constitution', but it had no representative government. The Ministry imposed upon the nation, up till 1870, the budget it chose to propose.

cultivating the land, which, freed from taxes and mortgages, would become so much dearer to them.

As to other countries, revolution would break out everywhere, but revolution under divers aspects; in one country state socialism, in another federation; everywhere more or less socialism, not conforming to any particular rule.

VI

Let us now return to our city in revolt, and consider how its citizens can provide foodstuffs for themselves. How are the necessary provisions to be obtained if the nation as a whole has not accepted communism? This is the question to be solved. Take, for example, one of the large French towns – take the capital itself, for that matter. Paris consumes every year thousands of tons of grain, 400,000 head of oxen, 300,000 calves, 400,000 swine, and more than 2 million sheep, besides great quantities of game. This huge city devours, besides, more than 20 million pounds of butter, 200 million eggs, and other produce in like proportion.

It imports flour and grain from the United States and from Russia, Hungary, Italy, Egypt and the Indies; livestock from Germany, Italy, Spain – even Romania and Russia; and as for groceries, there is not a country in the world that it does not lay under contribution.

Now, let us see how Paris or any other great town could be revictualled by home-grown produce, supplies of which could be readily and willingly sent in from the provinces.

To those who put their trust in 'authority' the question will appear quite simple. They would begin by establishing a strongly centralized government, furnished with all the machinery of coercion – the police, the army, the guillotine. This government would draw up a statement of all the produce contained in France. It would divide the country into districts of supply, and then *command* that a prescribed quantity of some particular foodstuff be sent to such a place on such a day, and delivered at such a station, to be there received on a given day by a specified official and stored in particular warehouses.

Now, we declare with the fullest conviction, not merely that such a solution is undesirable, but that it never could by any possibility be put into practice. It is wildly utopian!

Pen in hand, one may dream such a dream in the study, but in contact with reality it comes to nothing – this was proved in 1793; for, like all such theories, it leaves out of account the spirit of independence that is in man. The attempt would lead to a universal uprising, to three or four *Vendées,* to the villages rising against the towns, all the country up in arms defying the city for its arrogance in attempting to impose such a system upon the country.

We have already had too much of Jacobin utopias! Let us see if some other form of organization will meet the case.

During the great French Revolution, the provinces starved the large towns, and killed the Revolution. And yet it is a known fact that the production of grain in France during 1792–3 had not diminished; indeed, the evidence goes to show that it had increased. But after having taken possession of the manorial lands, after having reaped a harvest from them, the peasants would not part with their grain for paper-money. They withheld their produce, waiting for a rise in the price, or the introduction of gold. The most rigorous measures of the National Convention were without avail, and her executions failed to break up the ring, or force the farmers to sell their corn. For it is matter of history that the commissaries of the Convention did not scruple to guillotine those who withheld their grain from the market, and pitilessly executed those who speculated in foodstuffs. All the same, the corn was not forthcoming, and the townsfolk suffered from famine.

But what was offered to the husbandman in exchange for this hard toil? Assignats, scraps of paper decreasing in value every day, promises of payment, which could not be kept. A £40 note would not purchase a pair of boots, and the peasant, very naturally, was not anxious to barter a year's toil for a piece of paper with which he could not even buy a shirt.

As long as worthless paper-money – whether called assignats or labour notes – is offered to the peasant-producer it will always be the same. The country will withhold its produce, and the towns will suffer want, even if the recalcitrant peasants are guillotined as before.

We must offer to the peasant in exchange for his toil not worthless paper-money, but the manufactured articles of which he stands in immediate need. He lacks the proper implements to till the land, clothes to protect him properly from the inclemencies of the weather, lamps and oil to replace his miserable rushlight or tallow dip, spades, rakes, ploughs. All these things, under present conditions, the peasant is forced to do without, not because he does not feel the need of them, but because, in his life of struggle and privation, a thousand useful things are beyond his reach; because he has no money to buy them.

Let the town apply itself, without loss of time, to manufacturing all that the peasant needs, instead of fashioning gewgaws for the wives of rich citizens. Let the sewing machines of Paris be set to work on clothes for the country folk: workaday clothes and clothes for Sunday too, instead of costly evening dresses for the English and Russian landlords and the African gold-magnates' wives. Let the factories and foundries turn out agricultural implements, spades, rakes, and such-like, instead of waiting till the English send them to France, in exchange for French wines!

Let the towns send no more inspectors to the villages, wearing red, blue, or rainbow-coloured scarves, to convey to the peasant orders to take his produce to this place or that, but let them send friendly embassies to the country folk and bid them in brotherly fashion: 'Bring us your produce, and take from our stores and shops all the manufactured articles you please.' – Then provisions would pour in on every side. The peasant would only withhold what he needed for his own use, and would send the rest into the cities, feeling *for the first time in the course of history* that these toiling townsfolk were his comrades – his brethren, and not his exploiters.

We shall be told, perhaps, that this would necessitate a complete transformation of industry. Well, yes, that is true of certain departments; but there are other branches which could be rapidly modified in such a way as to furnish the peasant with clothes, watches, furniture and the simple implements for which the towns make him pay such exorbitant prices at the present time. Weavers, tailors, shoemakers, tinsmiths, cabinet-makers and many other trades and crafts could easily direct their energies to the manufacture of useful and necessary articles, and abstain from producing mere luxuries. All that is needed is that the public mind should be thoroughly convinced of the necessity of this transformation, and should come to look upon it as an act of justice and of progress, and that it should no longer allow itself to be cheated by that dream, so dear to the theorists – the dream of a revolution which confines itself to taking possession of the profits of industry, and leaves production and commerce just as they are now.

This, then, is our view of the whole question. Cheat the peasant no longer with scraps of paper – be the sums inscribed upon them ever so large; but offer him in exchange for his produce the very *things* of which he, the tiller of the soil, stands in need. Then the fruits of the land will be poured into the towns. If this is not done there will be famine in our cities, and reaction and despair will follow in its train.

VII

All the great towns, we have said, buy their grain, their flour and their meat, not only from the provinces, but also from abroad. Foreign countries send Paris not only spices, fish, and various dainties, but also immense quantities of corn and meat.

But when the revolution comes these cities will have to depend on foreign countries as little as possible. If Russian wheat, Italian or Indian rice, and Spanish or Hungarian wines abound in the markets of Western Europe, it is not that the countries which export them have a superabundance, or that such a produce grows there of itself, like the dandelion in the meadows. In Russia, for instance, the peasant works sixteen hours a day, and half starves from three to six months every year, in order to export the grain with which he pays the landlord and the state. Today the police appears in the Russian village as soon as the harvest is gathered in, and sells the peasant's last horse and last cow for arrears of taxes and rent due to the landlord, unless the victim immolates himself of his own accord by selling the grain to the exporters. Usually, rather than part with his livestock at a disadvantage, he keeps only a nine months' supply of grain, and sells the rest. Then, in order to sustain life until the next harvest, he mixes birch-bark and tares with his flour for three months, if it has been a good year, and for six if it has been bad, while in London they are eating biscuits made of his wheat.

But as soon as the revolution comes, the Russian peasant will keep bread enough for himself and his children; the Italian and Hungarian peasants will do the same; the Hindu, let us hope, will profit by these good examples; and the farmers of America will hardly be able to cover all the deficit in grain which Europe will experience. So it will not do to count on their contributions of wheat and maize satisfying all the wants.

Since all our middle-class civilization is based on the exploitation of inferior races and countries with less advanced industrial systems, the revolution will confer a boon at the very outset, by menacing that 'civilization', and allowing the so-called inferior races to free themselves.

But this great benefit will manifest itself by a steady and marked diminution of the food supplies pouring into the great cities of Western Europe.

It is difficult to predict the course of affairs in the provinces. On the one hand the slave of the soil will take advantage of the revolution to straighten his bowed back. Instead of working fourteen or fifteen hours a day, as he does at present, he will be at liberty to work only half that time, which of course would have the effect of decreasing the production of the principal articles of consumption – grain and meat.

But, on the other hand, there will be an increase of production as soon as the peasant realizes that he is no longer forced to support the idle rich by his toil. New tracts of land will be cleared, new and improved machines set agoing.

'Never was the land so energetically cultivated as in 1792, when the peasant had taken back from the landlord the soil which he had coveted so long,' Michelet tells us, speaking of the Great Revolution.

Of course, before long, intensive culture would be within the reach of all. Improved machinery, chemical manures, and all such matters would soon be supplied by the commune. But everything tends to indicate that at the outset there would be a falling off in agricultural products, in France and elsewhere.

In any case it would be wisest to count upon such a falling off of contributions from the provinces as well as from abroad. – How is this falling off to be made good?

Why! by setting to work ourselves! No need to rack our brains for far-fetched panaceas when the remedy lies close at hand!

The large towns, as well as the villages, must undertake to till the soil. We must return to what biology calls 'the integration of

72

functions' – after the division of labour, the taking up of it as a whole – this is the course followed throughout Nature.

Besides, philosophy apart, the force of circumstances would bring about this result. Let Paris see that at the end of eight months it will be running short of bread, and Paris will set to work to grow wheat.

Land will not be wanting, for it is round the great towns, and round Paris especially, that the parks and pleasure grounds of the landed gentry are to be found. These thousands of acres only await the skilled labour of the husbandman to surround Paris with fields infinitely more fertile and productive than the steppes of southern Russia, where the soil is dried up by the sun. Nor will labour be lacking. To what should the 2 million citizens of Paris turn their attention, when they would be no longer catering for the luxurious fads and amusements of Russian princes, Romanian grandees, and wives of Berlin financiers?

With all the mechanical inventions of the century; with all the intelligence and technical skill of the worker accustomed to deal with complicated machinery; with inventors, chemists, professors of botany, practical botanists like the market-gardeners of Gennevilliers; with all the plant that they could use for multiplying and improving machinery; and, finally, with the organizing spirit of the Parisian people, their pluck and energy – with all these at its command, the agriculture of the anarchist commune of Paris would be a very different thing from the rude husbandry of the Ardennes.

Steam, electricity, the heat of the sun, and the breath of the wind, will ere long be pressed into service. The steam plough and the steam harrow will quickly do the rough work of preparation, and the soil, thus cleaned and enriched, will only need the intelligent care of man, and of woman even more than man, to be clothed with luxuriant vegetation – not once but three or four times in the year.

Thus, learning the art of horticulture from experts, and trying experiments in different methods on small patches of soil reserved for the purpose, vying with each other to obtain the best returns, finding in physical exercise, without exhaustion or overwork, the health and strength which so often flags in cities – men, women and children will gladly turn to the labour of the fields, when it

73

is no longer a slavish drudgery, but has become a pleasure, a festival, a renewal of health and joy.

'There are no barren lands; the earth is worth what man is worth' – that is the last word of modern agriculture. Ask of the earth, and she will give you bread, provided that you ask aright.

A district, though it were as small as the two departments of the Seine and the Seine-et-Oise, and with so great a city as Paris to feed, would be practically sufficient to grow upon it all the food supplies, which otherwise might fail to reach it.

The combination of agriculture and industry, the husbandman and the mechanic in the same individual – this is what anarchist communism will inevitably lead us to, if it starts fair with expropriation.

Let the revolution only get so far, and famine is not the enemy it will have to fear. No, the danger which will menace it lies in timidity, prejudice and half-measures. The danger is where Danton saw it when he cried to France: 'De l'audace, de l'audace, et encore de l'audace.' The bold thought first, and the bold deed will not fail to follow.

CHAPTER VI
Dwellings

I

Those who have closely watched the growth of socialist ideas among the workers must have noticed that on one momentous question – the housing of the people – a definite conclusion is being imperceptibly arrived at. It is a fact that in the large towns of France, and in many of the smaller ones, the workers are coming gradually to the conclusion that dwelling-houses are in no sense the property of those whom the state recognizes as their owners.

This idea has evolved naturally in the minds of the people, and nothing will ever convince them again that the 'rights of property' ought to extend to houses.

The house was not built by its owner. It was erected, decorated and furnished by innumerable workers – in the timber yard, the brickfield and the workshop, toiling for dear life at a minimum wage.

The money spent by the owner was not the product of his own toil. It was amassed, like all other riches, by paying the workers two-thirds or only a half of what was their due.

Moreover – and it is here that the enormity of the whole proceeding becomes most glaring – the house owes its actual value to the profit which the owner can make out of it. Now, this profit results from the fact that his house is built in a town – that is, in an agglomeration of thousands of other houses, possessing paved streets, bridges, quays and fine public buildings, well lighted, and affording to its inhabitants a thousand comforts and conveniences

75

unknown in villages; a town in regular communication with other towns, and itself a centre of industry, commerce, science and art; a town which the work of twenty or thirty generations has made habitable, healthy and beautiful.

A house in certain parts of Paris is valued at many thousands of pounds sterling, not because thousands of pounds' worth of labour have been expended on that particular house, but because it is in Paris; because for centuries workmen, artists, thinkers and men of learning and letters have contributed to make Paris what it is today – a centre of industry, commerce, politics, art and science; because Paris has a past; because, thanks to literature, the names of its streets are household words in foreign countries as well as at home, because it is the fruit of eighteen centuries of toil, the work of fifty generations of the whole French nation.

Who, then, can appropriate to himself the tiniest plot of ground, or the meanest building in such a city, without committing a flagrant injustice? Who, then, has the right to sell to any bidder the smallest portion of the common heritage?

On that point, as we have said, the workers begin to be agreed. The idea of free dwellings showed its existence very plainly during the siege of Paris, when the cry was for an abatement pure and simple of the terms demanded by the landlords. It appeared again during the Commune of 1871, when the Paris workmen expected the Council of the Commune to decide boldly on the abolition of rent. And when the new revolution comes, it will be the first question with which the poor will concern themselves.

Whether in time of revolution or in time of peace, the worker must be housed somehow or other; he must have some sort of roof over his head. But, however tumbledown and squalid his dwelling may be, there is always a landlord who can evict him. True, during the revolution the landlord cannot find bailiffs and police-sergeants to throw the workman's rags and chattels into the street, but who knows what the new government will do tomorrow? Who can say that it will not call coercion to its aid again, and set the police pack upon the tenant to hound him out of his hovels? Have we not seen the Commune of Paris proclaim the remission of rents due up to the first of April only!ᶜ After that, rent had to

---

ᶜ The decree of the 30 March: by this decree rents due up to the terms of October 1870 and January and April 1871 were annulled.

be paid, though Paris was in a state of chaos, and industry at a standstill; so that the 'federate' who had taken arms to defend the independence of Paris had absolutely nothing to depend upon – he and his family – but an allowance of 15 pence a day!

Now the worker must be made to see clearly that in refusing to pay rent to a landlord or owner he is not simply profiting by the disorganization of authority. He must understand that the abolition of rent is a recognized principle, sanctioned, so to speak, by popular assent; that to be housed rent-free is a right proclaimed aloud by the people.

Are we going to wait till this measure, which is in harmony with every honest man's sense of justice, is taken up by the few socialists scattered among the middle-class elements, of which the provisionary government will be composed? If it were so, the people would have to wait long – till the return of reaction, in fact!

This is why, refusing uniforms and badges – those outward signs of authority and servitude – and remaining people among the people, the earnest revolutionists will work side by side with the masses, that the abolition of rent, the expropriation of houses, may become an accomplished fact. They will prepare the ground and encourage ideas to grow in this direction; and when the fruit of their labours is ripe, the people will proceed to expropriate the houses without giving heed to the theories which will certainly be thrust in their way – theories about paying compensation to landlords, and finding first the necessary funds.

On the day that the expropriation of houses takes place, on that day, the exploited workers will have realized that new times have come, that labour will no longer have to bear the yoke of the rich and powerful, that equality has been openly proclaimed, that this revolution is a real fact, and not a theatrical make-believe, like so many others preceding it.

II

If the idea of expropriation be adopted by the people it will be carried into effect in spite of all the 'insurmountable' obstacles with which we are menaced.

Of course, the good folk in new uniforms, seated in the official armchairs of the Hôtel de Ville, will be sure to busy themselves in heaping up obstacles. They will talk of giving compensation to the landlords, of preparing statistics, and drawing up long reports. Yes, they would be capable of drawing up reports long enough to outlast the hopes of the people, who, after waiting and starving in enforced idleness, and seeing nothing come of all these official researches, would lose heart and faith in the revolution and abandon the field to the reactionaries. The new bureaucracy would end by making expropriation hateful in the eyes of all.

Here, indeed, is a rock which might shipwreck our hopes. But if the people turn a deaf ear to the specious arguments used to dazzle them, and realize that new life needs new conditions, and if they undertake the task themselves, then expropriation can be effected without any great difficulty.

'But how? How can it be done?' you ask us. We shall try to reply to this question, but with a reservation. We have no intention of tracing out the plans of expropriation in their smallest details. We know beforehand that all that any man, or group of men, could suggest today would be far surpassed by the reality when it comes. Man will accomplish greater things, and accomplish them better and by simpler methods than those dictated to him beforehand. Thus we shall merely indicate the manner by which expropriation *might* be accomplished without the intervention of government. We do not propose to go out of our way to answer those who declare that the thing is impossible. We confine ourselves to replying that we are not the upholders of any particular method of organization. We are only concerned to demonstrate that expropriation *could* be effected by popular initiative, and *could not* be effected by any other means whatever.

It seems very likely that, as soon as expropriation is fairly started, groups of volunteers will spring up in every district, street and block of houses, and undertake to inquire into the number of flats and houses which are empty and of those which are overcrowded, the unwholesome slums, and the houses which are too spacious for their occupants and might well be used to house those who are stifled in swarming tenements. In a few days these volunteers would have drawn up complete lists for the street and the district of all the flats, tenements, family mansions and villa residences, all the rooms and suites of rooms, healthy and unhealthy, small and large, foetid dens and homes of luxury.

78

Freely communicating with each other, these volunteers would soon have their statistics complete. False statistics can be manufactured in board rooms and offices, but true and exact statistics must begin with the individual and mount up from the simple to the complex.

Then, without waiting for anyone's leave, those citizens will probably go and find their comrades who were living in miserable garrets and hovels and will say to them simply: 'It is a real revolution this time, comrades, and no mistake about it. Come to such a place this evening; all the neighbourhood will be there; we are going to redistribute the dwelling-houses. If you are tired of your slum-garret, come and choose one of the flats of five rooms that are to be disposed of, and when you have once moved in you shall stay, never fear. The people are up in arms, and he who would venture to evict you will have to answer to them.'

'But everyone will want a fine house or a spacious flat!' we are told. – No, you are quite mistaken. It is not the people's way to clamour for the moon. On the contrary, every time we have seen them set about repairing a wrong we have been struck by the good sense and instinct for justice which animates the masses. Have we ever known them demand the impossible? Have we ever seen the people of Paris fighting among themselves while waiting for their rations of bread or firewood during the two sieges or during the terrible years of 1792–4? The patience and resignation which prevailed among them in 1871 was constantly presented for admiration by the foreign press correspondents; and yet these patient waiters knew full well that the last comers would have to pass the day without food or fire.

We do not deny that there are plenty of egotistic instincts in isolated individuals. We are quite aware of it. But we contend that the very way to revive and nourish these instincts would be to confine such questions as the housing of the people to any board or committee, in fact, to the tender mercies of officialism in any shape or form. Then indeed all the evil passions spring up, and it becomes a case of who is the most influential person on the board. The least inequality causes wranglings and recriminations. If the smallest advantage is given to anyone, a tremendous hue and cry is raised – and not without reason.

But if the people themselves, organized by streets, districts and parishes, undertake to move the inhabitants of the slums into the half-empty dwellings of the middle classes, the trifling inconveniences, the little inequalities will be easily tided over. Rarely has appeal been made to the good instincts of the masses – only as a last resort, to save the sinking ship in times of revolution – but never has such an appeal been made in vain; the heroism, the self-devotion of the toiler has never failed to respond to it. And thus it will be in the coming revolution.

But, when all is said and done, some inequalities, some inevitable injustices, undoubtedly will remain. There are individuals in our societies whom no great crisis can lift out of the deep mire of egoism in which they are sunk. The question, however, is not whether there will be injustices or no, but rather how to limit the number of them.

Now all history, all the experience of the human race, and all social psychology, unite in showing that the best and fairest way is to trust the decision to those whom it concerns most nearly. It is they alone who can consider and allow for the hundred and one details which must necessarily be overlooked in any merely official redistribution.

III

Moreover, it is by no means necessary to make straightway an absolutely equal redistribution of all the dwellings. There will no doubt be some inconveniences at first, but matters will soon be righted in a society which has adopted expropriation.

When the masons and carpenters, and all who are concerned in house building, know that their daily bread is secured to them, they will ask nothing better than to work at their old trades a few hours a day. They will adapt the fine houses, which absorbed the time of a whole staff of servants, for giving shelter to several families, and in a few months homes will have sprung up, infinitely healthier and more conveniently arranged than those of today. And to those who are not yet comfortably housed the anarchist commune will be able to say: 'Patience, comrades! Palaces fairer and finer than any the capitalists built for themselves will spring from the ground of our enfranchised city. They will belong to those who have most need of them. The anarchist commune does not build with an eye to revenues. These monuments erected to its citizens, products of the collective spirit, will serve as models to all humanity; they will be yours.'

If the people of the revolution expropriate the houses and proclaim free lodgings – the communalizing of houses and the right of each family to a decent dwelling – then the revolution will have assumed a communistic character from the first, and started on a course from which it will be by no means easy to turn it. It will have struck a fatal blow at individual property.

For the expropriation of dwellings contains in germ the whole social revolution. On the manner of its accomplishment depends the character of all that follows. Either we shall start on a good road leading straight to anarchist communism, or we shall remain sticking in the mud of despotic individualism.

It is easy to see the numerous objections – theoretic on the one hand, practical on the other – with which we are sure to be met. As it will be a question of maintaining iniquity at any price, our opponents will of course protest 'in the name of justice'. 'Is it not a crying shame', they will exclaim, 'that the people of Paris should take possession of all these fine houses, while the peasants in the country have only tumbledown huts to live in?' But do not let us make a mistake. These enthusiasts for justice forget, by a lapse of memory to which they are subject, the 'crying shame' which they themselves are tacitly defending. They forget that in this same city the worker, with his wife and children, suffocates in a noisome garret, while from his window he sees the rich man's palace. They forget that whole generations perish in crowded slums, starving for air and sunlight, and that to redress this injustice ought to be the first task of the revolution.

Do not let these disingenuous protests hold us back. We know that any inequality which may exist between town and country in the early days of the revolution will be transitory and of a nature that will right itself from day to day; for the village will not fail to improve its dwellings as soon as the peasant has ceased to be the beast of burden of the farmer, the merchant, the money-lender, and the state. In order to avoid an accidental and transitory inequality, shall we stay our hand from righting an ancient wrong?

The so-called practical objections are not very formidable either. We are bidden to consider the hard case of some poor fellow who by dint of privation has contrived to buy a house just large enough to hold his family. And we are going to deprive him of his hard-earned happiness, to turn him into the street! Certainly not. If his house is only just large enough for his family, by all means let him stay there. Let him work in his little garden, too; our 'boys' will not hinder him – nay, they will lend him a helping hand if need be. But suppose he lets lodgings, suppose he has empty rooms in his house; then the people will make the lodger understand that he need not pay his former landlord any more rent. Stay where you are, but rent free. No more duns and collectors; socialism has abolished all that!

Or again, suppose that the landlord has a score of rooms all to himself, and some poor woman lives near by with five children in one room. In that case the people would see whether, with some alterations, these empty rooms could not be converted into a suitable home for the poor woman and her five children. Would not that be more just and fair than to leave the mother and her five little ones languishing in a garret, while Sir Gorgeous Midas sat at his ease in an empty mansion? Besides, good Sir Gorgeous would probably hasten to do it of his own accord; his wife will be delighted to be freed from half her big, unwieldy house when there is no longer a staff of servants to keep it in order.

'So you are going to turn everything upside down', say the defenders of law and order. 'There will be no end to the evictions and removals. Would it not be better to start fresh by turning everybody out of doors and redistributing the houses by lot?' Thus our critics; but we are firmly persuaded that if no government interferes in the matter, if all the changes are entrusted to those free groups which have sprung up to undertake the work, the evictions and removals will be less numerous than those which take place in one year under the present system, owing to the rapacity of landlords.

In the first place, there are in all large towns almost enough empty houses and flats to lodge all the inhabitants of the slums. As to the palaces and suites of fine apartments, many working people would not live in them if they could. One could not 'keep up' such houses without a large staff of servants. Their occupants would soon find themselves forced to seek less luxurious dwellings. The fine ladies would find that palaces were not well adapted to self-help in the kitchen. Gradually people would shake down. There would be no need to conduct Dives to a garret at the bayonet's point, or instal Lazarus in Dives's palace by the help of an armed escort. People would shake down amicably into the available dwellings with the least possible friction and disturbance. Have we not the example of the village communes redistributing fields and disturbing the owners of the allotments so little that one can only praise the intelligence and good sense of the methods they employ? Fewer fields change hands under the management of the Russian commune than where personal property holds sway and is for ever carrying its quarrels into courts of law. And are we to believe that the inhabitants of a great European city would be less intelligent and less capable of organization than Russian or Hindu peasants?

Moreover, we must not blink at the fact that every revolution means a certain disturbance to everyday life, and those who expect this tremendous climb out of the old grooves to be accomplished without so much as jarring the dishes on their dinner-tables will find themselves mistaken. It is true that governments can change without disturbing worthy citizens at dinner, but the crimes of society towards those who have nourished and supported it are not to be redressed by any such political sleight of parties.

Undoubtedly there will be a disturbance, but it must not be one of pure loss; it must be minimized. And again – it is impossible to lay too much stress on this maxim – it will be by addressing ourselves to the interested parties, and not to boards and committees, that we shall best succeed in reducing the sum of inconveniences for everybody.

The people commit blunder on blunder when they have to choose by ballot some hare-brained candidate who solicits the honour of representing them, and takes upon himself to know all, to do all, and to organize all. But when they take upon themselves to organize what they know, what touches them directly, they do it better than all the 'talking-shops' put together. Is not the Paris Commune an instance in point? and the great dockers' strike? and have we not constant evidence of this fact in every village commune?

CHAPTER VII

Clothing

When the houses have become the common heritage of the citizens, and when each man has his daily supply of food, another forward step will have to be taken. The question of clothing will of course demand consideration next, and again the only possible solution will be to take possession, in the name of the people, of all the shops and warehouses where clothing is sold or stored, and to throw open the doors to all, so that each can take what he needs. The communalization of clothing – the right of each to take what he needs from the communal stores, or to have it made for him at the tailors and outfitters – is a necessary corollary of the communalization of houses and food.

Obviously we shall not need for that to despoil all citizens of their coats, to put all the garments in a heap and draw lots for them, as our critics, with equal wit and ingenuity, suggest. Let him who has a coat keep it still – nay, if he have ten coats it is highly improbable that anyone will want to deprive him of them, for most folk would prefer a new coat to one that has already graced the shoulders of some fat bourgeois; and there will be enough new garments, and to spare, without having recourse to second-hand wardrobes.

If we were to take an inventory of all the clothes and stuff for clothing accumulated in the shops and stores of the large towns, we should find probably that in Paris, Lyons, Bordeaux and Marseilles, there was enough to enable the commune to offer garments to all the citizens, of both sexes; and if all were not suited at once, the communal outfitters would soon make good these shortcomings.

We know how rapidly our great tailoring and dressmaking establishments work nowadays, provided as they are with machinery specially adapted for production on a large scale.

'But every one will want a sable-lined coat or a velvet gown!' exclaim our adversaries.

Frankly, we do not believe it. Every woman does not dote on velvet, nor does every man dream of sable linings. Even now, if we were to ask each woman to choose her gown, we should find some to prefer a simple, practical garment to all the fantastic trimmings the fashionable world affects.

Tastes change with the times, and the fashion in vogue at the time of the revolution will certainly make for simplicity. Societies, like individuals, have their hours of cowardice, but also their heroic moments; and though the society of today cuts a very poor figure sunk in the pursuit of narrow personal interests and second-rate ideas, it wears a different air when great crises come. It has its moments of greatness and enthusiasm. Men of generous nature will gain the power which today is in the hand of jobbers. Self-devotion will spring up, and noble deeds beget their like; even the egotists will be ashamed of hanging back, and will be drawn in spite of themselves to admire, if not to imitate, the generous and brave.

The great Revolution of 1793 abounds in examples of this kind, and it is always during such times of spiritual revival – as natural to societies as to individuals – that the spring tide of enthusiasm sweeps humanity onwards.

We do not wish to exaggerate the part played by such noble passions, nor is it upon them that we would found our ideal of society. But we are not asking too much if we expect their aid in tiding over the first and most difficult moments. We cannot hope that our daily life will be continuously inspired by such exalted enthusiasms, but we may expect their aid at the first, and that is all we need.

It is just to wash the earth clean, to sweep away the shards and refuse, accumulated by centuries of slavery and oppression, that the new anarchist society will have need of this wave of brotherly love. Later on it can exist without appealing to the spirit of self-sacrifice, because it will have eliminated oppression, and thus created a new world instinct with all the feelings of solidarity.

Besides, should the character of the revolution be such as we have sketched here, the free initiative of individuals would find an extensive field of action in thwarting the efforts of the egotists. Groups would spring up in every street and quarter to undertake the charge of the clothing. They would make inventories of all that the city possessed, and would find out approximately what were the resources at their disposal. It is more than likely that in the matter of clothing the citizens would adopt the same principle as in the matter of provisions – that is to say, they would offer freely from the common store everything which was to be found in abundance, and dole out whatever was limited in quantity.

Not being able to offer to each man a sable-lined coat, and to every woman a velvet gown, society would probably distinguish between the superfluous and the necessary, and, provisionally at least, class sable and velvet among the superfluities of life, ready to let time prove whether what is a luxury today may not become common to all tomorrow. While the necessary clothing would be guaranteed to each inhabitant of the anarchist city, it would be left to private activity to provide for the sick and feeble those things, provisionally considered as luxuries, and to procure for the less robust such special articles, as would not enter into the daily consumption of ordinary citizens.

'But', it may be urged, 'this means grey uniformity and the end of everything beautiful in life and art.'

'Certainly not!' we reply. And, still basing our reasonings on what already exists, we are going to show how an anarchist society could satisfy the most artistic tastes of its citizens without allowing them to amass the fortunes of millionaires.

CHAPTER VIII
Ways and means

I

If a society, a city, or a territory, were to guarantee the necessaries of life to its inhabitants (and we shall see how the conception of the necessaries of life can be so extended as to include luxuries), it would be compelled to take possession of what is absolutely needed for production; that is to say – land, machinery, factories, means of transport, etc. Capital in the hands of private owners would be expropriated, to be returned to the community.

The great harm done by bourgeois society, as we have already mentioned, is not only that capitalists seize a large share of the profits of each industrial and commercial enterprise, thus enabling themselves to live without working, but that all production has taken a wrong direction, as it is not carried on with a view to securing well-being to all. There is the reason why it must be condemned.

It is absolutely impossible that mercantile production should be carried on in the interest of all. To desire it would be to expect the capitalist to go beyond his province and to fulfil duties that he *cannot* fulfil without ceasing to be what he is – a private manufacturer seeking his own enrichment. Capitalist organization, based on the personal interest of each individual employer of labour, has given to society all that could be expected of it: it has increased the productive force of labour. The capitalist, profiting by the revolution effected in industry by steam, by the sudden development of chemistry and machinery, and by other inventions of our century, has worked in his own interest to increase the yield of human labour, and in a great measure he has succeeded so far. But to attribute other duties to him would be unreasonable. For example, to expect that he should use this superior yield of labour in the interest of society as a whole, would be to ask philanthropy and charity of him, and a capitalist enterprise cannot be based on charity.

It now remains for society, first, to extend this greater productivity, which is limited to certain industries, and to apply it to the general good. But it is evident that to utilize this high productivity of labour, so as to guarantee well-being to all, society must itself take possession of all means of production.

Economists, as is their wont, will not fail to remind us of the comparative well-being of a certain category of young robust workmen, skilled in certain special branches of industry which has been obtained under the present system. It is always this minority that is pointed out to us with pride. But even this well-being, which is the exclusive right of a few, is it secure? Tomorrow, maybe, negligence, improvidence, or the greed of their employers, will deprive these privileged men of their work, and they will pay for the period of comfort they have enjoyed with months and years of poverty or destitution. How many important industries – the textiles, iron, sugar, etc. – without mentioning all sorts of short-lived trades, have we not seen decline or come to a standstill on account of speculations, or in consequence of natural displacement of work, or from the effects of competition amongst the capitalists themselves! If the chief textile and mechanical industries had to pass through such a crisis as they have passed through in 1886, we hardly need mention the small trades, all of which have their periods of standstill.

What, too, shall we say to the price which is paid for the relative well-being of certain categories of workmen? Unfortunately, it is paid for by the ruin of agriculture, the shameless exploitation of the peasants, the misery of the masses. In comparison with the feeble minority of workers who enjoy a certain comfort, how many millions of human beings live from hand to mouth, without a secure wage, ready to go wherever they are wanted; how many peasants work fourteen hours a day for a poor pittance! Capital depopulates the country, exploits the colonies and the countries where industries are but little developed, dooms the immense majority of workmen to remain without technical education, to remain mediocre even in their own trade.

This is not merely accidental, it is a *necessity* of the capitalist system. In order well to remunerate certain classes of workmen, peasants *must* become the beasts of burden of society; the country *must* be deserted for the town; small trades must agglomerate in the foul suburbs of large cities, and manufacture a thousand little things for next to nothing, so as to bring the goods of the greater industries within reach of buyers with small salaries. That bad cloth may be sold to ill-paid workers, garments are made by tailors who are satisfied with a starvation wage! Eastern lands in a backward state are exploited by the West, in order that, under the capitalist system, workers in a few privileged industries may obtain certain limited comforts of life.

The evil of the present system is therefore not that the 'surplus value' of production goes to the capitalist, as Rodbertus and Marx said, thus narrowing the socialist conception and the general view of the capitalist system; the surplus value itself is but a consequence of deeper causes. The evil lies *in the possibility of a surplus value existing*, instead of a simple surplus not consumed by each generation; for, that a surplus value should exist, means that men, women and children are compelled by hunger to sell their labour for a small part of what this labour produces, and still more so, of what their labour is capable of producing. But this evil will last as long as the instruments of production belong to the few. As long as men are compelled to pay a heavy tribute to property holders for the right of cultivating land or putting machinery into action, and the owners of the land and the machine are free to produce what bids fair to bring them in the largest profits – rather than the greatest amount of useful commodities – well-being can only be temporarily guaranteed to a very few; it is only to be bought by the poverty of a large section of society. It is not sufficient to distribute the profits realized by a trade in equal parts, if at the same time thousands of other workers are exploited. It is a case of *producing the greatest amount of goods necessary to the well-being of all, with the least possible waste of human energy*.

This generalized aim cannot be the aim of a private owner; and this is why society as a whole, if it takes this view of production as its ideal, will be compelled to expropriate all that enhances well-being while producing wealth. It will have to take possession of land, factories, mines, means of communication, etc., and besides, it will have to study what products will promote general well-being, as well as the ways and means of an adequate production.

II

How many hours a day will man have to work to produce nourishing food, a comfortable home, and necessary clothing for his family? This question has often preoccupied socialists, and they generally came to the conclusion that four or five hours a day would suffice, on condition, be it well understood, that all men work. At the end of last century, Benjamin Franklin fixed the limit at five hours; and if the need of comfort is greater now, the power of production has augmented too, and far more rapidly.

In speaking of agriculture further on, we shall see what the earth can be made to yield to man when he cultivates it in a reasonable way, instead of throwing seed haphazard in a badly ploughed soil as he mostly does today. In the great farms of western America, some of which cover 30 square miles, but have a poorer soil than the manured soil of civilized countries, only 10 to 15 English bushels per English acre are obtained; that is to say, half the yield of European farms or of American farms in the eastern states. And nevertheless, thanks to machines which enable two men to plough 4 English acres a day, 100 men can produce in a year all that is necessary to deliver the bread of 10,000 people at their homes during a whole year.

Thus it would suffice for a man to work under the same conditions for *30 hours, say 6 half-days of 5 hours each, to have bread for a whole year;* and to work 30 half-days to guarantee the same to a family of five people.

We shall also prove by results obtained nowadays, that if we took recourse to intensive agriculture, less than 6 half-days' work could procure bread, meat, vegetables and even luxurious fruit for a whole family.

Again, if we study the cost of workmen's dwellings, built in large towns today, we can ascertain that to obtain, in a large English city, a semi-detached little house, as they are built for workmen for £250, from 1,400 to 1,800 half-days' work of 5 hours would be sufficient. And as a house of that kind lasts 50 years at least, it follows that 28 to 36 half-days' work a year would provide well-furnished, healthy quarters, with all necessary comfort for a family. Whereas when hiring the same apartment from an employer, a workman pays from 75 to 100 days' work per year.

Mark that these figures represent the maximum of what a house costs in England today, being given the defective organization of our societies. In Belgium, workmen's houses in the *cités ouvrières* have been built at a much smaller cost. So that, taking everything into consideration, we are justified in affirming that in a well-organized society 30 or 40 half-days' work a year will suffice to guarantee a perfectly comfortable home.

There now remains clothing, the exact value of which is almost impossible to fix, because the profits realized by a swarm of middlemen cannot be estimated. Let us take cloth, for example, and add up all the tribute levied on every yard of it by the landowners, the sheep owners, the wool merchants, and all their intermediate agents, then by the railway companies, mill-owners, weavers, dealers in ready-made clothes, sellers and commission agents, and we shall get then an idea of what we pay to a whole swarm of capitalists for each article of clothing. That is why it is perfectly impossible to say how many days' work an overcoat that you pay £3 or £4 for in a large London shop represents.

What is certain is that with present machinery it is possible to manufacture an incredible amount of goods both cheaply and quickly.

A few examples will suffice. Thus in the United States, in 751 cotton mills (for spinning and weaving), 175,000 men and women produce 2,033,000,000 yards of cotton goods, besides a great quantity of thread. On the average, more than 12,000 yards of cotton goods alone are obtained by 300 days' work of $9\frac{1}{2}$ hours each, say 40 yards of cotton in 10 hours. Admitting that a family needs 200 yards a year at most, this would be equivalent to 50 hours' work, say *10 half-days of 5 hours each*. And we should have thread besides; that is to say, cotton to sew with, and thread to weave cloth with, so as to manufacture woollen stuffs mixed with cotton.

As to the results obtained by weaving alone, the official statistics of the United States teach us that in 1870, if workmen worked

13 to 14 hours a day, they made 10,000 yards of white cotton goods in a year; sixteen years later (1886) they wove 30,000 yards by working only 55 hours a week.

Even in printed cotton goods they obtained, weaving and printing included, 32,000 yards in 2,670 hours of work a year – say about 12 yards an hour. Thus to have your 200 yards of white and printed cotton goods *17 hours' work a year* would suffice. It is necessary to remark that raw material reaches these factories in about the same state as it comes from the fields, and that the transformations gone through by the piece before it is converted into goods are completed in the course of these 17 hours. But to *buy* these 200 yards from the tradesman, a well-paid workman must give *at the very least* 10 to 15 days' work of 10 hours each, say 100 to 150 hours. And as to the English peasant, he would have to toil for a month, or a little more, to obtain this luxury.

By this example we already see that by working *50 half-days per year* in a well-organized society we could dress better than the lower middle classes do today.

But with all this we have only required 60 half-days' work of 5 hours each to obtain the fruits of the earth, 40 for housing, and 50 for clothing, which only makes half a year's work, as the year consists of 300 working-days if we deduct holidays.

There remain still 150 half-days' work which could be made use of for other necessaries of life – wine, sugar, coffee, tea, furniture, transport, etc., etc.

It is evident that these calculations are only approximative, but they can also be proved in another way. When we take into account how many, in the so-called civilized nations, produce nothing, how many work at harmful trades, doomed to disappear, and lastly, how many are only useless middlemen, we see that in each nation the number of real producers could be doubled. And if, instead of every ten men, twenty were occupied in producing useful commodities, and if society took the trouble to economize human energy, those twenty people would only have to work 5 hours a day without production decreasing. And it would suffice to reduce the waste of human energy which is going on in the rich families with their scores of useless servants, or in the administrations which occupy one official to every ten or even six inhabitants, and to utilize those forces, to augment immensely the productivity of a nation. In fact, work could be reduced to four or even three hours a day, to produce all the goods that are produced now.

After studying all these facts together, we may arrive, then, at the following conclusion: Imagine a society, comprising a few million inhabitants, engaged in agriculture and a great variety of industries – Paris, for example, with the Department of Seine-et-Oise. Suppose that in this society all children learn to work with their hands as well as with their brains. Admit that all adults, save women, engaged in the education of their children, bind themselves to work *5 hours a day* from the age of 20 or 22 to 45 or 50, and that they follow occupations they have chosen themselves in any one of those branches of human work which in this city are considered *necessary*. Such a society could in return guarantee well-being to all its members, a well-being more substantial than that enjoyed today by the middle classes. And, moreover, each worker belonging to this society would have at his disposal at least 5 hours a day which he could devote to science, art and individual needs which do not come under the category of *necessities*, but will probably do so later on, when man's productivity will have augmented, and those objects will no longer appear luxurious or inaccessible.

CHAPTER IX

The need for luxury

I

Man is not a being whose exclusive purpose in life is eating, drinking, and providing a shelter for himself. As soon as his material wants are satisfied, other needs, which, generally speaking may be described as of an artistic character, will thrust themselves forward. These needs are of the greatest variety; they vary with each and every individual; and the more society is civilized, the more will individuality be developed, and the more will desires be varied.

Even today we see men and women denying themselves necessaries to acquire mere trifles, to obtain some particular gratification, or some intellectual or material enjoyment. A Christian or an ascetic may disapprove of these desires for luxury; but it is precisely these trifles that break the monotony of existence and make it agreeable. Would life, with all its inevitable drudgery and sorrows, be worth living, if, besides daily work, man could never obtain a single pleasure according to his individual tastes?

If we wish for a social revolution, it is no doubt, first of all, to give bread to everyone; to transform this execrable society, in which we can every day see capable workmen dangling their arms for want of an employer who will exploit them; women and children wandering shelterless at night; whole families reduced to dry bread; men, women and children dying for want of care and even for want of food. It is to put an end to these iniquities that we rebel.

But we expect more from the revolution. We see that the worker, compelled to struggle painfully for bare existence, is reduced to ignore the higher delights, the highest within man's reach, of science, and especially of scientific discovery; of art, and especially of artistic creation. It is in order to obtain for all of us joys that are now reserved to a few; in order to give leisure and the possibility of developing everyone's intellectual capacities, that the social revolution must guarantee daily bread to all. After bread has been secured, leisure is the supreme aim.

No doubt, nowadays, when hundreds and thousands of human beings are in need of bread, coal, clothing and shelter, luxury is a crime; to satisfy it, the worker's child must go without bread! But in a society in which all have the necessary food and shelter, the needs which we consider luxuries today will be the more keenly felt. And as all men do not and cannot resemble one another (the variety of tastes and needs is the chief guarantee of human progress) there will always be, and it is desirable that there should always be, men and women whose desire will go beyond those of ordinary individuals in some particular direction.

Everybody does not need a telescope, because, even if learning were general, there are people who prefer to examine things through a microscope to studying the starry heavens. Some like statues, some pictures. A particular individual has no other ambition than to possess a good piano, while another is pleased with an accordion. The tastes vary, but the artistic needs exist in all. In our present, poor capitalistic society, the man who has artistic needs cannot satisfy them unless he is heir to a large fortune, or by dint of hard work appropriates to himself an intellectual capital which will enable him to take up a liberal profession. Still he cherishes the *hope* of some day satisfying his tastes more or less, and for this reason he reproaches the idealist communist societies with having the material life of each individual as their sole aim. 'In your communal stores you may perhaps have bread for all', he says to us, 'but you will not have beautiful pictures, optical instruments, luxurious furniture, artistic jewellery – in short, the many things that minister to the infinite variety of human tastes. And you suppress the possibility of obtaining anything besides the bread and meat which the commune can offer to all, and the drab linen in which all your lady citizens will be dressed.'

These are the objections which all communist systems have to consider, and which the founders of new societies, established in

American deserts, never understood. They believed that if the community could procure sufficient cloth to dress all its members, a music-room in which the 'brothers' could strum a piece of music, or act a play from time to time, it was enough. They forgot that the feeling for art existed in the agriculturist as well as in the burgher, and, notwithstanding that the expression of artistic feeling varies according to the difference in culture, in the main it remains the same. In vain did the community guarantee the common necessaries of life, in vain did it suppress all education that would tend to develop individuality, in vain did it eliminate all reading save the Bible. Individual tastes broke forth, and caused general discontent; quarrels arose when somebody proposed to buy a piano or scientific instruments; and the elements of progress flagged. The society could only exist on condition that it crushed all individual feeling, all artistic tendency, and all development.

Will the anarchist commune be impelled by the same direction? – Evidently not, if it understands that while it produces all that is necessary to material life, it must also strive to satisfy all manifestations of the human mind.

II

We frankly confess that when we think of the abyss of poverty and suffering that surrounds us, when we hear the heartrending cry of the worker walking the streets begging for work, we are loath to discuss the question: How will men act in a society, whose members are properly fed, to satisfy certain individuals desirous of possessing a piece of Sèvres china or a velvet dress?

We are tempted to answer: Let us make sure of bread to begin with, we shall see to china and velvet later on.

But as we must recognize that man has other needs besides food, and as the strength of anarchy lies precisely in that it understands *all* human faculties and *all* passions, and ignores none, we shall, in a few words, explain how man can contrive to satisfy all his intellectual and artistic needs.

We have already mentioned that by working 4 or 5 hours a day till the age of 45 or 50, man could easily produce *all* that is necessary to guarantee comfort to society.

But the day's work of a man accustomed to toil does not consist of 5 hours; it is a 10-hour day for 300 days a year, and lasts all his life. Of course, when a man is harnessed to a machine, his health is soon undermined and his intelligence is blunted; but when man has the possibility of varying occupations, and especially of alternating manual with intellectual work, he can remain occupied without fatigue, and even with pleasure, for 10 or 12 hours a day. Consequently, the man who will have done the 4 or 5 hours of manual work that are necessary for his existence, will have before him 5 or 6 hours which he will seek to employ according to his tastes. And these 5 or 6 hours a day will fully enable him to procure for himself, if he associates with others, all he wishes for, in addition to the necessaries guaranteed to all.

He will discharge first his task in the field, the factory, and so on, which he owes to society as his contribution to the general production. And he will employ the second half of his day, his week, or his year, to satisfy his artistic or scientific needs, or his hobbies.

Thousands of societies will spring up to gratify every taste and every possible fancy.

Some, for example, will give their hours of leisure to literature. They will then form groups comprising authors, compositors, printers, engravers, draughtsmen, all pursuing a common aim – the propagation of ideas that are dear to them.

Nowadays an author knows that there is a beast of burden, the worker, to whom, for the sum of a few shillings a day, he can entrust the printing of his books; but he hardly cares to know what a printing office is like. If the compositor suffers from lead-poisoning, and if the child who sees to the machine dies of anaemia, are there not other poor wretches to replace them?

But when there will be no more starvelings ready to sell their work for a pittance, when the exploited worker of today will be educated, and will have his *own* ideas to put down in black and white and to communicate to others, then the authors and scientific men will be compelled to combine among themselves and with the printers, in order to bring out their prose and their poetry.

So long as men consider fustian and manual labour a mark of inferiority, it will appear amazing to them to see an author setting up his own book in type, for has he not a gymnasium or games by way of diversion? But when the opprobrium connected with manual labour has disappeared, when all will have to work with their hands, there being no one to do it for them, then the authors as well as their admirers will soon learn the art of handling composing-sticks and type; they will know the pleasure of coming together – all admirers of the work to be printed – to set up the type, to shape it into pages, to take it in its virginal purity from the press. These beautiful machines, instruments of torture to the child who attends on them from morn till night, will be a source of enjoyment for those who will make use of them in order to give voice to the thoughts of their favourite author.

Will literature lose by it? Will the poet be less a poet after having worked out of doors or helped with his hands to multiply his work? Will the novelist lose his knowledge of human nature after having rubbed shoulders with other men in the forest or the factory, in the laying out of a road or on a railway line? Can there be two answers to these questions?

Maybe some books will be less voluminous; but then, more will be said on fewer pages. Maybe fewer waste-sheets will be published; but the matter printed will be more attentively read and more appreciated. The book will appeal to a larger circle of better educated readers, who will be more competent to judge.

Moreover, the art of printing, that has so little progressed since Gutenberg, is still in its infancy. It takes two hours to compose in type what is written in ten minutes, but more expeditious methods of multiplying thought are being sought after and will be discovered.*

What a pity every author does not have to take his share in the printing of his works! What progress printing would have already made! We should no longer be using movable letters, as in the seventeenth century.

III

Is it a dream to conceive a society in which – all having become producers, all having received an education that enables them to cultivate science or art, and all having leisure to do so – men

*They *have* already been discovered since the above lines were written.

would combine to publish the works of their choice, by contributing each his share of manual work? We have already hundreds of learned, literary and other societies; and these societies are nothing but voluntary groups of men, interested in certain branches of learning, and associated for the purpose of publishing their works. The authors who write for the periodicals of these societies are not paid, and the periodicals, apart from a limited number of copies, are not for sale; they are sent gratis to all quarters of the globe, to other societies, cultivating the same branches of learning. This member of the society may insert in its review a one-page note summarizing his observations; another may publish therein an extensive work, the results of long years of study; while others will confine themselves to consulting the review as a starting-point for further research. It does not matter: all these authors and readers are associated for the production of works in which all of them take an interest.

It is true that a learned society, like the individual author, goes to a printing office where workmen are engaged to do the printing. Nowadays, those who belong to the learned societies despise manual labour which indeed is carried on under very bad conditions; but a community which would give a generous philosophic and *scientific* education to all its members, would know how to organize manual labour in such a way that it would be the pride of humanity. Its learned societies would become associations of explorers, lovers of science, and workers – all knowing a manual trade and all interested in science.

If, for example, the society is studying geology, all will contribute to the exploration of the earth's strata; each member will take his share in research, and ten thousand observers, where we have now only a hundred, will do more in a year than we can do in twenty years. And when their works are to be published, ten thousand men and women, skilled in different trades, will be ready to draw maps, engrave designs, compose, and print the books. With gladness will they give their leisure – in summer to exploration, in winter to indoor work. And when their works appear, they will find not only a hundred, but ten thousand readers interested in their common work.

This is the direction in which progress is already moving. Even today, when England felt the need of a complete dictionary of the English language, the birth of a Littré, who would devote his life to this work, was not waited for. Volunteers were appealed to, and a thousand men offered their services, spontaneously and gratuitously, to ransack the libraries, to take notes, and to accomplish in a few years a work which one man could not complete in his lifetime. In all branches of human intelligence the same spirit is breaking forth, and we should have a very limited knowledge of humanity could we not guess that the future is announcing itself in such tentative co-operation, which is gradually taking the place of individual work.

For this dictionary to be a really collective work, it would have been necessary that many volunteer authors, printers and printers' readers should have worked in common; but something in this direction is done already in the socialist press, which offers us examples of manual and intellectual work combined. It happens in our newspapers that a socialist author composes in lead his own article. True, such attempts are rare, but they indicate in which direction evolution is going.

They show the road of liberty. In future, when a man will have something useful to say – a word that goes beyond the thoughts of his century, he will not have to look for an editor who might advance the necessary capital. He will look for collaborators among those who know the printing trade, and who approve the idea of his new work. Together they will publish the new book or journal.

Literature and journalism will cease to be a means of money-making and living at the cost of others. But is there anyone who knows literature and journalism from within, and who does not ardently desire that literature should at last be able to free itself from those who formerly protected it, and who now exploit it, and from the multitude which, with rare exceptions, pays for it in proportion to its mediocrity, or to the ease with which it adapts itself to the bad taste of the greater number?

Letters and science will only take their proper place in the work of human development when, freed from all mercenary bondage, they will be exclusively cultivated by those who love them, and for those who love them.

IV

Literature, science and art must be cultivated by free men. Only on this condition will they succeed in emancipating themselves from the yoke of the state, of capital and of the bourgeois mediocrity which stifles them.

What means has the scientist of today to make researches that interest him? Should he ask help of the state, which can only be given to one candidate in a hundred, and which only he may obtain who promises ostensibly to keep to the beaten track? Let us remember how the Academy of Sciences of France repudiated Darwin, how the Academy of St Petersburg treated Mendeléeff with contempt, and how the Royal Society of London refused to publish Joule's paper, in which he determined the mechanical equivalent of heat, finding it 'unscientific'.[g]

It is why all great researches, all discoveries revolutionizing science, have been made outside academies and universities, either by men rich enough to remain independent, like Darwin and Lyell, or by men who undermined their health by working in poverty, and often in great straits, losing endless time for want of a laboratory, and unable to procure the instruments or books necessary to continue their researches, but persevering against hope, and often dying before they had reached the end in view. Their name is legion.

Altogether, the system of help granted by the state is so bad that science has always endeavoured to emancipate itself from it. For this very reason there are thousands of learned societies organized and maintained by volunteers in Europe and America – some having developed to such a degree that all the resources of subventioned societies, and all the wealth of millionaires, would not buy their treasures. No governmental institution is as rich as the Zoological Society of London, which is supported by voluntary contributions.

It does not buy the animals which in thousands people its gardens: they are sent by other societies and by collectors of the entire world. The Zoological Society of Bombay will send an elephant as a gift; another time a hippopotamus or a rhinoceros is offered by Egyptian naturalists. And these magnificent presents are pouring in every day, arriving from all quarters of the globe – birds, reptiles, collections of insects, etc. Such consignments often comprise animals that could not be bought for all the gold in the world; thus, a traveller who has captured an animal at life's peril, and now loves it as he would love a child, will give it to the Society

---

[g] We know this from Playfair, who mentioned it at Joule's death.

because he is sure it will be cared for. The entrance fee paid by visitors, and they are numberless, suffices for the maintenance of that immense institution.

What is defective in the Zoological Society of London, and in other kindred societies, is that the member's fee cannot be paid in work; that the keepers and numerous employees of this large institution are not recognized as members of the Society, while many have no other incentive to joining the society than to put the cabalistic letters FZS (Fellow of the Zoological Society) on their cards. In a word, what is needed is a more perfect co-operation.

We may say the same about inventors, that we have said of scientists. Who does not know what sufferings nearly all great inventions have cost? Sleepless nights, families deprived of bread, want of tools and materials for experiments, this is the history of nearly all those who have enriched industry with inventions which are the truly legitimate pride of our civilization.

But what are we to do to alter conditions that everybody is convinced are bad? Patents have been tried, and we know with what results. The inventor sells his patent for a few pounds, and the man who has only lent the capital pockets the enormous profits often resulting from the invention. Besides, patents isolate the inventor. They compel him to keep secret his researches which therefore end in failure; whereas the simplest suggestion, coming from a brain less absorbed in the fundamental idea, sometimes suffices to fertilize the invention and make it practical. Like all state control, patents hamper the progress of industry. Thought being incapable of being patented, patents are a crying injustice in theory, and in practice they result in one of the great obstacles to the rapid development of invention.

What is needed to promote the spirit of invention is, first of all, the awakening of thought, the boldness of conception, which our entire education causes to languish; it is the spreading of a scientific education, which would increase the number of enquirers a hundredfold; it is faith that humanity is going to take a step forward, because it is enthusiasm, the hope of doing good, that has inspired all the great inventors. The social revolution alone can give this impulse to thought, this boldness, this knowledge, this conviction of working for all.

Then we shall have vast institutes supplied with motor-power and tools of all sorts, immense industrial laboratories open to all enquirers, where men will be able to work out their dreams, after having acquitted themselves of their duty towards society; machinery palaces where they will spend their five or six hours of leisure; where they will make their experiments; where they will find other comrades, experts in other branches of industry, likewise coming to study some difficult problem, and therefore able to help and enlighten each other, the encounter of their ideas and experience causing the longed-for solution to be found. And yet again, this is no dream. Solanóy Gorodók, in Petersburg, has already partially realized it as regards technical matters. It is a factory well furnished with tools and free to all; tools and motor-power are supplied gratis, only metals and wood are charged for at cost price. Unfortunately, workmen only go there at night when worn out by ten hours' labour in the workshop. Moreover, they carefully hide their inventions from each other, as they are hampered by patents and capitalism – that bane of present society, that stumbling-block in the path of intellectual and moral progress.

V

And what about art? From all sides we hear lamentations about the decadence of art. We are, indeed, far behind the great masters of the Renaissance. The technicalities of art have recently made great progress; thousands of people gifted with a certain amount of talent cultivate every branch, but art seems to fly from civilization! Technicalities make headway, but inspiration frequents artists' studios less than ever.

Where, indeed, should it come from? Only a grand idea can inspire art. *Art* is in our ideal synonymous with creation, it must look ahead; but save a few rare, very rare exceptions, the professional artist remains too philistine to perceive new horizons.

Moreover, this inspiration cannot come from books; it must be drawn from life, and present society cannot arouse it.

Raphael and Murillo painted at a time when the search for a new ideal could be pursued while retaining the old religious traditions. They painted to decorate churches which themselves represented the pious work of several generations of a given city. The basilica with its mysterious aspect, its grandeur, was connected with the life itself of the city, and could inspire a painter. He worked for a popular monument; he spoke to his fellow citizens, and in return he received inspiration; he appealed to the multitude in the same way as did the nave, the pillars, the stained windows, the statues, and the carved doors. Nowadays the greatest honour a painter can aspire to is to see his canvas, framed in gilded wood, hung in a museum, a sort of old curiosity shop, where you see, as in the Prado, Murillo's Ascension next to a beggar of Velázquez and the dogs of Philip II. Poor Velázquez and poor Murillo! Poor Greek statues which *lived* in the acropolis of their cities, and are now stifled beneath the red cloth hangings of the Louvre!

When a Greek sculptor chiselled his marble he endeavoured to express the spirit and heart of the city. All its passions, all its traditions of glory, were to live again in the work. But today the *united* city has ceased to exist; there is no more communion of ideas. The town is a chance agglomeration of people who do not know one another, who have no common interest, save that of enriching themselves at the expense of one another. The fatherland does not exist ... What fatherland can the international banker and the rag-picker have in common? Only when cities, territories, nations, or groups of nations, will have renewed their harmonious life, will art be able to draw its inspiration from *ideals held in common*. Then will the architect conceive the city's monument which will no longer be a temple, a prison, or a fortress; then will the painter, the sculptor, the carver, the ornament-worker know where to put their canvases, their statues and their decorations; deriving their power of execution from the same vital source, and gloriously marching all together towards the future.

But till then art can only vegetate. The best canvases of modern artists are those that represent nature, villages, valleys, the sea with its dangers, the mountain with its splendours. But how can the painter express the poetry of work in the field if he has only contemplated it, imagined it, if he has never delighted in it himself? If he only knows it as a bird of passage knows the country he soars over in his migrations? If, in the vigour of early youth, he has not followed the plough at dawn, and enjoyed mowing grass with a large sweep of the scythe next to hardy haymakers vying in energy with lively young girls who fill the air with their songs?

The love of the soil and of what grows on it is not acquired by sketching with a paintbrush – it is only in its service; and without loving it, how paint it? This is why all that the best painters have produced in this direction is still so imperfect, not true to life, nearly always merely sentimental. There is no *strength* in it.

You must have seen a sunset when returning from work. You must have been a peasant among peasants to keep the splendour of it in your eye. You must have been at sea with fishermen at all hours of the day and night, have fished yourself, struggled with the waves, faced the storm, and after rough work experienced the joy of hauling a heavy net, or the disappointment of seeing it empty, to understand the poetry of fishing. You must have spent time in a factory, known the fatigues and the joys of creative work, forged metals by the vivid light of a blast furnace, have felt the life in a machine, to understand the power of man and to express it in a work of art. You must, in fact, be permeated with popular feelings, to describe them.

Besides, the works of future artists who will have lived the life of the people, like the great artists of the past, will not be destined for sale. They will be an integral part of a living whole that would not be complete without them, any more than they would be complete without it. Men will go to the artist's own city to gaze at his work, and the spirited and serene beauty of such creations will produce its beneficial effect on heart and mind.

Art, in order to develop, must be bound up with industry by a thousand intermediate degrees, blended, so to say, as Ruskin and the great socialist poet Morris have proved so often and so well. Everything that surrounds man, in the street, in the interior and exterior of public monuments, must be of a pure artistic form.

But this can only be realized in a society in which all enjoy comfort and leisure. Then only shall we see art associations, of which each member will find room for his capacity; for art cannot dispense with an infinity of purely manual and technical supplementary works. These artistic associations will undertake to embellish the houses of their members, as those kind volunteers, the young painters of Edinburgh, did in decorating the walls and ceilings of the great hospital for the poor in their city.

A painter or sculptor who has produced a work of personal feeling will offer it to the woman he loves, or to a friend. Executed for love's sake – will his work, inspired by love, be inferior to the art that today satisfies the vanity of the philistine, because it has cost much money?

The same will be done as regards all pleasures not comprised in the necessaries of life. He who wishes for a grand piano will enter the association of musical instrument makers. And by giving the association part of his half-days' leisure, he will soon possess the piano of his dreams. If he is fond of astronomical studies he will join the association of astronomers, with its philosophers, its observers, its calculators, with its artists in astronomical instruments, its scientists and amateurs, and he will have the telescope he desires by taking his share of the associated work, for it is especially the rough work that is needed in an astronomical observatory – bricklayer's, carpenter's, founder's, mechanic's work, the last touch being given to the instrument of precision by the artist.

In short, the five or seven hours a day which each will have at his disposal, after having consecrated several hours to the production of necessities, would amply suffice to satisfy all longings for luxury, however varied. Thousands of associations would undertake to supply them. What is now the privilege of an insignificant minority would be accessible to all. Luxury, ceasing to be a foolish and ostentatious display of the bourgeois class, would become an artistic pleasure.

Everyone would be the happier for it. In collective work, performed with a light heart to attain a desired end, a book, a work of art or an object of luxury, each will find an incentive and the necessary relaxation that makes life pleasant.

In working to put an end to the division between master and slave, we work for the happiness of both, for the happiness of humanity.

CHAPTER X
Agreeable work

I

When socialists maintain that a society, freed from the rule of the capitalists, would make work agreeable, and would suppress all repugnant and unhealthy drudgery, they are laughed at. And yet even today we can see the striking progress that is being made in this direction; and wherever this progress has been achieved, employers congratulate themselves on the economy of energy obtained thereby.

It is evident that a factory could be made as healthy and pleasant as a scientific laboratory. And it is no less evident that it would be advantageous to make it so. In a spacious and well-ventilated factory the work is better; it is easy to introduce many small ameliorations, of which each represents an economy of time or of manual labour. And if most of the workshops we know are foul and unhealthy, it is because the workers are of no account in the organization of factories, and because the most absurd waste of human energy is the distinctive feature of the present industrial organization.

Nevertheless, now and again, we already find, even now, some factories so well managed that it would be a real pleasure to work in them, if the work, be it well understood, were not to last more than four or five hours a day, and if everyone had the possibility of varying it according to his tastes.

There are immense works, which I know, in one of the midland counties, unfortunately consecrated to engines of war. They are perfect as regards sanitary and intelligent organization. They occupy

50 English acres of land, 15 of which are roofed with glass. The pavement of fireproof bricks is as clean as that of a miner's cottage, and the glass roof is carefully cleaned by a gang of workmen who do nothing else. In these works are forged steel ingots or blooms weighing as much as 20 tons; and when you stand 30 feet from the immense furnace, whose flames have a temperature of more than 1,000 degrees, you do not guess its presence save when its great doors open to let out a steel monster. And the monster is handled by only three or four workmen, who now here, now there, open a tap causing immense cranes to move one way or another by the pressure of water.

You enter these works expecting to hear the deafening noise of stampers, and you find that there are no stampers. The immense hundred-ton guns and the crankshafts of transatlantic steamers are forged by hydraulic pressure, and the worker has but to turn a tap to give shape to the immense mass of steel, which makes a far more homogeneous metal, without crack or flaw, of the blooms, whatever be their thickness.

I expected an infernal grating, and I saw machines which cut blocks of steel 30 feet long with no more noise than is needed to cut cheese. And when I expressed my admiration to the engineer who showed us round, he answered –

'A mere question of economy! This machine, that planes steel, has been in use for forty-two years. It would not have lasted ten years if its parts, badly adjusted, "interfered" and creaked at each movement of the plane!

'And the blast-furnaces? It would be a waste to let heat escape instead of utilizing it. Why roast the founders, when heat lost by radiation represents tons of coal?

'The stampers that made buildings shake five leagues off were also waste. Is it not better to forge by pressure than by impact, and it costs less – there is less loss.

'In these works, light, cleanliness, the space allotted to each bench, are but a simple question of economy. Work is better done when you can see what you do, and have elbow-room.

'It is true', he said, 'we were very cramped before coming here. Land is so expensive in the vicinity of large towns – landlords are so grasping!'

It is even so in mines. We know what mines are like nowadays from Zola's descriptions and from newspaper reports. But the mine of the future will be well ventilated, with a temperature as easily regulated as that of a library; there will be no horses doomed to die below the earth: underground traction will be carried on by means of an automatic cable put in motion at the pit's mouth. Ventilators will be always working, and there will never be explosions. This is no dream. Such a mine is already to be seen in England; I went down it. Here again the excellent organization is simply a question of economy. The mine of which I speak, in spite of its immense depth (466 yards), has an output of 1,000 tons of coal a day, with only 200 miners – 5 tons a day per worker, whereas the average for the 2,000 pits in England at the time I visited this mine in the early nineties, was hardly 300 tons a year per man.

If necessary, it would be easy to multiply examples proving that as regards the material organization Fourier's dream was not a utopia.

This question has, however, been so frequently discussed in socialist newspapers that public opinion should already be educated on this point. Factory, forge and mine *can* be as healthy and magnificent as the finest laboratories in modern universities, and the better the organization the more will man's labour produce.

If it be so, can we doubt that work will become a pleasure and a relaxation in a society of equals, in which 'hands' will not be compelled to sell themselves to toil, and to accept work under any conditions? Repugnant tasks will disappear, because it is evident that these unhealthy conditions are harmful to society as a whole. Slaves can submit to them, but free men will create new conditions, and their work will be pleasant and infinitely more productive. The exceptions of today will be the rule of tomorrow.

The same will come to pass as regards domestic work, which today society lays on the shoulders of that drudge of humanity – woman.

II

A society regenerated by the revolution will make domestic slavery disappear – this last form of slavery, perhaps the most tenacious, because it is also the most ancient. Only it will not come about in the way dreamt of by phalansterians, nor in the manner often imagined by authoritarian communists.

Phalansteries are repugnant to millions of human beings. The most reserved man certainly feels the necessity of meeting his fellows for the purpose of common work, which becomes the more attractive the more he feels himself a part of an immense whole. But it is not so for the hours of leisure, reserved for rest and intimacy. The phalanstery and the familystery do not take this into account, or else they endeavour to supply this need by artificial groupings.

A phalanstery, which is in fact nothing but an immense hotel, can please some, and even all at a certain period of their life, but the great mass prefers family life (family life of the future, be it understood). They prefer isolated apartments, Anglo-Saxons even going as far as to prefer houses of from six to eight rooms, in which the family, or an agglomeration of friends, can live apart. Sometimes a phalanstery is a necessity, but it would be hateful, were it the general rule. Isolation, alternating with time spent in society, is the normal desire of human nature. This is why one of the greatest tortures in prison is the impossibility of isolation, much as solitary confinement becomes torture in its turn, when not alternated with hours of social life.

As to considerations of economy, which are sometimes laid stress on in favour of phalansteries, they are those of a petty tradesman. The most important economy, the only reasonable one, is to make life pleasant for all, because the man who is satisfied with his life produces infinitely more than the man who curses his surroundings.[h]

Other socialists reject the phalanstery. But when you ask them how domestic work can be organized, they answer: 'Each can do "his own work". My wife manages the house; the wives of bourgeois will do as much.' And if it is a bourgeois playing at socialism who speaks, he will add, with a gracious smile to his wife: 'Is it not true, darling, that you would do without a servant in a socialist society? You would work like the wife of our good comrade Paul or the wife of John the carpenter?'

[h] It seems that the communists of Young Icaria had understood the importance of a free choice in their daily relations apart from work. The ideal of religious communists has always been to have meals in common; it is by meals in common that early Christians manifested their adhesion to Christianity. Communion is still a vestige of it. Young Icarians had given up this religious tradition. They dined in a common dining room, but at small separate tables, at which they sat according to the attractions of the moment. The communists of Amana have each their house and dine at home, while taking their provisions at will at the communal stores.

Servant or wife, man always reckons on woman to do the housework.

But woman, too, at last claims her share in the emancipation of humanity. She no longer wants to be the beast of burden of the house. She considers it sufficient work to give many years of her life to the rearing of her children. She no longer wants to be the cook, the mender, the sweeper of the house! And, owing to American women taking the lead in obtaining their claims, there is a general complaint of the dearth of women who will condescend to domestic work in the United States. My lady prefers art, politics, literature, or the gaming tables; as to the work-girls, they are few, those who consent to submit to apron-slavery, and servants are only found with difficulty in the States. Consequently, the solution, a very simple one, is pointed out by life itself. Machinery undertakes three-quarters of the household cares.

You black your boots, and you know how ridiculous this work is. What can be more stupid than rubbing a boot twenty or thirty times with a brush? A tenth of the European population must be compelled to sell itself in exchange for a miserable shelter and insufficient food, and woman must consider herself a slave, in order that millions of her sex should go through this performance every morning.

But hairdressers have already machines for brushing glossy or woolly heads of hair. Why should we not apply, then, the same principle to the other extremity? So it has been done, and nowadays the machine for blacking boots is in general use in big American and European hotels. Its use is spreading outside hotels. In large English schools, where the pupils are boarding in the houses of the teachers, it has been found easier to have one single establishment which undertakes to brush a thousand pairs of boots every morning.

As to washing up! Where can we find a housewife who has not a horror of this long and dirty work, that is usually done by hand, solely because the work of the domestic slave is of no account?

In America they do better. There are already a number of cities in which hot water is conveyed to the houses as cold water is in Europe. Under these conditions the problem was a simple one, and a woman – Mrs Cochrane – solved it. Her machine washes twelve dozen plates or dishes, wipes them and dries them, in less than three minutes. A factory in Illinois manufactures these machines and sells them at a price within reach of the average middle-class purse. And why should not small households send their crockery to an establishment as well as their boots? It is even probable that the two functions, brushing and washing up, will be undertaken by the same association.

Cleaning, rubbing the skin off your hands when washing and wringing linen; sweeping floors and brushing carpets, thereby raising clouds of dust which afterwards occasion much trouble to dislodge from the places where they have settled down, all this work is still done because woman remains a slave, but it tends to disappear as it can be infinitely better done by machinery. Machines of all kinds will be introduced into households, and the distribution of motor-power in private houses will enable people to work them without muscular effort.

Such machines cost little to manufacture. If we still pay very much for them, it is because they are not in general use, and chiefly because an exorbitant tax is levied upon every machine by the gentlemen who wish to live in grand style and who have speculated on land, raw material, manufacture, sale, patents, and duties.

But emancipation from domestic toil will not be brought about by small machines only. Households are emerging from their present state of isolation; they begin to associate with other households to do in common what they did separately.

In fact, in the future we shall not have a brushing machine, a machine for washing up plates, a third for washing linen, and so on, in each house. To the future, on the contrary, belongs the common heating apparatus that sends heat into each room of a whole district and spares the lighting of fires. It is already so in a few American cities. A great central furnace supplies all houses and all rooms with hot water, which circulates in pipes; and to regulate the temperature you need only turn a tap. And should you care to have a blazing fire in any particular room you can light the gas specially supplied for heating purposes from a central reservoir. All the immense work of cleaning chimneys and keeping up fires – and woman knows what time it takes – is disappearing.

Candles, lamps, and even gas have had their day. There are entire cities in which it is sufficient to press a button for light to burst forth, and, indeed, it is a simple question of economy and of knowledge to give yourself the luxury of electric light. And lastly, also in America, they speak of forming societies for the almost complete suppression of household work. It would only be necessary to create a department for every block of houses. A cart would come to each door and take the boots to be blacked, the crockery to be washed up, the linen to be washed, the small things to be mended (if it were worth while), the carpets to be brushed, and the next morning would bring back the things entrusted to it, all well cleaned. A few hours later your hot coffee and your eggs done to a nicety would appear on your table. It is a fact that between twelve and 2 o'clock there are more than 20 million Americans and as many Englishmen who eat roast beef or mutton, boiled pork, potatoes and a seasonable vegetable. And at the lowest figure 8 million fires burn during two or three hours to roast this meat and cook these vegetables; 8 million women spend their time preparing a meal which, taking all households, represents at most a dozen different dishes.

'Fifty fires burn', wrote an American woman the other day, 'where one would suffice!' Dine at home, at your own table, with your children, if you like; but only think yourself, why should these fifty women waste their whole morning to prepare a few cups of coffee and a simple meal! Why fifty fires, when two people and one single fire would suffice to cook all these pieces of meat and all these vegetables? Choose your own beef or mutton to be roasted if you are particular. Season the vegetables to your taste if you prefer a particular sauce! But have a single kitchen with a single fire, and organize it as beautifully as you are able to.

Why has woman's work never been of any account? Why in every family are the mother and three or four servants obliged to spend so much time at what pertains to cooking? Because those who want to emancipate mankind have not included woman in their dream of emancipation, and consider it beneath their superior masculine dignity to think 'of those kitchen arrangements' which they have put on the shoulders of that drudge – woman.

To emancipate woman is not only to open the gates of the university, the law courts or the parliaments to her, for the 'emancipated' woman will always throw domestic toil on to another woman. To emancipate woman is to free her from the brutalizing toil of kitchen and wash-house; it is to organize your household in such a way as to enable her to rear her children, if she be so minded, while still retaining sufficient leisure to take her share of social life.

It will come. As we have said, things are already improving. Only let us fully understand that a revolution, intoxicated with the beautiful words, Liberty, Equality, Solidarity, would not be a revolution if it maintained slavery at home. Half humanity subjected to the slavery of the hearth would still have to rebel against the other half.

CHAPTER XI
Free agreement

I

Accustomed as we are by hereditary prejudices and our unsound education and training to represent ourselves the beneficial hand of government, legislation and magistracy everywhere, we have come to believe that man would tear his fellow man to pieces like a wild beast the day the police took his eye off him; that absolute chaos would come about if authority were overthrown during a revolution. And with our eyes shut we pass by thousands and thousands of human groupings which form themselves freely, without any intervention of the law, and attain results infinitely superior to those achieved under governmental tutelage.

If you open a daily paper you find that its pages are entirely devoted to government transactions and to political jobbery. A man from another world, reading it, would believe that, with the exception of the Stock Exchange transactions, nothing gets done in Europe save by order of some master. You find nothing in the paper about institutions that spring up, grow up, and develop without ministerial prescription! Nothing – or almost nothing! Even where there is a heading, 'Sundry Events' (*Faits divers*, a favourite column in the French papers), it is because they are connected with the police. A family drama, an act of rebellion, will only be mentioned if the police have appeared on the scene.

Three hundred and fifty million Europeans love or hate one another, work, or live on their incomes; but, apart from literature, theatre or sport, their lives remain ignored by newspapers if governments have not intervened in it in some way or other. It is even so with history. We know the least details of the life of a king or of a parliament; all good and bad speeches pronounced by the politicians have been preserved: 'speeches that have never had the least influence on the vote of a single member', as an old parliamentarian said. Royal visits, the good or bad humour of politicians, their jokes and intrigues, are all carefully recorded for posterity. But we have the greatest difficulty to reconstitute a city of the Middle Ages, to understand the mechanism of that immense commerce that was carried on between Hanseatic cities, or to know how the city of Rouen built its cathedral. If a scholar spends his life in studying these questions, his works remain unknown, and parliamentary histories – that is to say, the defective ones, as they only treat of one side of social life – multiply; they are circulated, they are taught in schools.

In this way we do not even perceive the prodigious work accomplished every day by spontaneous groups of men, which constitutes the chief work of our century.

We therefore propose to point out some of these most striking manifestations, and to show how men, as soon as their interests do not absolutely clash, act in concert, harmoniously, and perform collective work of a very complex nature.

It is evident that in present society, based on individual property – that is to say, on plunder, and on a narrow-minded, and therefore foolish individualism – facts of this kind are necessarily limited; agreements are not always perfectly free, and often they have a mean, if not execrable aim.

But what concerns us is not to give examples which might be blindly followed, and which, moreover, present society could not possibly give us. What we have to do is to show that, in spite of the authoritarian individualism which stifles us, there remains in our life, taken as a whole, a very great part in which we only act by free agreement; and that therefore it would be much easier than is usually thought, to dispense with government.

In support of our view we have already mentioned railways, and we will now return to them.

We know that Europe has a system of railways, over 175,000 miles long, and that on this network you can nowadays travel from north to south, from east to west, from Madrid to Petersburg, and from Calais to Constantinople, without delays, without even changing carriages (when you travel by express). More than that: a parcel deposited at a station will find its addressee anywhere, in Turkey or in Central Asia, without more formality needed for sending it than writing its destination on a bit of paper.

This result might have been obtained in two ways. A Napoleon, a Bismarck, or some potentate having conquered Europe, would from Paris, Berlin or Rome, draw a railway map and regulate the hours of the trains. The Russian Tsar Nicholas I dreamt of such a power. When he was shown rough drafts of railways between Moscow and Petersburg, he seized a ruler and drew on the map of Russia a straight line between these two capitals, saying, 'Here is the plan.' And the road was built in a straight line, filling in deep ravines, building bridges of a giddy height, which had to be abandoned a few years later, after the railway had cost about £120,000 to £150,000 per English mile.

This is one way, but happily things were managed differently. Railways were constructed piece by piece, the pieces were joined together, and the hundred different companies, to whom these pieces belonged, gradually came to an understanding concerning the arrival and departure of their trains, and the running of carriages on their rails, from all countries, without unloading merchandise as it passes from one network to another.

All this was done by free agreement, by exchange of letters and proposals, and by congresses at which delegates met to discuss well-specified special points, and to come to an agreement about them, but not to make laws. After the congress was over, the delegates returned to their respective companies, not with a law, but with the draft of a contract to be accepted or rejected.

Of course difficulties were met in the way. There were obstinate men who would not be convinced. But a common interest compelled them to agree in the end, without invoking the help of armies against the refractory members.

This immense network of railways connected together, and the enormous traffic it has given rise to, no doubt constitutes the most striking trait of the nineteenth century; and it is the result of free agreement. If somebody had foretold it eighty years ago, our grandfathers would have thought him idiotic or mad. They would have said: 'Never will you be able to make the shareholders of a hundred companies listen to reason! It is a utopia, a fairy tale. A central government, with an "iron" director, can alone enforce it.'

And the most interesting thing in this organization is, that there is no European central government of railways! Nothing! No minister of railways, no dictator, not even a continental parliament, not even a directing committee! Everything is done by free agreement.

So we ask the believers in the state, who pretend that 'we can never do without a central government, were it only for regulating the traffic', we ask them: 'But how do European railways manage without them? How do they continue to convey millions of travellers and mountains of luggage across a continent? If companies owning railways have been able to agree, why should railway workers, who would take possession of railways, not agree likewise? And if the Petersburg–Warsaw Company and that of Paris–Belfort can act in harmony, without giving themselves the luxury of a common commander, why, in the midst of our societies, consisting of groups of free workers, should we need a government?'

II

When we endeavour to prove by examples that even today, in spite of the iniquitous organization of society as a whole, men, provided their interests be not diametrically opposed, agree without the intervention of authority, we do not ignore the objections that will be put forth.

All such examples have their defective side, because it is impossible to quote a single organization exempt from the exploitation of the weak by the strong, the poor by the rich. This is why the statists will not fail to tell us with their wonted logic: 'You see that the intervention of the state is necessary to put an end to this exploitation!'

Only they forget the lessons of history; they do not tell us to what extent the state itself has contributed towards the existing order by creating proletarians and delivering them up to exploiters. They forget to prove to us that it is possible to put an end to exploitation while the primal causes – private capital and poverty, two-thirds of which are artificially created by the state – continue to exist.

When we speak of the accord established among the railway companies, we expect them, the worshippers of the bourgeois state, to say to us: 'Do you not see how the railway companies oppress and ill-use their employees and the travellers! The only way is, that the state should intervene to protect the workers and the public!'

But have we not said and repeated over and over again, that as long as there are capitalists, these abuses of power will be perpetuated. It is precisely the state, the would-be benefactor, that has given to the companies that monopoly and those rights upon us which they possess today. Has it not created concessions, guarantees? Has it not sent its soldiers against railwaymen on strike? And during the first trials (quite lately we saw it still in Russia), has it not extended the privilege of the railway magnates as far as to forbid the press to mention railway accidents, so as not to depreciate the shares it guaranteed? Has it not favoured the monopoly which has anointed the Vanderbilts and the Polyakoffs, the directors of the PLM, the CPR, the St Gothard, 'the kings of our days'?

Therefore, if we give as an example the tacit agreement come to between railway companies, it is by no means as an ideal of economical management, nor even an ideal of technical organization. It is to show that if capitalists, without any other aim than that of augmenting their dividends at other people's expense, can exploit railways successfully without establishing an international department – societies of working men will be able to do it just as well, and even better, without nominating a ministry of European railways.

Another objection is raised that is more serious at first sight. We may be told that the agreement we speak of is not perfectly *free*, that the large companies lay down the law to the small ones. It might be mentioned, for example, that a certain rich German company, supported by the state, compels travellers who go from Berlin to Basle to pass via Cologne and Frankfort, instead of taking the Leipzig route; or that such a company carries goods 130 miles in a roundabout way (on a long distance) to favour its influential shareholders, and thus ruins the secondary lines. In the United States travellers and goods are sometimes compelled to travel impossibly circuitous routes so that dollars may flow into the pocket of a Vanderbilt.

Our answer will be the same: As long as capital exists, the greater capital will oppress the lesser. But oppression does not result from capital only. It is also owing to the support given them by the state, to monopoly created by the state in their favour, that the large companies oppress the small ones.

The early English and French socialists have shown long since how English legislation did all in its power to ruin the small industries, drive the peasant to poverty, and deliver over to wealthy industrial employers battalions of men, compelled to work for no matter what salary. Railway legislation did exactly the same. Strategic lines, subsidized lines, companies which received the international mail monopoly, everything was brought into play to forward the interests of wealthy financiers. When Rothschild, creditor to all European states, puts capital in a railway, his faithful subjects, the ministers, will do their best to make him earn more.

In the United States, in the democracy that authoritarians hold up to us as an ideal, the most scandalous fraudulency has crept into everything that concerns railroads. Thus, if a company ruins its competitors by cheap fares, it is often enabled to do so because it is reimbursed by land given to it by the state for a gratuity. Documents recently published concerning the American wheat trade have fully shown up the part played by the state in the exploitation of the weak by the strong. Here, too, the power of accumulated capital has increased tenfold and a hundredfold by means of state help. So that, when we see syndicates of railway companies (a product of free agreement) succeeding in protecting their small companies against big ones, we are astonished at the intrinsic force of free agreement that can hold its own against all-powerful capital favoured by the state.

It is a fact that little companies exist, in spite of the state's partiality. If in France, land of centralization, we only see five or six large companies, there are more than a hundred and ten in Great Britain who agree remarkably well, and who are certainly better organized for the rapid transit of travellers and goods than the French and German companies.

Moreover, that is not the question. Large capital, favoured by the state, can always, *if it be to its advantage*, crush the lesser one. What is of importance to us is this: The agreement between hundreds of capitalist companies to whom the railways of Europe belong, *was established without intervention of a central government* to lay down the law to the divers societies; it has subsisted by means of congresses composed of delegates, who discuss among themselves, and submit *proposals*, not *laws*, to their constituents. It is a new principle that differs completely from all governmental principle, monarchical or republican, absolute or parliamentarian. It is an innovation that has been timidly introduced into the customs of Europe, but has come to stay.

III

How often have we not read in the writings of state-loving socialists: 'Who, then, will undertake the regulation of canal traffic in the future society? Should it enter the mind of one of your anarchist "comrades" to put his barge across a canal and obstruct thousands of boats, who will force him to yield to reason?'

Let us confess the supposition to be somewhat fanciful. Still, it might be said, for instance: 'Should a certain commune, or a group of communes, want to make their barges pass before others, they might perhaps block the canal in order to carry stones, while wheat, needed in another commune, would have to stand by. Who, then, would regulate the traffic if not the government?'

But real life has again demonstrated that government can be very well dispensed with here as elsewhere. Free agreement, free organization, replace that noxious and costly system, and do better.

We know what canals mean to Holland. They are its highways. We also know how much traffic there is on the canals. What is carried along our highroads and railroads is transported on canal-boats in Holland. There you could find cause to fight, in order to make your boats pass before others. There the government might really interfere to keep the traffic in order.

Yet it is not so. The Dutch settled matters in a more practical way, long ago, by founding guilds, or syndicates of boatmen. These were free associations sprung from the very needs of navigation. The right of way for the boats was adjusted by the order of inscription in a navigation register; they had to follow one another in turn. Nobody was allowed to get ahead of the others under pain of being excluded from the guild. None could station more than a certain number of days along the quay; and if the owner found no goods to carry during that time, so much the worse for him; he had to depart with his empty barge to leave room for newcomers. Obstruction was thus avoided, even though the competition between the private owners of the boats continued to exist. Were the latter suppressed, the agreement would have been only the more cordial.

It is unnecessary to add that the shipowners could adhere or not to the syndicate. That was their business, but most of them elected to join it. Moreover, these syndicates offered such great advantages that they spread also along the Rhine, the Weser, the Oder, and as far as Berlin. The boatmen did not wait for a great Bismarck to annex Holland to Germany, and to appoint an Ober Haupt General Staats Canal Navigation's Rath (Supreme Head Councillor of the General States Canal Navigation), with a number of gold stripes on his sleeves, corresponding to the length of the title. They preferred coming to an international understanding. Besides, a number of shipowners, whose sailing-vessels ply between Germany and Scandinavia, as well as Russia, have also joined these syndicates, in order to regulate traffic in the Baltic, and to bring about a certain harmony in the *chassé-croisé* of vessels. These associations have sprung up freely, recruiting volunteer adherents, and have nought in common with governments.

It is, however, more than probable that here too greater capital oppresses lesser. Maybe the syndicate has also a tendency to become a monopoly, especially where it receives the precious patronage of the state that surely did not fail to interfere with it. Let us not forget either that these syndicates represent associations whose members have only private interests at stake, and that if at the same time each shipowner were compelled – by the socializing of production, consumption and exchange – to belong to federated communes, or to a hundred other associations for the satisfying of his needs, things would have a different aspect. A group of ship-owners, powerful on sea, would feel weak on land, and they would be obliged to lessen their claims in order to come to terms with railways, factories, and other groups.

At any rate, without discussing the future, here is another spontaneous association that has dispensed with government. Let us quote more examples.

As we are talking of ships and boats, let us mention one of the most splendid organizations that the nineteenth century has brought forth, one of those we may with right be proud of – the English Lifeboat Association.

It is known that every year more than a thousand ships are wrecked on the shores of England. At sea a good ship seldom fears a storm. It is near the coasts that danger threatens – rough seas that shatter her sternpost, squalls that carry off her masts and sails, currents that render her unmanageable, reefs and sandbanks on which she runs aground.

Even in olden times, when it was a custom among inhabitants of the coasts to light fires in order to attract vessels on to reefs, in order to plunder their cargoes, they always strove to save the crew. Seeing a ship in distress, they launched their boats and went to the rescue of shipwrecked sailors, only too often finding a watery grave themselves. Every hamlet along the sea shore has its legends of heroism, displayed by woman as well as by man, to save crews in distress.

No doubt the state and men of science have done something to diminish the number of casualties. Lighthouses, signals, charts, meteorological warnings have diminished them greatly, but there remains a thousand ships and several thousand human lives to be saved every year.

To this end a few men of goodwill put their shoulders to the wheel. Being good sailors and navigators themselves, they invented a lifeboat that could weather a storm without being torn to pieces or capsizing, and they set to work to interest the public in their venture, to collect the necessary funds for constructing boats, and for stationing them along the coasts, wherever they could be of use.

These men, not being Jacobins, did not turn to the government. They understood that to bring their enterprise to a successful issue they must have the co-operation, the enthusiasm, the local knowledge and especially the self-sacrifice of the local sailors. They also understood that to find men who at the first signal would launch their boat at night, in a chaos of waves, not suffering themselves to be deterred by darkness or breakers, and struggling five, six, ten hours against the tide before reaching a vessel in distress – men ready to risk their lives to save those of others – there must be a feeling of solidarity, a spirit of sacrifice not to be bought with galloon. It was therefore a perfectly spontaneous movement, sprung from agreement and individual initiative. Hundreds of local groups arose along the coasts. The initiators had the common sense not to pose as masters. They looked for sagacity in the fishermen's hamlets, and when a rich man sent £1,000 to a village on the coast to erect a lifeboat station, and his offer was accepted, he left the choice of a site to the local fishermen and sailors.

Models of new boats were not submitted to the Admiralty. We read in a Report of the Association: 'As it is of importance that lifeboatmen should have full confidence in the vessel they man, the Committee will make a point of constructing and equipping the boats according to the lifeboatmen's expressed wish.' In consequence every year brings with it new improvements.

The work is wholly conducted by volunteers organizing in committees and local groups; by mutual aid and agreement! – Oh, anarchists! Moreover, they ask nothing of the ratepayers, and in a year they may receive £40,000 in spontaneous subscriptions.

As to the results, here they are: In 1891 the Association possessed 293 lifeboats. The same year it saved 601 shipwrecked sailors and 33 vessels. Since its foundation it has saved 32,671 human beings.

In 1886, three lifeboats with all their men having perished at sea, hundreds of new volunteers entered their names, organized themselves into local groups, and the agitation resulted in the construction of twenty additional boats. As we proceed, let us note that every year the Association sends to the fishermen and sailors excellent barometers at a price three times less than their sale price in private shops. It propagates meteorological knowledge, and warns the parties concerned of the sudden changes of weather predicted by men of science.

Let us repeat that these hundreds of committees and local groups are not organized hierarchically, and are composed exclusively of volunteers, lifeboatmen, and people interested in the work. The Central Committee, which is more of a centre for correspondence, in no wise interferes.

It is true that when a voting on some question of education or local taxation takes place in a district, these committees of the National Lifeboat Association do not, as such, take part in the deliberations – a modesty which unfortunately the members of elected bodies do not imitate. But, on the other hand, these brave men do not allow those who have never faced a storm to legislate for them about saving life. At the first signal of distress they rush to their boats, and go ahead. There are no embroidered uniforms, but much goodwill.

Let us take another society of the same kind, that of the Red Cross. The name matters little; let us examine it.

Imagine somebody saying fifty years ago: 'The state, capable as it is of massacring twenty thousand men in a day, and of wounding fifty thousand more, is incapable of helping its own victims; consequently, as long as war exists private initiative must intervene, and men of goodwill must organize internationally for this humane work!' What mockery would not have met the man who would have dared to speak thus! To begin with, he would have been called a utopian, and if that did not silence him he would have been told: 'What nonsense! Your volunteers will be found wanting precisely where they are most needed, your volunteer hospitals will be centralized in a safe place, while everything will be wanting in the ambulances. Utopians like you forget the national rivalries which will cause the poor soldiers to die without any help.' Such disheartening remarks would have only been equalled by the number of speakers. Who of us has not heard men hold forth in this strain?

Now we know what happened. Red Cross societies organized themselves freely, everywhere, in all countries, in thousands of localities; and when the war of 1870–1 broke out, the volunteers set to work. Men and women offered their services. Thousands of hospitals and ambulances were organized; trains were started carrying ambulances, provisions, linen and medicaments for the wounded. The English committees sent entire convoys of food, clothing, tools, grain to sow, beasts of draught, even steam-ploughs with their attendants to help in the tillage of departments devastated by the war! Only consult *La Croix Rouge*, by Gustave Moynier, and you will be really struck by the immensity of the work performed.

As to the prophets ever ready to deny other men's courage, good sense and intelligence, and believing themselves to be the only ones capable of ruling the world with a rod, none of their predictions were realized. The devotion of the Red Cross volunteers was beyond all praise. They were only too eager to occupy the most dangerous posts; and whereas the salaried doctors of the Napoleonic state fled with their staff when the Prussians approached, the Red Cross volunteers continued their work under fire, enduring the brutalities of Bismarck's and Napoleon's officers, lavishing their care on the wounded of all nationalities. Dutch, Italians, Swedes, Belgians, even Japanese and Chinese agreed remarkably well. They distributed their hospitals and their ambulances according to the needs of the occasion. They vied with one another especially in the hygiene of their hospitals. And there is many a Frenchman who still speaks with deep gratitude of the tender care he received from the Dutch or German volunteers in the Red Cross ambulances. But what is this to an authoritarian? His ideal is the regiment doctor, salaried by the state. What does he care for the Red Cross and its hygienic hospitals, if the nurses be not functionaries!

Here is then an organization, sprung up but yesterday, and which reckons its members by hundreds of thousands; possesses ambulances, hospital trains, elaborates new processes for treating wounds, and so on, and is due to the spontaneous initiative of a few devoted men.

Perhaps we shall be told that the state has something to do with this organization. Yes, states have laid hands on it to seize it. The directing committees are presided over by those whom flunkeys call princes of the blood. Emperors and queens lavishly patronize the national committees. But it is not to this patronage that the success of the organization is due. It is to the thousand local committees of each nation; to the activity of individuals, to the devotion of all those who try to help the victims of war. And this devotion would be far greater if the state did not meddle with it.

In any case, it was not by the order of an international directing committee that Englishmen and Japanese, Swedes and Chinamen bestirred themselves to send help to the wounded in 1871. It was not by order of an international ministry that hospitals rose on the invaded territory and that ambulances were carried on to the battlefield. It was by the initiative of volunteers from each country. Once on the spot, they did not get hold of one another by the hair as was foreseen by the Jacobinists of all nations; they all set to work without distinction of nationality.

We may regret that such great efforts should be put to the service of so bad a cause, and we may ask ourselves like the poet's child: 'Why inflict wounds if you are to heal them afterwards?' In striving to destroy the power of capitalist and middle-class authority, we work to put an end to the massacres called wars, and we would far rather see the Red Cross volunteers put forth their activity to bring about (with us) the suppression of war; but we had to mention this immense organization as another illustration of results produced by free agreement and free aid.

If we wished to multiply examples taken from the art of exterminating men we should never end. Suffice to quote the numerous societies to which the German army owes its force, that does not only depend on discipline, as is generally believed. I mean the societies whose aim is to propagate military knowledge.

At one of the last congresses of the Military Alliance (*Kriegerbund*), delegates from 2,452 federated societies, comprising 151,712 members, were present. But there are besides very numerous shooting, military games, strategical games, topographical studies societies – these are the workshops in which the technical knowledge of the German army is developed, not in regimental schools. It is a formidable network of all kinds of societies, including military men and civilians, geographers and gymnasts, sportsmen and technologists, which rise up spontaneously, organize, federate, discuss and explore the country. It is these voluntary and free associations that go to make the real backbone of the German army.

Their aim is execrable. It is the maintenance of the empire. But what concerns us is to point out that, in spite of military organization being the 'Great Mission of the State', success in this branch is the more certain the more it is left to the free agreement of groups and to the free initiative of individuals.

Even in matters pertaining to war, free agreement is thus appealed to; and to further prove our assertion let us mention the Volunteer Topographers' Corps of Switzerland who study in detail the mountain passes, the Aeroplane Corps of France, the three hundred thousand British volunteers, the British National Artillery Association, and the society, now in course of organization, for the defence of England's coasts, as well as the appeals made to the commercial fleet, the Bicyclists' Corps, and the new organizations of private motor-cars and steam launches.

Everywhere the state is abdicating and abandoning its holy functions to private individuals. Everywhere free organization trespasses on its domain. And yet, the facts we have quoted give us only a glimpse of what free agreement has in store for us in the future, when there will be no more state.

CHAPTER XII

Objections

I

Let us now examine the principal objections put forth against communism. Most of them are evidently caused by a simple misunderstanding, yet they raise important questions and merit our attention.

It is not for us to answer the objections raised by authoritarian communism – we ourselves hold with them. Civilized nations have suffered too much in the long, hard struggle for the emancipation of the individual, to disown their past work and to tolerate a government that would make itself felt in the smallest details of a citizen's life, even if that government had no other aim than the good of the community. Should an authoritarian socialist society ever succeed in establishing itself, it could not last; general discontent would soon force it to break up, or to reorganize itself on principles of liberty.

It is of an anarchist-communist society we are about to speak, a society that recognizes the absolute liberty of the individual, that does not admit of any authority, and makes use of no compulsion to drive men to work. Limiting our studies to the economic side of the question, let us see if such a society, composed of men as they are today, neither better nor worse, neither more nor less industrious, would have a chance of successful development.

The objection is known. 'If the existence of each is guaranteed, and if the necessity of earning wages does not compel men to work, nobody will work. Every man will lay the burden of his work on another if he is not forced to do it himself.' Let us first note the incredible levity with which this objection is raised, without even realizing that the real question raised by this objection is merely to know, on the one hand, whether you effectively obtain by wage-work the results that are said to be obtained, and, on the other hand, whether voluntary work is not already now more productive than work stimulated by wages. A question which, to be dealt with properly, would require a serious study. But whereas in exact sciences men give their opinion on subjects infinitely less important and less complicated after serious research, after carefully collecting and analysing facts – on this question they will pronounce judgement without appeal, resting satisfied with any one particular event, such as, for example, the want of success of some communist association in America. They act like the barrister who does not see in the counsel for the opposite side a representative of a cause, or an opinion contrary to his own, but a simple nuisance – an adversary in an oratorical debate; and if he be lucky enough to find a repartee, does not otherwise care to justify his cause. Therefore the study of this essential basis of all political economy, *the study of the most favourable conditions for giving society the greatest amount of useful products with the least waste of human energy*, does not advance. People either limit themselves to repeating commonplace assertions, or else they pretend ignorance of our assertions.

What is most striking in this levity is that even in capitalist political economy you already find a few writers compelled by facts to doubt the axiom put forth by the founders of their science, that the threat of hunger is man's best stimulant for productive work. They begin to perceive that in production a certain *collective element* is introduced, which has been too much neglected up till now, and which might be more important than personal gain. The inferior quality of wage-work, the terrible waste of human energy in modern agricultural and industrial labour, the ever-growing quantity of pleasure-seekers, who shift their burden on to others' shoulders, the absence of a certain animation in production that is becoming more and more apparent; all this is beginning to preoccupy the economists of the 'classical' school. Some of them ask themselves if they have not got on the wrong track: if the imaginary evil being, that was supposed to be tempted exclusively by a bait of lucre or wages, really exists. This heresy penetrates even into universities; it is found in books of orthodox economy.

But this does not prevent a great many socialist reformers from remaining partisans of individual remuneration, and defending the old citadel of wagedom, notwithstanding that it is being delivered over stone by stone to the assailants by its former defenders.

They fear that without compulsion the masses will not work.

But during our own lifetime, have we not heard the same fears expressed twice? Once, by the anti-abolitionists in America before the emancipation of the Negroes, and, for a second time, by the Russian nobility before the liberation of the serfs? 'Without the whip the Negro will not work', said the anti-abolitionist. 'Free from their master's supervision the serfs will leave the fields uncultivated', said the Russian serf-owners. It was the refrain of the French noblemen in 1789, the refrain of the Middle Ages, a refrain as old as the world, and we shall hear it every time there is a question of sweeping away an injustice. And each time actual facts give it the lie. The liberated peasant of 1792 ploughed with an eager energy, unknown to his ancestors; the emancipated Negro works more than his fathers; and the Russian peasant, after having honoured the honeymoon of his emancipation by celebrating Fridays as well as Sundays, has taken up work with an eagerness proportionate to the completeness of his liberation. There, where the soil is his, he works desperately; that is the exact word for it. The anti-abolitionist refrain can be of value to slave-owners; as to the slaves themselves, they know what it is worth, as they know its motive.

Moreover, who but the economists themselves taught us that while a wage-earner's work is very often indifferent, an intense and productive work is only obtained from a man who sees his wealth increase in proportion to his efforts? All hymns sung in honour of private property can be reduced to this axiom.

For it is remarkable that when economists, wishing to celebrate the blessings of property, show us how an unproductive, marshy or stony soil is clothed with rich harvests when cultivated by the peasant proprietor, they in nowise prove their thesis in favour of private property. By admitting that the only guarantee not to be robbed of the fruits of your labour is to possess the instruments of labour – which is true – the economists only prove that man really produces most when he works in freedom, when he has a certain choice in his occupations, when he has no overseer to impede him, and lastly, when he sees his work bringing in a profit to him and to others who work like him, but bringing in little to idlers. Nothing else can be deducted from their argumentation, and this is what we maintain ourselves.

As to the form of possession of the instruments of labour, the economists only mention it *indirectly* in their demonstration, as a guarantee to the cultivator that he shall not be robbed of the profits of his yield nor of his improvements. Besides, in support of their thesis in favour of *private property* against all other forms of *possession*, should not the economists demonstrate that under the form of communal property land never produces such rich harvests as when the possession is private? But this they could not prove; in fact, it is the contrary that has been observed.

Take for example a commune in the canton of Vaud, in the winter time, when all the men of the village go to fell wood in the forest, which belongs to them all. It is precisely during these festivals of labour that the greatest ardour for work and the most considerable display of human energy are apparent. No salaried labour, no effort of a private owner can bear comparison with it.

Or let us take a Russian village, when all its inhabitants mow a field belonging to the commune, or farmed by it. There you will see what man *can* produce when he works in common for communal production. Comrades vie with one another in cutting the widest swathe, women bestir themselves in their wake so as not to be distanced by the mowers. It is a festival of labour, in which a hundred people accomplish in a few hours a work that would not have been finished in a few days had they worked separately. What a miserable contrast compared to them is offered by the work of the isolated owner!

In fact, we might quote scores of examples among the pioneers of America, in Swiss, German, Russian, and in certain French villages; or the work done in Russia by gangs (*artels*) of masons, carpenters, boatmen, fishermen, etc., who undertake a task and divide the produce or the remuneration among themselves, without it passing through the intermediary of middlemen; or else the amount of work I saw performed in English shipyards when the remuneration was paid on the same principle. We could also mention the great communal hunts of nomadic tribes, and an infinite number of successful collective enterprises. And in every case we could show the unquestionable superiority of communal work compared to that of the wage-earner or the isolated private owner.

Well-being – that is to say, the satisfaction of physical, artistic, and moral needs, has always been the most powerful stimulant to work. And where a hireling hardly succeeds to produce the bare necessities with difficulty, a free worker, who sees ease and luxury increasing for him and for others in proportion to his efforts, spends infinitely far more energy and intelligence, and obtains first-class products in a far greater abundance. The one feels riveted to misery, the other hopes for ease and luxury in the future. In this lies the whole secret. Therefore a society aiming at the well-being of all, and at the possibility of all enjoying life in all its manifestations, will give voluntary work, which will be infinitely superior and yield far more than work has produced up till now under the goad of slavery, serfdom, or wagedom.

II

Nowadays, whoever can load on others his share of labour indispensable to existence, does so, and it is believed that it will always be so.

Now, work indispensable to existence is essentially manual. We may be artists or scientists; but none of us can do without things obtained by manual work – bread, clothes, roads, ships, light, heat, etc. And, moreover, however highly artistic or however subtly metaphysical are our pleasures, they all depend on manual labour. And it is precisely this labour – the basis of life – that everyone tries to avoid.

We understand perfectly well that it must be so nowadays.

Because, to do manual work now, means in reality to shut yourself up for ten or twelve hours a day in an unhealthy workshop, and to remain chained to the same task for twenty or thirty years, and maybe for your whole life.

It means to be doomed to a paltry wage, to the uncertainty of the morrow, to want of work, often to destitution, more often than not to death in a hospital, after having worked forty years to feed, clothe, amuse and instruct others than yourself and your children.

It means to bear the stamp of inferiority all your life; because, whatever the politicians tell us, the manual worker is always considered inferior to the brain worker, and the one who has toiled ten hours in a workshop has not the time, and still less the means, to give himself the high delights of science and art, nor even to prepare himself to appreciate them; he must be content with the crumbs from the table of privileged persons.

We understand that under these conditions manual labour is considered a curse of fate.

We understand that all men have but one dream – that of emerging from, or enabling their children to emerge from, this inferior state; to create for themselves an 'independent' position, which means what? – To also live by other men's work!

As long as there will be a class of manual workers and a class of 'brain' workers, black hands and white hands, it will be thus.

What interest, in fact, can this depressing work have for the worker, when he knows that the fate awaiting him from the cradle to the grave will be to live in mediocrity, poverty and insecurity of the morrow? Therefore, when we see the immense majority of men take up their wretched task every morning, we feel surprised at their perseverance, at their zeal for work, at the habit that enables them, like machines blindly obeying an impetus given, to lead this life of misery without hope for the morrow; without foreseeing ever so vaguely that some day they, or at least their children, will be part of a humanity rich in all the treasures of a bountiful nature, in all the enjoyments of knowledge, scientific and artistic creation, reserved today to a few privileged favourites.

It is precisely to put an end to this separation between manual and brain work that we want to abolish wagedom, that we want the social revolution. Then work will no longer appear a curse of fate: it will become what it should be – the free exercise of *all* the faculties of man.

Moreover, it is time to submit to a serious analysis this legend about superior work, supposed to be obtained under the lash of wagedom.

It would be sufficient to visit, not the model factory and workshop that we find now and again, but a number of the ordinary factories, to conceive the immense waste of human energy that characterizes modern industry. For one factory more or less rationally organized, there are a hundred or more which waste man's labour, without any more substantial motive than that of perhaps bringing in a few pounds more per day to the employer.

Here you see youths from 20 to 25 years of age, sitting all day long on a bench, their chests sunken in, feverishly shaking their heads and bodies, to tie, with the speed of conjurers, the two ends of worthless scraps of cotton, the refuse of the lace-looms. What progeny will these trembling and rickety bodies bequeath to their country? 'But they occupy so little room in the factory, and each of them brings me in sixpence net every day', will say the employer.

In an immense London factory we saw girls, bald at 17 from carrying trays of matches on their heads from one room to another, when the simplest machine could wheel the matches to their tables. But 'It costs so little, the work of women who have no special trade! Why should we use a machine? When these can do no more, they will be easily replaced, there are so many of them in the street!'

On the steps of a mansion on an icy night you will find a barefoot child asleep, with its bundle of papers in its arms ... child-labour costs so little that it may well be employed, every evening, to sell ten pennyworth of papers, of which the poor boy will receive a penny, or a penny half-penny. And continually in all big cities you may see robust men tramping about who have been out of work for months, while their daughters grow pale in the overheated vapours of the workshop for dressing stuffs, and their sons are filling blacking-pots by hand, or spend those years during which they ought to have learned a trade, in carrying about baskets for a greengrocer, and at the age of 18 or 20 become regular unemployed.

And so it is everywhere, from San Francisco to Moscow, and from Naples to Stockholm. The waste of human energy is the distinguishing and predominant trait of our industry, not to mention trade where it attains still more colossal proportions.

What a sad satire is that name, political *economy*, given to the science of waste of energy under the system of wagedom!

This is not all. If you speak to the director of a well-organized factory, he will naively explain to you that it is difficult nowadays to find a skilful, vigorous and energetic workman, who works with a will. 'Should such a man present himself among the twenty or thirty who call every Monday asking us for work, he is sure to be received, even if we are reducing the number of our hands. We recognize him at the first glance, and he is always accepted, even though we have to get rid of an older and less active worker the next day.' And the one who has just received notice to quit, and all those who will receive it tomorrow, go to reinforce that immense reserve-army of capital – workmen out of work – who are only called to the loom or the bench when there is pressure of work, or to oppose strikers. And those others – the average workers who are sent away by the better-class factories as soon as business is slackened? They also join the formidable army of aged and indifferent workers who continually circulate among the second-class factories – those which barely cover their expenses and make their way in the world by trickery and snares laid for the buyer, and especially for the consumer in distant countries.

And if you talk to the workmen themselves, you will soon learn that the rule in such factories is – never to do your best. 'Shoddy pay – shoddy work!' this is the advice which the working man receives from his comrades upon entering such a factory.

For the workers know that if in a moment of generosity they give way to the entreaties of an employer and consent to intensify the work in order to carry out a pressing order, this nervous work will be exacted in the future as a rule in the scale of wages. Therefore in all such factories they prefer never to produce as much as they can. In certain industries production is limited so as to keep up high prices, and sometimes the password, 'Go canny', is given, which signifies, 'Bad work for bad pay!'

Wage-work is serf-work; it cannot, it must not, produce all that it could produce. And it is high time to disbelieve the legend which represents wagedom as the best incentive to productive work. If industry nowadays brings in a hundred times more than it did in the days of our grandfathers, it is due to the sudden awakening of physical and chemical sciences towards the end of the last century; not to the capitalist organization of wagedom, but *in spite of* that organization.

III

Those who have seriously studied the question do not deny any of the advantages of communism, on condition, be it well understood, that communism be perfectly free, that is to say, anarchist. They recognize that work paid with money, even disguised under the name of 'labour cheques', to workers' associations governed by the state, would keep up the characteristics of wagedom and would retain its disadvantages. They agree that the whole system would soon suffer from it, even if society came into possession of the instruments of production. And they admit that, thanks to an 'integral' complete education given to all children, to the laborious habits of civilized societies, with the liberty of choosing and varying their occupations and the attractions of work done by equals for the well-being of all, a communist society would not be wanting in producers who would soon make the fertility of the soil triple and tenfold, and give a new impulse to industry.

This our opponents agree to. 'But the danger', they say, 'will come from that minority of loafers who will not work, and will not have regular habits, in spite of the excellent conditions that would make work pleasant. Today the prospect of hunger compels the most refractory to move along with the others. The one who does not arrive in time is dismissed. But one black sheep suffices to contaminate the whole flock, and two or three sluggish or refractory workmen would lead the others astray and bring a spirit of disorder and rebellion into the workshop that would make work impossible; so that in the end we should have to return to a system of compulsion that would force such ringleaders back into the ranks. And then, is not the system of wages, paid in proportion to work performed, the only one that enables compulsion to be employed, without hurting the feelings of independence of the worker? All other means would imply the continual intervention of an authority that would be repugnant to free men.' This, we believe, is the objection fairly stated.

To begin with, such an objection belongs to the category of arguments which try to justify the state, the penal law, the judge and the gaoler.

'As there are people, a feeble minority, who will not submit to social customs', the authoritarians say, 'we must maintain magistrates, tribunals and prisons, although these institutions become a source of new evils of all kinds.'

Therefore we can only repeat what we have so often said concerning authority in general: 'To avoid a possible evil you have recourse to means which in themselves are a greater evil, and become the source of those same abuses that you wish to remedy. For, do not forget that it is wagedom, the impossibility of living otherwise than by selling your labour, which has created the present capitalist system, whose vices you begin to recognize.' Besides, this way of reasoning is merely a sophistical justification of the evils of the present system. Wagedom was *not* instituted to remove the disadvantages of communism; its origin, like that of the state and private ownership, is to be found elsewhere. It is born of slavery and serfdom imposed by force, and only wears a more modern garb. Thus the argument in favour of wagedom is as valueless as those by which they seek to apologize for private property and the state.

We are, nevertheless, going to examine the objection, and see if there is any truth in it.

First of all, is it not evident that if a society, founded on the principle of free work, were really menaced by loafers, it could protect itself without the authoritarian organization we have nowadays, and without having recourse to wagedom?

Let us take a group of volunteers, combining for some particular enterprise. Having its success at heart, they all work with a will, save one of the associates, who is frequently absent from his post. Must they on his account dissolve the group, elect a president to impose fines, and work out a code of penalties? It is evident that neither the one nor the other will be done, but that some day the comrade who imperils their enterprise will be told: 'Friend, we should like to work with you; but as you are often absent from your post, and you do your work negligently, we must part. Go and find other comrades who will put up with your indifference!'

This way is so natural that it is practised everywhere, even nowadays, in all industries, in competition with all possible systems of fines, docking of wages, supervision, etc.; a workman may enter the factory at the appointed time, but if he does his work badly, if he hinders his comrades by his laziness or other defects, if he is quarrelsome, there is an end of it; he is compelled to leave the workshop.

Authoritarians pretend that it is the almighty employer and his overseers who maintain regularity and quality of work in factories. In reality, in every somewhat complicated enterprise, in which the goods produced pass through many hands before being finished, it is the factory itself, the workmen as a unity, who see to the good quality of the work. Therefore the best factories of British private industry have few overseers, far less on an average than the French factories, and less than the British state factories.

A certain standard of public morals is maintained in the same way. Authoritarians say it is due to rural guards, judges and policemen, whereas in reality it is maintained *in spite of* judges, policemen and rural guards. 'Many are the laws producing criminals!' was said long ago.

Not only in industrial workshops do things go on in this way; it happens everywhere, every day, on a scale that only bookworms have as yet no notion of. When a railway company, federated with other companies, fails to fulfil its engagements, when its trains are late and goods lie neglected at the stations, the other companies threaten to cancel the contract, and that threat usually suffices.

It is generally believed, at any rate it is taught in state-approved schools, that commerce only keeps to its engagements from fear of lawsuits. Nothing of the sort; nine times in ten the trader who has not kept his word will not appear before a judge. There, where trade is very active, as in London, the sole fact of having driven a creditor to bring a lawsuit suffices for the immense majority of merchants to refuse for good to have any dealings with a man who has compelled one of them to go to law.

This being so, why should means that are used today among workers in the workshop, traders in the trade, and railway companies in the organization of transport, not be made use of in a society based on voluntary work?

Take, for example, an association stipulating that each of its members should carry out the following contract: 'We undertake to give you the use of our houses, stores, streets, means of transport, schools, museums, etc., on condition that, from 20 to 45 or 50 years of age, you consecrate four or five hours a day to some work recognized as necessary to existence. Choose yourself the producing groups which you wish to join, or organize a new group, provided that it will undertake to produce necessaries. And as for the remainder of your time, combine together with whomsoever you like, for recreation, art or science, according to the bent of your taste.

'Twelve or fifteen hundred hours of work a year, in one of the groups producing food, clothes, or houses, or employed in public sanitation, transport, and so on, is all we ask of you. For this amount of work we guarantee to you the free use of all that these groups produce, or will produce. But if not one, of the thousands of groups of our federation, will receive you, whatever be their motive; if you are absolutely incapable of producing anything useful, or if you refuse to do it, then live like an isolated man or like an invalid. If we are rich enough to give you the necessaries of life we shall be delighted to give them to you. You are a man, and you have the right to live. But as you wish to live under special conditions, and leave the ranks, it is more than probable that you will suffer for it in your daily relations with other citizens. You will be looked upon as a ghost of bourgeois society, unless some friends of yours, discovering you to be a talent, kindly free you from all moral obligation towards society by doing all the necessary work for you.

'And finally, if it does not please you, go and look for other conditions elsewhere in the wide world, or else seek adherents and organize with them on novel principles. We prefer our own.'

This is what could be done in a communal society in order to turn away sluggards if they became too numerous.

IV

We very much doubt that we need fear this contingency in a society really based on the entire freedom of the individual.

In fact, in spite of the premium on idleness offered by the private ownership of capital, the really lazy man is comparatively rare, unless his laziness be due to illness.

Among workmen it is often said that the bourgeois are idlers. There are certainly enough of them, but they, too, are the exception. On the contrary, in every industrial enterprise, you are sure to find one or more bourgeois who work very hard. It is true that the majority of bourgeois profit by their privileged position to award themselves the least unpleasant tasks, and that they work under hygienic conditions of air, food, etc., which permit them to do their business without too much fatigue. But these are precisely the conditions which we claim for all workers, without exception.

It must also be said that if, thanks to their privileged position, rich people often perform absolutely useless or even harmful work in society, nevertheless the ministers, heads of departments, factory owners, traders, bankers, etc., subject themselves for a number of hours every day to work which they find more or less tiresome, all preferring their hours of leisure to this obligatory work. And if in nine cases out of ten this work is a harmful work, they find it none the less tiring for that. But it is precisely because the middle class put forth great energy, even in doing harm (knowingly or not) and defending their privileged position, that they have succeeded in defeating the landed nobility, and that they continue to rule the masses. If they were idlers, they would long since have ceased to exist, and would have disappeared like the aristocracy. In a society that would expect only four or five hours a day of useful, pleasant and hygienic work, these same middle-class people would perform their task perfectly well, and they certainly would not put up with the horrible conditions in which men toil nowadays without reforming them. If a Huxley spent only five hours in the sewers of London, rest assured that he would have found the means of making them as sanitary as his physiological laboratory.

As to the laziness of the great majority of workers, only philistine economists and philanthropists can utter such nonsense.

If you ask an intelligent manufacturer, he will tell you that if workmen only put it into their heads to be lazy, all factories would have to be closed, for no measure of severity, no system of spying, would be of any use. You should have seen the terror caused in 1887 among British employers when a few agitators started preaching the 'go canny' theory – 'Bad pay, bad work'; 'Take it easy, do not overwork yourselves, and waste all you can.' – 'They demoralize the worker, they want to kill our industry!' cried those same people who the day before inveighed against the immorality of the worker and the bad quality of his work. But if the workers were what they are represented to be – namely, the idlers whom the employer is supposed continually to threaten with dismissal from the workshop – what would the word 'demoralization' signify?

So when we speak of possible idlers, we must well understand that it is a question of a small minority in society; and before legislating for that minority, would it not be wise to study the origin of that idleness? Whoever observes with an intelligent eye, sees well enough that the child reputed lazy at school is often the one who simply does not understand, because he is being badly taught. Very often, too, he is suffering from cerebral anaemia, caused by poverty and an anti-hygienic education. A boy who is lazy at Greek or Latin would work admirably were he taught science, especially if he were taught with the aid of manual labour. A girl who is stupid at mathematics becomes the first mathematician of her class if she by chance meets somebody who can explain to her the elements of arithmetic which she did not understand. And a workman, lazy in the workshop, cultivates his garden at dawn, while gazing at the rising sun, and will be at work again at nightfall, when all nature goes to its rest.

Somebody has said that dust is matter in the wrong place. The same definition applies to nine-tenths of those called lazy. They are people gone astray in a direction that does not answer to their temperament nor to their capacities. In reading the biography of great men, we are struck with the number of 'idlers' among them. They were lazy so long as they had not found the right path; afterwards they became laborious to excess. Darwin, Stephenson and many others belonged to this category of idlers.

Very often the idler is but a man to whom it is repugnant to spend all his life making the eighteenth part of a pin, or the hundredth part of a watch, while he feels he has exuberant energy which he would like to expend elsewhere. Often, too, he is a rebel who cannot submit to being fixed all his life to a work-bench in order to procure a thousand pleasures for his employer, while knowing himself to be far the less stupid of the two, and knowing his only fault to be that of having been born in a hovel instead of coming into the world in a castle.

Lastly, an immense number of 'idlers' are idlers because they do not know well enough the trade by which they are compelled to earn their living. Seeing the imperfect thing they make with their own hands, striving vainly to do better, and perceiving that they never will succeed on account of the bad habits of work already acquired, they begin to hate their trade, and, not knowing any other, hate work in general. Thousands of workmen and artists who are failures suffer from this cause.

On the other hand, he who since his youth has learned to play the piano *well*, to handle the plane *well*, the chisel, the brush or the file, so that he feels that what he does is *beautiful*, will never give up the piano, the chisel or the file. He will find pleasure in his work which does not tire him, so long as he is not overdriven.

Under the one name, *idleness,* a series of results due to different causes have been grouped, of which each one could be a source of good, instead of being a source of evil to society. Like all questions concerning criminality and related to human faculties, facts have been collected having nothing in common with one another. People speak of laziness or crime, without giving themselves the trouble to analyse the cause. They are in a hurry to punish these faults without enquiring if the punishment itself does not contain a premium on 'laziness' or 'crime'.[i]

This is why a free society, if it saw the number of idlers increasing in its midst, would no doubt think of looking first for the *cause* of laziness, in order to suppress it, before having recourse to punishment. When it is a case, as we have already mentioned, of simple bloodlessness, then before stuffing the brain of a child with science, nourish his system so as to produce blood, strengthen him, and, that he shall not waste his time, take him to the country or to the seaside; there, teach him in the open air, not in books – geometry, by measuring the distance to a spire, or the height of a tree; natural sciences, while picking flowers and fishing in the sea; physical science, while building the boat he will go to fish in. But for mercy's sake do not fill his brain with classical sentences and dead languages. Do not make an idler of him! ...

Or, here is a child which has neither order nor regular habits. Let the children first inculcate order among themselves, and later on, the laboratory, the workshop, the work that will have to be done in a limited space, with many tools about, under the guidance of an intelligent teacher, will teach them method. But do not make disorderly beings out of them by your school, whose only order is the symmetry of its benches, and which – true image of the chaos in its teachings – will never inspire anybody with the love of harmony, of consistency, and method in work.

Do not you see that by your methods of teaching, framed by a ministry for 8 million scholars, who represent 8 million different capacities, you only impose a system good for mediocrities, conceived by an average of mediocrities? Your school becomes a university of laziness, as your prison is a university of crime. Make the school free, abolish your university grades, appeal to the

[i] See my book, *In Russian and French Prisons.* London, 1887.

volunteers of teaching; begin that way, instead of making laws against laziness which only serve to increase it.

Give the workman who cannot condemn himself to make all his life a minute particle of some object, who is stifled at his little tapping machine, which he ends by loathing, give him the chance of tilling the soil, of felling trees in the forest, sailing the seas in the teeth of a storm, dashing through space on an engine, but do not make an idler of him by forcing him all his life to attend to a small machine, to plough the head of a screw, or to drill the eye of a needle.

Suppress the cause of idleness, and you may take it for granted that few individuals will really hate work, especially voluntary work, and that there will be no need to manufacture a code of laws on their account.

CHAPTER XIII
The collectivist wages system

I

In their plans for the reconstruction of society the collectivists commit, in our opinion, a twofold error. While speaking of abolishing capitalist rule, they intend nevertheless to retain two institutions which are the very basis of this rule – representative government and the wages' system.

As regards so-called representative government, we have often spoken about it. It is absolutely incomprehensible to us that intelligent men – and such are not wanting in the collectivist party – can remain partisans of national or municipal parliaments after all the lessons history has given them – in France, in England, in Germany or in the United States.

While we see parliamentary rule breaking up, and from all sides criticism of this rule growing louder – not only of its results, but also of *its principles* – how is it that the revolutionary socialists defend a system already condemned to die?

Built up by the middle classes to hold their own against royalty, sanctioning, and, at the same time strengthening, their sway over the workers, parliamentary rule is pre-eminently a middle-class rule. The upholders of this system have never seriously maintained that a parliament or a municipal council represent a nation or a city. The most intelligent among them know that this is impossible. The middle classes have simply used the parliamentary system to raise a protecting barrier against the pretensions of royalty, without giving the people liberty. But gradually, as the people become conscious of their real interests, and the variety of their interests is growing, the system can no longer work. Therefore democrats of all countries vainly imagine various palliatives. The referendum is tried and found to be a failure; proportional representation is spoken of, the representation of minorities, and other parliamentary utopias. In a word, they strive to find what is not to be found, and after each new experiment they are bound to recognize that it was a failure; so that confidence in representative government vanishes more and more.

It is the same with the wages' system; because, once the abolition of private property is proclaimed, and the possession in common of all means of production is introduced – how can the wages' system be maintained in any form? This is, nevertheless, what collectivists are doing when they recommend the use of the *labour-cheques* as a mode of remuneration for labour accomplished for the great collectivist employer – the state.

It is easy to understand why the early English socialists, since the time of Robert Owen, came to the system of labour-cheques. They simply tried to make capital and labour agree. They repudiated the idea of laying hands on capitalist property by means of revolutionary measures.

It is also easy to understand why Proudhon took up later on the same idea. In his mutualist system he tried to make capital less offensive, notwithstanding the retaining of private property, which he detested from the bottom of his heart, but which he believed to be necessary to guarantee individuals against the state.

Neither is it astonishing that certain economists, more or less bourgeois, admit labour-cheques. They care little whether the worker is paid in labour-notes or in coin stamped with the effigy of the republic or the empire. They only care to save from destruction the individual ownership of dwelling-houses, of land, of factories; in any case – that, at least, of dwelling-houses and the capital that is necessary for manufacturing. And labour-notes would just answer the purpose of upholding this private property.

As long as labour-notes can be exchanged for jewels or carriages, the owner of the house will willingly accept them for rent. And as long as dwelling-houses, fields and factories belong to isolated owners, men will have to pay these owners, in one way or another, for being allowed to work in the fields or factories, or for living in the houses. The owners will agree to be paid by the workers in gold, in paper-money, or in cheques exchangeable for all sorts of commodities, once that toll upon labour is maintained, and the right to levy it is left with them. But how can we defend labour-notes, this new form of wagedom, when we admit that the houses, the fields, and the factories will no longer be private property – that they will belong to the commune or the nation?

II

Let us closely examine this system of remuneration for work done, preached by the French, German, English and Italian collectivists (the Spanish anarchists, who still call themselves collectivists, imply by collectivism the possession in common of all instruments of production, and the 'liberty of each group to divide the produce, as they think fit, according to communist or any other principles').

It amounts to this: everybody works in field, factory, school, hospital, etc. The working day is fixed by the state, which owns the land, the factories, the roads, etc. Every work-day is paid for with a *labour-note*, which is inscribed with these words: *Eight hours' work*. With this cheque the worker can procure all sorts of merchandise in the stores owned by the state or by divers corporations. The cheque is divisible, so that you can buy an hour's-work worth of meat, ten minutes' worth of matches, or half an hour of tobacco. After the collectivist revolution, instead of saying 'twopence worth of soap', we shall say 'five minutes' worth of soap'.

Most collectivists, true to the distinction laid down by middle-class economists (and by Marx as well) between *qualified* work and *simple* work, tell us, moreover, that *qualified* or professional work must be paid a certain quantity more than *simple* work. Thus one hour's work of a doctor will have to be considered as equivalent to two or three hours' work of a hospital nurse, or to three or five hours' work of a navvy. 'Professional, or qualified work, will be a multiple of simple work', says the collectivist Grönlund, 'because this kind of work needs a more or less long apprenticeship.'

Some other collectivists, such as the French Marxist, Guesde, do not make this distinction. They proclaim the 'equality of wages'.

The doctor, the schoolmaster and the professor will be paid (in labour-cheques) at the same rate as the navvy. Eight hours visiting the sick in a hospital will be worth the same as eight hours spent in earthworks or else in mines or factories.

Some make a greater concession; they admit that disagreeable or unhealthy work – such as sewerage – could be paid for at a higher rate than agreeable work. One hour's work of a sewerman would be worth, they say, two hours of a professor's work.

Let us add that certain collectivists admit of corporations being paid a lump sum for work done. Thus a corporation would say: 'Here are a hundred tons of steel. A hundred workmen were required to produce them, and it took them ten days. Their work-day being an eight-hour day, it has taken them eight thousand working hours to produce a hundred tons of steel – eight hours a ton.' For this the state would pay them eight thousand labour-notes of one hour each, and these eight thousand cheques would be divided among the members of the iron-works as they themselves thought proper.

On the other hand, a hundred miners having taken twenty days to extract eight thousand tons of coal, coal would be worth two hours a ton, and the sixteen thousand cheques of one hour each, received by the Guild of Miners, would be divided among their members according to their own appreciation.

If the miners protested and said that a ton of steel should only cost six hours' work instead of eight; if the professor wished to have his day paid four times more than the nurse, then the state would interfere and would settle their differences.

Such is, in a few words, the organization the collectivists wish to see arise out of the social revolution. As we see, their principles are: collective property of the instruments of production, and remuneration to each according to the time spent in producing, while taking into account the productivity of his labour. As to the political system, it would be the parliamentary system, modified by *positive instructions* given to those elected, and by the referendum – a vote, taken by *noes* or *ayes* by the nation.

Let us own that this system appears to us simply unrealizable.

Collectivists begin by proclaiming a revolutionary principle – the abolition of private property – and then they deny it, no sooner than proclaimed, by upholding an organization of production and consumption which originated in private property.

They proclaim a revolutionary principle, and ignore the consequences that this principle will inevitably bring about. They forget that the very fact of abolishing individual property in the instruments of work – land, factories, road, capital – must launch society into absolutely new channels; must completely overthrow the present system of production, both in its aim as well as in its means; must modify daily relations between individuals, as soon as land, machinery, and all other instruments of production are considered common property.

They say, 'No private property', and immediately after strive to maintain private property in its daily manifestations. 'You shall be a commune as far as regards production: fields, tools, machinery, all that has been invented up till now – factories, railways, harbours, mines, etc., all are yours. Not the slightest distinction will be made concerning the share of each in this collective property.

'But from tomorrow you will minutely debate the share you are going to take in the creation of new machinery, in the digging of new mines. You will carefully weigh what part of the new produce belongs to you. You will count your minutes of work, and you will take care that a minute of your neighbours should not buy more than yours.

'And as an hour measures nothing, as in some factories a worker can see to six power-looms at a time, while in another he only tends two, you will weigh the muscular force, the brain energy, and the nervous energy you have expended. You will accurately calculate the years of apprenticeship in order to appraise the amount each will contribute to future production. And this – after having declared that you do not take into account his share in *past* production.'

Well, for us it is evident that a society cannot be based on two absolutely opposed principles, two principles that contradict one another continually. And a nation or a commune which would have such an organization would be compelled to revert to private property in the instruments of production, or to transform itself into a communist society.

III

We have said that certain collectivist writers desire that a distinction should be made between *qualified* or professional work and *simple* work. They pretend that an hour's work of an engineer, an architect or a doctor, must be considered as two or three hours' work of a blacksmith, a mason or a hospital nurse. And the same distinction must be made between all sorts of trades necessitating apprenticeship, and the simple toil of day-labourers.

Well, to establish this distinction would be to maintain all the inequalities of present society. It would mean fixing a dividing line, from the beginning, between the workers and those who pretend to govern them. It would mean dividing society into two very distinct classes – the aristocracy of knowledge placed above the horny-handed lower orders – the one doomed to serve the other; the one working with its hands to feed and clothe those who, profiting by their leisure, study how to govern their fosterers.

It would mean reviving one of the distinct peculiarities of present society and giving it the sanction of the social revolution. It would mean setting up as a principle an abuse already condemned in our ancient crumbling society.

We know the answer we shall get. They will speak of 'scientific socialism'; they will quote bourgeois economists, and Marx too, to prove that a scale of wages has its *raison d'être*, as 'the labour force' of the engineer will have cost more to society than the 'labour force' of the navvy. In fact – have not economists tried to prove to us that if an engineer is paid twenty times more than a navvy it is *because* the 'necessary' outlay to make an engineer is greater than that necessary to make a navvy? And has not Marx asserted that the same distinction is equally logical between two branches of manual labour? He could not conclude otherwise, having taken up on his own account Ricardo's theory of value, and upheld that goods *are* exchanged in proportion to the quantity of work socially necessary for their production.

But we know what to think of this. We know that if engineers, scientists or doctors are paid ten or a hundred times more than a labourer, and if a weaver earns three times more than an agricultural labourer, and ten times more than a girl in a match factory, it is not by reason of their 'cost of production', but by reason of a monopoly of education, or a monopoly of industry. Engineers, scientists and doctors merely exploit their capital – their diplomas – as middle-class employers exploit a factory, or as nobles used to exploit their titles of nobility.

As to the employer who pays an engineer twenty times more than a labourer, it is simply due to personal interest; if the engineer can economize £4,000 a year on the cost of production, the employer pays him £800. And if the employer has a foreman who saves £400 on the work by cleverly sweating workmen, he gladly gives him £80 or £120 a year. He parts with an extra £40 when he expects to gain £400 by it; and this is the essence of the capitalist system. The same differences obtain among different manual trades.

Let them, therefore, not talk to us of 'the cost of production' which raises the cost of skilled labour, and tell us that a student who has gaily spent his youth in a university has a *right* to a wage ten times greater than the son of a miner who has grown pale in a mine since the age of 11; or that a weaver has a *right* to a wage three or four times greater than that of an agricultural labourer. The cost of teaching a weaver his work is not four times greater than the cost of teaching a peasant his. The weaver simply benefits by the advantages his industry reaps in international trade, from countries that have as yet no industries, and in consequence of the privileges accorded by all states to industries in preference to the tilling of the soil.

Nobody has ever calculated the *cost of production* of a producer; and if a noble loafer costs far more to society than a worker, it remains to be seen whether a robust day-labourer does not cost more to society than a skilled artisan, when we have taken into account infant mortality among the poor, the ravages of anaemia, and premature deaths.

Could they, for example, make us believe that the 1s. 3d. paid to a Paris workwoman, the 3d. paid to an Auvergne peasant girl who grows blind at lace-making, or the 1s. 8d. paid to the peasant represent their 'cost of production'? We know full well that people work for less, but we also know that they do so exclusively because, thanks to our wonderful organization, they would die of hunger did they not accept these mock wages.

For us the scale of remuneration is a complex result of taxes, of governmental tutelage, of capitalist monopoly. In a word, of state and capital. Therefore, we say that all wages' theories have been invented after the event to justify injustices at present existing, and that we need not take them into consideration.

Neither will they fail to tell us that the collectivist scale of wages would be an improvement. 'It would be better', so they say, 'to see certain artisans receiving a wage two or three times higher than common labourers, than to see a minister receiving in a day what a workman cannot earn in a year. It would be a great step towards equality.'

For us this step would be the reverse of progress. To make a distinction between simple and professional work in a new society would result in the revolution sanctioning and recognizing as a principle a brutal fact we submit to nowadays, but that we nevertheless find unjust. It would mean imitating those gentlemen of the French Assembly who proclaimed on August 4th, 1789, the abolition of feudal rights, but who on August 8th sanctioned these same rights by imposing dues on the peasants to compensate the noblemen, placing these dues under the protection of the Revolution. It would mean imitating the Russian government, which proclaimed, at the time of the emancipation of the serfs, that certain lands should henceforth belong to the nobility, while formerly these lands were considered as belonging to the serfs.

Or else, to take a better known example, when the Commune of 1871 decided to pay members of the Commune Council 12s. 6d. a day, while the Federates on the ramparts received only 1s. 3d., this decision was hailed as an act of superior democratic equality. In reality, the Commune only ratified the former inequality between functionary and soldier, government and governed. Coming from an Opportunist Chamber of Deputies, such a decision would have appeared admirable, but the Commune doomed her own revolutionary principles when she failed to put them into practice.

Under our existing social system, when a minister gets paid £4,000 a year, while a workman must content himself with £40 or less; when a foreman is paid two or three times more than a workman, and among workmen there is every gradation, from 8s. a day down to the peasant girl's 3d., we disapprove of the high salary of the minister as well as of the difference between the 8s. of the workman and the 3d. of the poor woman. And we say, 'Down with the privileges of education, as well as with those of birth!' We are anarchists precisely because these privileges revolt us.

They revolt us already in this authoritarian society. Could we endure them in a society that began by proclaiming equality?

This is why some collectivists, understanding the impossibility of maintaining a scale of wages in a society inspired by the breath of the revolution, hasten to proclaim equality of wage. But they meet with new difficulties, and their equality of wages becomes the same unrealizable utopia as the scale of wages of other collectivists.

A society having taken possession of all social wealth, having boldly proclaimed the right of all to this wealth – whatever share they may have taken in producing it – will be compelled to abandon any system of wages, whether in currency or labour-notes.

IV

The collectivists say, 'To each according to his deeds'; or, in other terms, according to his share of services rendered to society. They think it expedient to put this principle into practice, as soon as the social revolution will have made all instruments of production common property. But we think that if the social revolution had the misfortune of proclaiming such a principle, it would mean its necessary failure; it would mean leaving the social problem, which past centuries have burdened us with, unsolved.

Of course, in a society like ours, in which the more a man works the less he is remunerated, this principle, at first sight, may appear to be a yearning for justice. But in reality it is only the perpetuation of injustice. It was by proclaiming this principle that wagedom began, to end in the glaring inequalities and all the abominations of present society; because, from the moment work done began to be appraised in currency, or in any other form of wage, the day it was agreed upon that man would only receive the wage he should be able to secure to himself, the whole history of a state-aided capitalist society was as good as written; it was contained in germ in this principle.

Shall we, then, return to our starting-point, and go through the same evolution again? Our theorists desire it, but fortunately it is impossible. The revolution, we maintain, must be communist; if not, it will be drowned in blood, and have to be begun over again.

Services rendered to society, be they work in factory or field, or mental services, *cannot be* valued in money. There can be no exact measure of value (of what has been wrongly termed exchange value), nor of use value, in terms of production. If two individuals work for the community five hours a day, year in year out, at different work which is equally agreeable to them, we may say that on the whole their labour is approximately equivalent. But we cannot divide their work, and say that the result of any particular day, hour or minute of work of the one is worth the result of one day, one hour or one minute of the other.

We may roughly say that the man who during his lifetime has deprived himself of leisure during ten hours a day has given far more to society than the one who has only deprived himself of leisure during five hours a day, or who has not deprived himself at all. But we cannot take what he has done during two hours, and say that the yield of his two hours' work is worth twice as much as the yield of another individual, who has worked only one hour, and remunerate the two in proportion. It would be disregarding all that is complex in industry, in agriculture, in the whole life of present society; it would be ignoring to what extent all individual work is the result of the past and the present labour of society as a whole. It would mean believing ourselves to be living in the Stone Age, whereas we are living in an age of steel.

If you enter a modern coal-mine you will see a man in charge of a huge machine that raises and lowers a cage. In his hand he holds a lever that stops and reverses the course of the machine; he lowers it and the cage reverses its course in the twinkling of an eye; he sends it upwards or downwards into the depths of the shaft with a giddy swiftness. All attention, he follows with his eyes fixed on an indicator which shows him, on a small scale, at which point of the shaft the cage is at each second of its progress; and as soon as the indicator has reached a certain level, he suddenly stops the course of the cage, not a yard higher nor lower than the required spot. And no sooner have the colliers unloaded their coal-wagonettes, and pushed empty ones instead, than he reverses the lever and again sends the cage back into space.

During eight or ten consecutive hours every day he must keep the same strain of attention. Should his brain relax for a moment, the cage would inevitably strike against the gear, break its wheels, snap the rope, crush men, and put a stop to all work in the mine. Should he waste three seconds at each touch of the lever, the extraction, in our modern perfected mines, would be reduced by from twenty to fifty tons a day.

Is it he who is the most necessary man in the mine? Or, is it perhaps the boy who signals to him from below to raise the cage? Is it the miner at the bottom of the shaft, who risks his life every instant, and who will some day be killed by fire-damp? Or is it the engineer, who would lose the layer of coal, and would cause the miners to dig on rock by a simple mistake in his calculations? Or, is it the mine owner who has put his capital into the mine, and who has perhaps, contrary to expert advice, asserted that excellent coal would be found there?

All those who are engaged in the mine contribute to the extraction of coal in proportion to their strength, their energy, their knowledge, their intelligence and their skill. And we may say that all have the right to *live*, to satisfy their needs, and even their whims, when the necessaries of life have been secured for all. But how can we appraise the work of each one of them?

And, moreover, is the coal they have extracted entirely *their* work? Is it not also the work of the men who have built the railway leading to the mine and the roads that radiate from all the railway stations? Is it not also the work of those that have tilled and sown the fields, extracted iron, cut wood in the forest, built the machines that burn coal, slowly developed the mining industry altogether, and so on?

It is utterly impossible to draw a distinction between the work of each of those men. To measure the work by its results leads us to an absurdity; to divide the total work, and to measure its fractions by the number of hours spent on the work also leads us to absurdity. One thing remains: to put the *needs* above the *works*, and first of all to recognize *the right to live*, and later on *the right to well-being* for all those who took their share in production.

But take any other branch of human activity – take the manifestations of life as a whole. Which one of us can claim the higher remuneration for his work? Is it the doctor who has found out the illness, or the nurse who has brought about recovery by her hygienic care? Is it the inventor of the first steam-engine, or the boy, who, one day getting tired of pulling the rope that formerly opened the valve to let steam enter under the piston, tied the rope to the lever of the machine, without suspecting that he had invented the essential mechanical part of all modern machinery – the automatic valve?

Is it the inventor of the locomotive, or the workman of Newcastle, who suggested replacing the stones formerly laid under the rails by wooden sleepers, as the stones, for want of elasticity, caused the trains to derail? Is it the engineer on the locomotive? The signalman who stops the trains, or lets them pass by? The switchman who transfers a train from one line to another?

Again, to whom do we owe the transatlantic cable? Is it to the electrical engineer who obstinately affirmed that the cable would transmit messages while learned men of science declared it to be impossible? Is it to Maury, the learned physical geographer, who advised that thick cables should be set aside for others as thin as a walking-cane? Or else to those volunteers, come from nobody knows where, who spent their days and nights on deck minutely examining every yard of the cable, and removed the nails that the shareholders of steamship companies stupidly caused to be driven into the non-conducting wrapper of the cable, so as to make it unserviceable?

And in a wider sphere, the true sphere of life, with its joys, its sufferings and its accidents, cannot each one of us recall someone who has rendered him so great a service that we should be indignant if its equivalent in coin were mentioned? The service may have been but a word, nothing but a word spoken at the right time, or else it may have been months and years of devotion, and are we going to appraise these 'incalculable' services in 'labour-notes'?

'The works of each!' But human society would not exist for more than two consecutive generations if everyone did not give infinitely more than that for which he is paid in coin, in 'cheques', or in civic rewards. The race would soon become extinct if mothers did not sacrifice their lives to take care of their children, if men did not give continually, without demanding an equivalent reward, if men did not give most precisely when they expect no reward.

If middle-class society is decaying, if we have got into a blind alley from which we cannot emerge without attacking past institutions with torch and hatchet, it is precisely because we have given too much to counting. It is because we have let ourselves be influenced into *giving* only to *receive*. It is because we have aimed at turning society into a commercial company based on *debit* and *credit*.

After all, the collectivists know this themselves. They vaguely understand that a society could not exist if it carried out the principle of 'each according to his deeds'. They have a notion that *necessaries* – we do not speak of whims – the needs of the individual, do not always correspond to his *works*. Thus De Paepe tells us: 'The principle – the eminently individualist principle – would, however, be *tempered* by social intervention for the education of children and young persons (including maintenance and lodging), and by the social organization for assisting the infirm and the sick, for retreats for aged workers, etc.' They understand that a man of 40, father of three children, has other needs than a young man of 20. They know that the woman who suckles her infant and spends sleepless nights at its bedside, cannot do as much *work* as the man who has slept peacefully. They seem to take in that men and women, worn out maybe by dint of overwork for society, may be incapable of doing as much *work* as those who have spent their time leisurely and pocketed their 'labour-notes' in the privileged career of state functionaries.

They are eager to temper their principle. They say: 'Society will not fail to maintain and bring up its children; to help both aged and infirm. Without doubt *needs* will be the measure of the cost that society will burden itself with, to temper the principle of deeds.'

Charity, charity, always Christian charity, organized by the state this time. They believe in improving the asylums for foundlings, in effecting old-age and sick insurances – so as to *temper* their principle. But they cannot yet throw aside the idea of 'wounding first and healing afterwards'!

Thus, after having denied communism, after having laughed at their ease at the formula – 'To each according to his needs' – these great economists discover that they have forgotten something, the needs of the producers, which they now admit. Only it is for the state to estimate them, for the state to verify if the needs are not disproportionate to the work.

The state will dole out charity. Thence to the English poor law and the workhouse is but a step.

There is but a slight difference, because even this stepmother of a society against whom we are in revolt has also been compelled to *temper* her individualist principles; she, too, has had to make concessions in a communist direction and under the same form of charity.

She, too, distributes halfpenny dinners to prevent the pillaging of her shops; builds hospitals – often very bad ones, but sometimes splendid ones – to prevent the ravages of contagious diseases. She, too, after having paid the hours of labour, shelters the children of those she has wrecked. She takes their needs into consideration and doles out charity.

Poverty, we have said elsewhere, was the primary cause of wealth. It was poverty that created the first capitalist; because, before accumulating 'surplus value', of which we hear so much, men had to be sufficiently destitute to consent to sell their labour, so as not to die of hunger. It was poverty that made capitalists. And if the number of the poor increased so rapidly during the Middle Ages, it was due to the invasions and wars that followed the founding of states, and to the increase of riches resulting from the exploitation of the East. These two causes tore asunder the bonds that kept men together in the agrarian and urban communities, and taught them to proclaim the principle of *wages*, so dear to the exploiters, instead of the solidarity they formerly practised in their tribal life.

And it is this principle that is to spring from a revolution which men dare to call by the name of social revolution – a name so dear to the starved, the oppressed, and the sufferers!

It can never be. For the day on which old institutions will fall under the proletarian axe, voices will cry out: 'Bread, shelter, ease for all!' And those voices will be listened to; the people will say: 'Let us begin by allaying our thirst for life, for happiness, for liberty, that we have never quenched. And when we shall have tasted of this joy, we will set to work to demolish the last vestiges of middle-class rule: its morality drawn from account-books, its "debit and credit" philosophy, its "mine and yours" institutions. "In demolishing we shall build," as Proudhon said; and we shall build in the name of communism and anarchy.'

CHAPTER XIV
Consumption and production

I

Looking at society and its political organization from a different standpoint than that of all the authoritarian schools – for we start from a free individual to reach a free society, instead of beginning by the state to come down to the individual – we follow the same method in economic questions. We study the needs of the individuals, and the means by which they satisfy them, before discussing production, exchange, taxation, government, and so on.

At first sight the difference may appear trifling, but in reality it upsets all the canons of official political economy.

If you open the works of any economist you will find that he begins with *production*, i.e., by the analysis of the means employed nowadays for the creation of wealth: division of labour, the factory, its machinery, the accumulation of capital. From Adam Smith to Marx, all have proceeded along these lines. Only in the latter parts of their books do they treat of *consumption*, that is to say, of the means resorted to in our present society to satisfy the needs of the individuals; and even there they confine themselves to explaining how riches *are* divided among those who vie with one another for their possession.

Perhaps you will say this is logical. Before satisfying needs you must create the wherewithal to satisfy them. But, before producing anything, must you not feel the need of it? Was it not necessity that first drove man to hunt, to raise cattle, to cultivate land, to

158

make implements, and later on to invent machinery? Is it not the study of the needs that should govern production? To say the least, it would therefore be quite as logical to begin by considering the needs, and afterwards to discuss how production is, and ought to be, organized, in order to satisfy these needs.

This is precisely what we mean to do.

But as soon as we look at political economy from this point of view, it entirely changes its aspect. It ceases to be a simple description of facts, and becomes a *science*, and we may define this science as: *The study of the needs of mankind, and the means of satisfying them with the least possible waste of human energy*. Its true name should be *physiology of society*. It constitutes a parallel science to the physiology of plants and animals, which is the study of the needs of plants and animals, and of the most advantageous ways of satisfying them. In the series of sociological sciences, the economy of human societies takes the place occupied in the series of biological sciences by the physiology of organic bodies.

We say, here are human beings, united in a society. All of them feel the need of living in healthy houses. The savage's hut no longer satisfies them; they require a more or less comfortable solid shelter. The question is, then: whether, taking the present capacity of men for production, every man can have a house of his own? and what is hindering him from having it?

And as soon as we ask *this* question, we see that every family in Europe could perfectly well have a comfortable house, such as are built in England, in Belgium, or in Pullman City, or else an equivalent set of rooms. A certain number of days' work would suffice to build a pretty little airy house, well fitted up and lighted by electricity.

But nine-tenths of Europeans have never possessed a healthy house, because at all times common people have had to work day after day to satisfy the needs of their rulers, and have never had the necessary leisure or money to build, or to have built, the home of their dreams. And they can have no houses, and will inhabit hovels as long as present conditions remain unchanged.

It is thus seen that our method is quite contrary to that of the economists, who immortalize the so-called *laws* of production, and, reckoning up the number of houses built every year, demonstrate by statistics, that as the number of the new-built houses *is* too small to meet all demands, nine-tenths of Europeans *must* live in hovels.

Let us pass on to food. After having enumerated the benefits accruing from the division of labour, economists tell us the division of labour requires that some men should work at agriculture and others at manufacture. Farmers producing so much, factories so much, exchange being carried on in such a way, they analyse the sale, the profit, the net gain or the surplus value, the wages, the taxes, banking, and so on.

But after having followed them so far, we are none the wiser, and if we ask them: 'How is it that millions of human beings are in want of bread, when every family could grow sufficient wheat to feed ten, twenty, and even a hundred people annually?' they answer us by droning the same anthem – division of labour, wages, surplus value, capital, etc. – arriving at the same conclusion, that production is insufficient to satisfy all needs; a conclusion which, if true, does not answer the question: 'Can or cannot man by his labour produce the bread he needs? And if he cannot, what is it that hinders him?'

Here are 350 million Europeans. They need so much bread, so much meat, wine, milk, eggs and butter every year. They need so many houses, so much clothing. This is the minimum of their needs. Can they produce all this? and if they can, will sufficient leisure be left them for art, science and amusement? – in a word, for everything that is not comprised in the category of absolute necessities? If the answer is in the affirmative, what hinders them going ahead? What must they do to remove the obstacles? Is it time that is needed to achieve such a result? Let them take it! But let us not lose sight of the aim of production – the satisfaction of the needs of all.

If the most imperious needs of man remain unsatisfied now, what must we do to increase the productivity of our work? But is there no other cause? Might it not be that production, having lost sight of the *needs* of man, has strayed in an absolutely wrong direction, and that its organization is at fault? And as we can prove that such is the case, let us see how to reorganize production so as to really satisfy all needs.

This seems to us the only right way of facing things. The only way that would allow of political economy becoming a science – the science of social physiology.

It is evident that so long as science treats of production, as *it
is* carried on at present by civilized nations, by Hindu communes,
or by savages, it can hardly state facts otherwise than the economists
state them now; that is to say, as a simple *descriptive* chapter,
analogous to the descriptive chapters of zoology and botany. But
if this chapter were written so as to throw some light on the
economy of the energy that is necessary to satisfy human needs,
the chapter would gain in precision, as well as in descriptive value.
It would clearly show the frightful waste of human energy under
the present system, and it would prove that as long as this system
exists, the needs of humanity will never be satisfied.

The point of view, we see, would be entirely changed. Behind
the loom that weaves so many yards of cloth, behind the steel-plate
perforator, and behind the safe in which dividends are hoarded,
we should see man, the artisan of production, more often than not
excluded from the feast he has prepared for others. We should
also understand that the standpoint being wrong, the so-called
'laws' of value and exchange are but a very false explanation of
events, as they happen nowadays; and that things will come to pass
very differently when production is organized in such a manner as
to meet all needs of society.

II

There is not one single principle of political economy that does
not change its aspect if you look at it from our point of view.

Take, for instance, overproduction, a word which every day
re-echoes in our ears. Is there a single economist, academician or
candidate for academical honours who has not supported arguments,
proving that economic crises are due to overproduction – that at
a given moment more cotton, more cloth, more watches are produced than are needed! Have we not, all of us, thundered against
the rapacity of the capitalists who are obstinately bent on producing
more than can possibly be consumed!

However, on careful examination all these reasonings prove
unsound. In fact, is there one single commodity among those in
universal use which is produced in greater quantity than need be?
Examine one by one all commodities sent out by countries exporting
on a large scale, and you will see that nearly all are produced in

insufficient quantities for the inhabitants of the countries exporting them.

It is not a surplus of wheat that the Russian peasant sends to Europe. The most plentiful harvests of wheat and rye in European Russia only yield *enough* for the population. And as a rule, the peasant deprives himself of what he actually needs when he sells his wheat or rye to pay rent and taxes.

It is not a surplus of coal that England sends to the four corners of the globe, because only three-quarters of a ton, per head of population, annually, remains for home domestic consumption, and millions of Englishmen are deprived of fire in the winter, or have only just enough to boil a few vegetables. In fact, setting aside useless luxuries, there is in England, which exports more than any other country, one single commodity in universal use – cottons – whose production is sufficiently great to *perhaps* exceed the needs of the community. Yet when we look upon the rags that pass for wearing apparel worn by over a third of the inhabitants of the United Kingdom, we are led to ask ourselves whether the cottons exported would not, on the whole, suit the *real* needs of the population?

As a rule it is not a surplus that is exported, though it may have been so originally. The fable of the barefooted shoemaker is as true of nations as it was formerly of individual artisans. We export the *necessary* commodities. And we do so, because the workmen cannot buy with their wages what they have produced, *and pay besides the rent and interest to the capitalist and the banker.*

Not only does the ever-growing need of comfort remain unsatisfied, but the strict necessities of life are often wanting. Therefore, 'surplus production' does *not* exist, at least not in the sense given to it by the theorists of political economy.

Taking another point – all economists tell us that there is a well-proved law: 'Man produces more than he consumes.' After he has lived on the proceeds of his toil, there remains a surplus. Thus, a family of cultivators produces enough to feed several families, and so forth.

For us, this oft-repeated sentence has no sense. If it meant that each generation leaves something to future generations, it would be true; thus, for example, a farmer plants a tree that will live, maybe, for thirty, forty, or a hundred years, and whose fruits will still be gathered by the farmer's grandchildren. Or he clears a few acres of virgin soil, and we say that the heritage of future generations has been increased by that much. Roads, bridges, canals, his house and his furniture are so much wealth bequeathed to succeeding generations.

But this is not what is meant. We are told that the cultivator produces more than he *need* consume. Rather should they say that, the state having always taken from him a large share of his produce for taxes, the priest for tithe, and the landlord for rent, a whole class of men has been created, who formerly consumed what they produced – save what was set aside for unforeseen accidents, or expenses incurred in afforestation, roads, etc. – but who today are compelled to live very poorly, from hand to mouth, the remainder having been taken from them by the state, the landlord, the priest and the usurer.

Therefore we prefer to say: the agricultural labourer, the industrial worker and so on *consume less than they produce* because they are *compelled* to sell most of the produce of their labour and to be satisfied with but a small portion of it.

Let us also observe that if the needs of the individual are taken as the starting-point of our political economy, we cannot fail to reach communism, an organization which enables us to satisfy all needs in the most thorough and economical way. While if we start from our present method of production, and aim at gain and surplus value, without asking whether our production corresponds to the satisfaction of needs, we necessarily arrive at capitalism, or at most at collectivism – both being but two different forms of the present wages' system.

In fact, when we consider the needs of the individual and of society, and the means which man has resorted to in order to satisfy them during his varied phases of development, we see at once the necessity of systematizing our efforts, instead of producing haphazard as we do nowadays. It becomes evident that the appropriation by a few of all riches not consumed, and transmitted from one generation to another, is not in the general interest. And we see as a fact that owing to these methods the needs of three-quarters of society are *not* satisfied, so that the present waste of human strength in useless things is only the more criminal.

We discover, moreover, that the most advantageous use of all commodities would be, for each of them, to go, first, for satisfying those needs which are the most pressing: that, in other words, the so-called 'value in use' of a commodity does not depend on a simple whim, as has often been affirmed, but on the satisfaction it brings to *real* needs.

Communism – that is to say, an organization which would correspond to a view of consumption, production, and exchange, taken as a whole – therefore becomes the logical consequence of such a comprehension of things – the only one, in our opinion, that is really scientific.

A society that will satisfy the needs of all, and which will know how to organize production to answer to this aim will also have to make a clean sweep of several prejudices concerning industry, and first of all of the theory often preached by economists – *the division of labour* theory – which we are going to discuss in the next chapter.

CHAPTER XV
The division of labour

I

Political economy has always confined itself to stating facts occurring in society, and justifying them in the interest of the dominant class. Therefore, it pronounces itself in favour of the division of labour in industry. Having found it profitable to capitalists, it has set it up as a *principle*.

Look at the village smith, said Adam Smith, the father of modern political economy. If he has never been accustomed to making nails he will only succeed by hard toil in forging two or three hundred a day, and even then they will be bad. But if this same smith has never made anything but nails, he will easily supply as many as two thousand three hundred in the course of a day. And Smith hastened to the conclusion – 'Divide labour, specialize, go on specializing; let us have smiths who only know how to make heads or points of nails, and by this means we shall produce more. We shall grow rich.'

That a smith condemned for life to make the heads of nails would lose all interest in his work, that he would be entirely at the mercy of his employer with his limited handicraft, that he would be out of work four months out of twelve, and that his wages would fall very low down, when it would be easy to replace him by an apprentice, Smith did not think of all this when he exclaimed – 'Long live the division of labour. This is the real gold-mine that will enrich the nation!' And all joined him in this cry.

And later on, when a Sismondi or a J. B. Say began to understand that the division of labour, instead of enriching the whole nation, only enriches the rich, and that the worker, who is doomed for life to making the eighteenth part of a pin, grows stupid and sinks into poverty – what did official economists propose? Nothing! They did not say to themselves that by a lifelong grind at one and the same mechanical toil the worker would lose his intelligence and his spirit of invention, and that, on the contrary, a variety of occupations would result in considerably augmenting the productivity of a nation. But this is the very issue we have now to consider.

If, however, learned economists were the only ones to preach the permanent and often hereditary division of labour, we might allow them to preach it as much as they pleased. But the ideas taught by doctors of science filter into men's minds and pervert them; and from repeatedly hearing the division of labour, profits, interest, credit, etc., spoken of as problems long since solved, all middle-class people, and workers too, end by arguing like economists; they venerate the same fetishes.

Thus we see most socialists, even those who have not feared to point out the mistakes of economical science, justifying the division of labour. Talk to them about the organization of work during the revolution, and they answer that the division of labour must be maintained; that if you sharpened pins before the revolution you must go on sharpening them after. True, you will not have to work more than five hours a day, but you will have to sharpen pins all your life, while others will make designs for machines that will enable you to sharpen hundreds of millions of pins during your lifetime; and others again will be specialists in the higher branches of literature, science and art, etc. You were born to sharpen pins while Pasteur was born to invent the inoculation against anthrax, and the revolution will leave you both to your respective employments. Well, it is this horrible principle, so noxious to society, so brutalizing to the individual, source of so much harm, that we propose to discuss in its divers manifestations.

We know the consequences of the division of labour full well. It is evident that, first of all, we are divided into two classes: on the one hand, producers, who consume very little and are exempt from thinking because they only do physical work, and who work badly because their brains remain inactive; and on the other hand, the consumers, who, producing little or hardly anything, have the privilege of thinking for the others, and who think badly because the whole world of those who toil with their hands is unknown to them. Then, we have the labourers of the soil who know nothing of machinery, while those who work at machinery ignore everything about agriculture. The idea of modern industry is a child *tending* a machine that he cannot and must not understand, and a foreman who fines him if his attention flags for a moment. The ideal of industrial agriculture is to do away with the agricultural labourer altogether and to set a man who does odd jobs to tend a steam-plough or a threshing-machine. The division of labour means labelling and stamping men for life – some to splice ropes in factories, some to be foremen in a business, others to shove huge coal-baskets in a particular part of a mine; but none of them to have any idea of machinery as a whole, nor of business, nor of mines. And thereby they destroy the love of work and the capacity for invention that, at the beginning of modern industry, created the machinery on which we pride ourselves so much.

What they have done for individuals, they also wanted to do for nations. Humanity was to be divided into national workshops, having each its speciality. Russia, we were taught, was destined by nature to grow corn; England to spin cotton; Belgium to weave cloth; while Switzerland was to train nurses and governesses. Moreover, each separate city was to establish a speciality. Lyons was to weave silk, Auvergne to make lace, and Paris fancy articles. In this way, economists said, an immense field was opened for production and consumption, and in this way an era of limitless wealth for mankind was at hand.

However, these great hopes vanished as fast as technical knowl-edge spread abroad. As long as England stood alone as a weaver of cotton and as a metal-worker on a large scale; as long as only Paris made artistic fancy articles, etc., all went well, economists could preach the so-called division of labour without being refuted.

But a new current of thought induced by and by all civilized nations to manufacture for themselves. They found it advantageous to produce what they formerly received from other countries, or from their colonies, which in their turn aimed at emancipat-ing themselves from the mother-country. Scientific discoveries universalized the methods of production, and henceforth it was useless to pay an exorbitant price abroad for what could easily be produced at home. And now we see already that this industrial revolution strikes a crushing blow at the theory of the division of labour which for a long time was supposed to be so sound.

CHAPTER XVI

The decentralization of industry[j]

I

After the Napoleonic wars Britain had nearly succeeded in ruining the main industries which had sprung up in France at the end of the preceding century. She also became mistress of the seas and had no rivals of importance. She took in the situation, and knew how to turn its privileges and advantages to account. She established an industrial monopoly, and, imposing upon her neighbours her prices for the goods she alone could manufacture, accumulated riches upon riches.

But as the middle-class Revolution of the eighteenth century had abolished serfdom and created a proletariat in France, French industry, hampered for a time in its flight, soared again, and from the second half of the nineteenth century France ceased to be a tributary of England for manufactured goods. Today she too has grown into a nation with an export trade. She sells far more than 60 million pounds' worth of manufactured goods, and two-thirds of these goods are fabrics. The number of Frenchmen working for export or living by their foreign trade, is estimated at 3 million.

France is therefore no longer England's tributary. In her turn she has striven to monopolize certain branches of foreign industry, such as silks and ready-made clothes, and has reaped immense profits therefrom; but she is on the point of losing this monopoly

---

[j] A fuller development of these ideas will be found in my book, *Fields, Factories, and Workshops*, published by Messrs Thomas Nelson and Sons in their popular series in 1912.

for ever, just as England is on the point of losing the monopoly of cotton goods.

Travelling eastwards, industry has reached Germany. Fifty years ago Germany was a tributary of England and France for most manufactured commodities in the higher branches of industry. It is no longer so. In the course of the last fifty years, and especially since the Franco-German War, Germany has completely reorganized her industry. The new factories are stocked with the best machinery; the latest creations of industrial art in cotton goods from Manchester, or in silks from Lyons, etc., are now realized in new German factories. It took two or three generations of workers, at Lyons and Manchester, to construct the modern machinery; but Germany adopted it in its perfected state. Technical schools, adapted to the needs of industry, supply the factories with an army of intelligent workmen – practical engineers, who can work with both hand and brain. German industry starts at the point which was only reached by Manchester and Lyons after fifty years of groping in the dark, of exertion and experiments.

It follows that since Germany manufactures so well at home, she diminishes her imports from France and England year by year. She has not only become their rival in manufactured goods in Asia and in Africa, but also in London and in Paris. Shortsighted people in France may cry out against the Frankfort Treaty; English manufacturers may explain German competition by little differences in railway tariffs; they may linger on the petty side of questions, and neglect great historical facts. But it is none the less certain that the main industries, formerly in the hands of England and France, have progressed eastward, and in Germany they have found a country, young, full of energy, possessing an intelligent middle class, and eager in its turn to enrich itself by foreign trade.

While Germany has freed herself from subjection to France and England, has manufactured her own cotton cloth, and constructed her own machines – in fact, manufactured all commodities – the main industries have also taken root in Russia, where the development of manufacture is the more instructive as it sprang up but yesterday.

At the time of the abolition of serfdom in 1861, Russia had hardly any factories. Everything needed in the way of machines, rails, railway-engines, fine dress materials, came from the West. Twenty years later she already possessed 85,000 factories, and the value of the goods manufactured in Russia had increased fourfold.

The old machinery was superseded, and now nearly all the steel in use in Russia, three-quarters of the iron, two-thirds of the coal, all railway-engines, railway-carriages, rails, nearly all steamers, are made in Russia.

Russia, destined – so wrote economists – to remain an agricultural territory, has rapidly developed into a manufacturing country. She orders hardly anything from England, and very little from Germany.

Economists hold the customs responsible for these facts, and yet cottons manufactured in Russia are sold at the same price as in London. Capital taking no cognizance of fatherlands, German and English capitalists, accompanied by engineers and foremen of their own nationalities, have introduced in Russia and in Poland manufactories whose goods compete in excellence with the best from England. If customs were abolished tomorrow, manufacture would only gain by it. Not long ago the British manufacturers delivered another hard blow to the import of cloth and woollens from the West. They set up in southern and middle Russia immense wool factories, stocked with the most perfect machinery from Bradford, and already now Russia imports only the highest sorts of cloth and woollen fabrics from England, France and Austria. The remainder is fabricated at home, both in factories and as domestic industries.

The main industries not only move eastward, they are spreading also to the southern peninsulas. The Turin Exhibition of 1884 already demonstrated the progress made in Italian manufactured produce; and, let us not make any mistake about it, the mutual hatred of the French and Italian middle classes has no other origin than their industrial rivalry. Spain is also becoming an industrial country; while in the East, Bohemia has suddenly sprung into importance as a new centre of manufactures, provided with perfected machinery and applying the best scientific methods.

We might also mention Hungary's rapid progress in the main industries, but let us rather take Brazil as an example. Economists sentenced Brazil to cultivate cotton for ever, to export it in its raw state, and to receive cotton cloth from Europe in exchange. In fact, forty years ago Brazil had only nine wretched little cotton factories with 385 spindles. Today there are 160 cotton mills, possessing 1,500,000 spindles and 50,000 looms, which throw 500 million yards of textiles on the market annually.

Even Mexico is now very successful in manufacturing cotton cloth, instead of importing it from Europe. As to the United States, they have quite freed themselves from European tutelage, and have triumphally developed their manufacturing powers to an enormous extent.

But it was India which gave the most striking proof against the specialization of national industry.

We all know the theory: the great European nations need colonies, for colonies send raw material – cotton fibre, unwashed wool, spices, etc., to the motherland. And the motherland, under pretence of sending them manufactured wares, gets rid of her damaged stuffs, her machine scrap-iron and everything which she no longer has any use for. It costs her little or nothing, and none the less the articles are sold at exorbitant prices.

Such was the theory – such was the practice for a long time. In London and Manchester fortunes were made, while India was being ruined. In the India Museum in London unheard-of riches, collected in Calcutta and Bombay by English merchants, are to be seen.

But other English merchants and capitalists conceived the very simple idea that it would be more expedient to exploit the natives of India by making cotton cloth in India itself, than to import from 20 to 24 million pounds' worth of goods annually.

At first a series of experiments ended in failure. Indian weavers – artists and experts in their own craft – could not inure themselves to factory life; the machinery sent from Liverpool was bad; the climate had to be taken into account; and merchants had to adapt themselves to new conditions, now fully mastered, before British India could become the menacing rival of the motherland she is today.

She now possesses more than 200 cotton mills which employ about 230,000 workmen, and contain more than 6,000,000 spindles and 80,000 looms, and 40 jute mills, with 400,000 spindles. She exports annually to China, to the Dutch Indies, and to Africa, nearly 8 million pounds' worth of the same white cotton cloth, said to be England's speciality. And while English workmen are often unemployed and in great want, Indian women weave cotton by machinery for the Far East at wages of sixpence a day. In short, intelligent manufacturers are fully aware that the day is not far off when they will not know what to do with the 'factory hands' who formerly wove cotton cloth for export from England. Besides which it is becoming more and more evident that India will not import a single ton of iron from England. The initial difficulties in using the coal and the iron-ore obtained in India have been overcome; and foundries, rivalling those in England, have been built on the shores of the Indian Ocean.

Colonies competing with the motherland in its production of manufactured goods, such is the factor which will regulate economy in the twentieth century.

And why should India not manufacture? What should be the hindrance? Capital? – But capital goes wherever there are men, poor enough to be exploited. Knowledge? But knowledge recognizes no national barriers. Technical skill of the worker? – No. Are, then, Hindu workmen inferior to the hundreds of thousands of boys and girls, not 18 years old, at present working in the English textile factories?

II

After having glanced at national industries it would be very interesting to turn to some special branches.

Let us take silk, for example, an eminently French produce in the first half of the nineteenth century. We all know how Lyons became the emporium of the silk trade. At first raw silk was gathered in southern France, till little by little they ordered it from Italy, from Spain, from Austria, from the Caucasus and from Japan, for the manufacture of their silk fabrics. In 1875, out of 5 million kilos of raw silk converted into stuffs in the vicinity of Lyons, there were only 400,000 kilos of French silk. But if Lyons manufactured imported silk, why should not Switzerland, Germany, Russia, do as much? Consequently, silk-weaving began to develop in the villages round Zurich. Basle became a great centre of the silk trade. The Caucasian administration engaged women from Marseilles and workmen from Lyons to teach Georgians the perfected rearing of silk-worms, and the art of converting silk into fabrics to the Caucasian peasants. Austria followed. Then Germany, with the help of Lyons workmen, built great silk factories. The United States did likewise in Paterson.

And today the silk trade is no longer a French monopoly. Silks are made in Germany, in Austria, in the United States and in England, and it is now reckoned that one-third of the silk stuffs used in France are imported. In winter, Caucasian peasants weave silk handkerchiefs at a wage that would mean starvation to the silk-weavers of Lyons. Italy and Germany send silks to France; and Lyons, which in 1870–4 exported 460 million francs' worth of silk fabrics, exports now only one-half of that amount. In fact, the time is not far off when Lyons will only send higher class goods and a few novelties as patterns to Germany, Russia and Japan.

And so it is in all industries. Belgium has no longer the cloth monopoly; cloth is made in Germany, in Russia, in Austria, in the United States. Switzerland and the French Jura have no longer a clockwork monopoly; watches are made everywhere. Scotland no longer refines sugar for Russia: refined Russian sugar is imported into England. Italy, although possessing neither coal nor iron, makes her own ironclads and engines for her steamers. Chemical industry is no longer an English monopoly; sulphuric acid and soda are made even in the Urals. Steam-engines, made at Winterthur, have acquired everywhere a wide reputation, and at the present moment, Switzerland, which has neither coal nor iron, and no seaports to import them – nothing but excellent technical schools – makes machinery better and cheaper than England. So ends the theory of exchange.

The tendency of trade, as for all else, is towards decentralization.

Every nation finds it advantageous to combine agriculture with the greatest possible variety of factories. The specialization, of which economists spoke so highly, certainly has enriched a number of capitalists, but is now no longer of any use. On the contrary, it is to the advantage of every region, every nation, to grow their own wheat, their own vegetables, and to manufacture at home most of the produce they consume. This diversity is the surest pledge of the complete development of production by mutual co-operation, and the moving cause of progress, while specialization is now a hindrance to progress.

Agriculture can only prosper in proximity to factories. And no sooner does a single factory appear than an infinite variety of other factories *must* spring up around, so that, mutually supporting and stimulating one another by their inventions, they increase their productivity.

III

It is foolish indeed to export wheat and to import flour, to export wool and import cloth, to export iron and import machinery; not only because transportation is a waste of time and money, but, above all, because a country with no developed industry inevitably remains behind the times in agriculture; because a country with no large factories to bring steel to a finished condition is doomed to be backward in all other industries; and lastly, because the industrial and technical capacities of the nation remain undeveloped, if they are not exercised in a variety of industries.

Nowadays everything holds together in the world of production. Cultivation of the soil is no longer possible without machinery, without great irrigation works, without railways, without manure factories. And to adapt this machinery, these railways, these irrigation engines, etc., to local conditions, a certain spirit of invention, and a certain amount of technical skill must be developed, while they necessarily lie dormant so long as spades and ploughshares are the only implements of cultivation.

If fields are to be properly cultivated, if they are to yield the abundant harvests that man has the right to expect, it is essential that workshops, foundries and factories develop within the reach of the fields. A variety of occupations, and a variety of skills arising therefrom, both working together for a common aim – these are the true forces of progress.

And now let us imagine the inhabitants of a city or a territory – whether vast or small – stepping for the first time on to the path of the social revolution.

We are sometimes told that 'nothing will have changed': that the mines, the factories, etc., will be expropriated, and proclaimed national or communal property, that every man will go back to his usual work, and that the revolution will then be accomplished.

But this is a mere dream: the social revolution cannot take place so simply.

We have already mentioned that should the revolution break out tomorrow in Paris, Lyons, or any other city – should the workers lay hands on factories, houses and banks, present production would be completely revolutionized by this simple fact.

International commerce will come to a standstill; so also will the importation of foreign breadstuffs; the circulation of commodities and of provisions will be paralysed. And then, the city or territory in revolt will be compelled to provide for itself, and to reorganize its production, so as to satisfy its own needs. If it fails to do so, it is death. If it succeeds, it will revolutionize the economic life of the country.

The quantity of imported provisions having decreased, consumption having increased, a million Parisians working for exportation purposes having been thrown out of work, a great number of things imported today from distant or neighbouring countries not reaching their destination, fancy-trade being temporarily at a standstill, what will the inhabitants have to eat six months after the revolution?

We think that when the stores containing foodstuffs are empty, the masses will seek to obtain their food from the land. They will see the necessity of cultivating the soil, of combining agricultural production with industrial production in the suburbs of Paris itself and its environs. They will have to abandon the merely ornamental trades and consider their most urgent need – bread.

A great number of the inhabitants of the cities will have to become agriculturists. Not in the same manner as the present peasants who wear themselves out, ploughing for a wage that barely provides them with sufficient food for the year, but by following the principles of the intensive agriculture, of the market-gardeners, applied on a large scale by means of the best machinery that man has invented or can invent. They will till the land – not, however, like the country beast of burden: a Paris jeweller would object to that. They will organize cultivation on better principles; and not in the future, but at once, during the revolutionary struggles, from fear of being worsted by the enemy.

Agriculture will have to be carried out on intelligent lines, by men and women availing themselves of the experience of the present time, organizing themselves in joyous gangs for pleasant work, like those who, a hundred years ago, worked in the Champ de Mars for the Feast of the Federation – a work of delight, when not carried to excess, when scientifically organized, when man invents and improves his tools and is conscious of being a useful member of the community.

Of course, they will not only cultivate wheat and oats – they will also produce those things which they formerly used to order from foreign parts. And let us not forget that for the inhabitants of a revolted territory, 'foreign parts' may include all districts that have not joined in the revolutionary movement. During the revolutions of 1793 and 1871 Paris was made to feel that 'foreign parts' meant even the country district at her very gates. The speculator in grains at Troyes starved in 1793 and 1794 the sans-culottes of Paris as badly, and even worse, than the German armies brought on to French soil by the Versailles conspirators. The revolted city will be compelled to do without these 'foreigners', and why not? France invented beet-root sugar when sugar-cane ran short during the continental blockade. Parisians discovered saltpetre in their cellars when they no longer received any from abroad. Shall we be inferior to our grandfathers, who hardly lisped the first words of science?

A revolution is more than a mere change of the prevailing political system. It implies the awakening of human intelligence, the increasing of the inventive spirit tenfold, a hundredfold; it is the dawn of a new science – the science of men like Laplace, Lamarck, Lavoisier. It is a revolution in the minds of men, as deep as, and deeper still than, in their institutions.

And there are still economists who tell us that, once the 'revolution is made', everyone will return to his workshop, as if passing through a revolution were going home after a walk in the Epping forest!

To begin with, the sole fact of having laid hands on middle-class property will imply the necessity of completely reorganizing the whole of economic life in the workshops, the dockyards, the factories.

And the revolution surely will not fail to act in this direction. Should Paris, during the social revolution, be cut off from the world for a year or two by the supporters of middle-class rule, its millions of intellects, not yet depressed by factory life – that city of little trades which stimulate the spirit of invention – will show the world what man's brain can accomplish without asking any help from without, but the motor force of the sun that gives light, the power of the wind that sweeps away impurities, and the silent life-forces at work in the earth we tread on.

We shall see then what a variety of trades, mutually co-operating on a spot of the globe and animated by a revolution, can do to feed, clothe, house, and supply with all manner of luxuries millions of intelligent men.

We need write no fiction to prove this. What we are sure of, what has already been experimented upon, and recognized as practical, would suffice to carry it into effect, if the attempt were fertilized, vivified by the daring inspiration of the revolution and the spontaneous impulse of the masses.

CHAPTER XVII

Agriculture

I

Political economy has often been reproached with drawing all its deductions from the decidedly false principle, that the only incentive capable of forcing a man to augment his power of production is personal interest in its narrowest sense.

The reproach is perfectly true; so true that epochs of great industrial discoveries and true progress in industry are precisely those in which the happiness of all was inspiring men, and in which personal enrichment was least thought of. The great investigators in science and the great inventors aimed, above all, at giving greater freedom of mankind. And if Watt, Stephenson, Jacquard, etc., could have only foreseen what a state of misery their sleepless nights would bring to the workers, they certainly would have burned their designs and broken their models.

Another principle that pervades political economy is just as false. It is the tacit admission, common to all economists, that if there is often overproduction in certain branches, a society will nevertheless never have sufficient products to satisfy the wants of all, and that consequently the day will never come when nobody will be forced to sell his labour in exchange for wages. This tacit admission is found at the basis of all theories and all the so-called 'laws' taught by economists.

And yet it is certain that the day when any civilized association of individuals would ask itself, *what are the needs of all, and the means of satisfying them*, it would see that, in industry as in agriculture, it already possesses sufficient to provide abundantly for all needs, on condition that it knows how to apply these means to satisfy real needs.

That this is true as regards industry no one can contest. Indeed, it suffices to study the processes already in use to extract coals and ore, to obtain steel and work it, to manufacture on a great scale what is used for clothing, etc., in order to perceive that we could already increase our production fourfold or more, and yet use for that *less* work than we are using now.

We go further. We assert that agriculture is in the same position: those who cultivate the soil, like the manufacturers, already could increase their production, not only fourfold but tenfold, and they can put it into practice as soon as they feel the need of it – as soon as a socialist organization of work will be established instead of the present capitalistic one.

Each time agriculture is spoken of, men imagine a peasant bending over the plough, throwing badly sorted corn haphazard into the ground and waiting anxiously for what the good or bad season will bring forth; they think of a family working from morn to night and reaping as reward a rude bed, dry bread and coarse beverage. In a word, they picture 'the savages' of La Bruyère.

And for these men, ground down to such a misery, the utmost relief that society proposes is to reduce their taxes or their rent. But even most social reformers do not dare to imagine a cultivator standing erect, taking leisure, and producing by a few hours' work per day sufficient food to nourish, not only his own family, but a hundred men more at the least. In their most glowing dreams of the future socialists do not go beyond American extensive culture, which, after all, is but the infancy of agricultural art.

But the thinking agriculturist has broader ideas today – his conceptions are on a far grander scale. He only asks for a fraction of an acre in order to produce sufficient vegetables for a family; and to feed twenty-five horned beasts he needs no more space than he formerly required to feed one; his aim is to make his own soil, to defy seasons and climate, to warm both air and earth around the young plant; to produce, in a word, on one acre what he used to gather from fifty acres, and that without any excessive fatigue – by greatly reducing, on the contrary, the total of former labour. He knows that we will be able to feed everybody by giving to the culture of the fields no more time than what each can give with pleasure and joy.

This is the present tendency of agriculture.

While scientific men, led by Liebig, the creator of the chemical theory of agriculture, often got on the wrong tack in their love of mere theories, unlettered agriculturists opened up new roads to prosperity. Market-gardeners of Paris, Troyes, Rouen, Scotch and English gardeners, Flemish and Lombardian farmers, peasants of Jersey, Guernsey, and farmers on the Scilly Isles have opened up such large horizons that the mind hesitates to grasp them. While up till lately a family of peasants needed at least seventeen to twenty acres to live on the produce of the soil – and we know how peasants live – we can now no longer say what is the minimum area on which all that is necessary to a family can be grown, even including articles of luxury, if the soil is worked by means of intensive culture.

Twenty years ago it could already be asserted that a population of 30 million individuals could live very well, without importing anything, on what could be grown in Great Britain. But now, when we see the progress recently made in France, in Germany, in England, and when we contemplate the new horizons which open before us, we can say that in cultivating the earth as it is already cultivated in many places, even on poor soils, 50 or 60 million inhabitants to the territory of Great Britain would still be a very feeble proportion to what man could exact from the soil.

In any case (as we are about to demonstrate) we may consider it as absolutely proved that if tomorrow Paris and the two departments of Seine and of Seine-et-Oise organized themselves as an anarchist commune, in which all worked with their hands, and if the entire universe refused to send them a single bushel of wheat, a single head of cattle, a single basket of fruit, and left them only the territory of the two departments, they could not only produce all the corn, meat, and vegetables necessary for themselves, but also vegetables and fruit which are now articles of luxury, in sufficient quantities for all.

And, in addition, we affirm that the sum total of this labour would be far less than that expended at present to feed these people with corn harvested in Auvergne and Russia, with vegetables produced a little everywhere by extensive agriculture, and with fruit grown in the South.

It is self-evident that we in nowise desire all exchange to be suppressed, nor that each region should strive to produce that which will only grow in its climate by a more or less artificial culture. But we care to draw attention to the fact that the theory of exchange, such as is understood today, is strangely exaggerated – that exchange is often useless and even harmful. We assert, moreover, that people have never had a right conception of the immense labour of southern wine growers, nor that of Russian and Hungarian corn growers, whose excessive labour could also be very much reduced if they adopted intensive culture, instead of their present system of extensive agriculture.

II

It would be impossible to quote here the mass of facts on which we base our assertions. We are therefore obliged to refer our readers who want further information to another book, *Fields, Factories, and Workshops.*[k] Above all we earnestly invite those who are interested in the question to read several excellent works published in France and elsewhere, and of which we give a list at the close of this book.[1] As to the inhabitants of large towns, who have as yet no real notion of what agriculture can be, we advise them to explore the surrounding market-gardens. They need but observe and question the market-gardeners, and a new world will be open to them. They will then be able to see what European agriculture may be in the twentieth century; and they will understand with what force the social revolution will be armed when we know the secret of taking everything we need from the soil.

A few facts will suffice to show that our assertions are in no way exaggerated. We only wish them to be preceded by a few general remarks.

We know in what a wretched condition European agriculture is. If the cultivator of the soil is not plundered by the landowner, he

---

[k] A new enlarged edition of it has been published last year by Thomas Nelson and Sons in their Shilling Library.

is robbed by the state. If the state taxes him moderately, the money-lender enslaves him by means of promissory notes, and soon turns him into the simple tenant of a soil belonging in reality to a financial company. The landlord, the state and the banker thus plunder the cultivator by means of rent, taxes and interest. The sum varies in each country, but it never falls below the quarter, very often the half of the raw produce. In France and in Italy agriculturists paid the state quite recently as much as 44 per cent of the gross produce.

Moreover, the share of the owner and the state always goes on increasing. As soon as the cultivator has obtained more plentiful crops by prodigies of labour, invention or initiative, the tribute he will owe to the landowner, the state, and the banker will augment in proportion. If he doubles the number of bushels reaped per acre, rent will be doubled, and taxes too, and the state will take care to raise them still more if the prices go up. And so on. In short, everywhere the cultivator of the soil works twelve to sixteen hours a day; these three vultures take from him everything he might lay by; they rob him everywhere of what would enable him to improve his culture. This is why agriculture progresses so slowly.

The cultivator can only occasionally make some progress, in some exceptional regions, under quite exceptional circumstances, following upon a quarrel between the three vampires. And yet we have said nothing about the tribute every cultivator pays to the manufacturer. Every machine, every spade, every barrel of chemical manure, is sold to him at three or four times its real cost. Nor let us forget the middleman, who levies the lion's share of the earth's produce.

This is why, during all this century of invention and progress, agriculture has only improved from time to time on very limited areas.

Happily there have always been small oases, neglected for some time by the vultures; and here we learn what intensive agriculture can produce for mankind. Let us mention a few examples.

In the American prairies (which, however, only yield meagre spring wheat crops, from 7 to 15 bushels an acre, and even these are often marred by periodical droughts), 500 men, working only during eight months, produce the annual food of 50,000 people. With all the improvements of the last three years, one man's yearly

labour (300 days) yields, delivered in Chicago as flour, the yearly
food of 250 men. Here the result is obtained by a great economy
in manual labour: on those vast plains, ploughing, harvesting,
threshing, are organized in almost military fashion. There is no
useless running to and fro, no loss of time – all is done with
parade-like precision.

This is agriculture on a large scale – extensive agriculture, which
takes the soil from nature without seeking to improve it. When the
earth has yielded all it can, they leave it; they seek elsewhere for
a virgin soil, to be exhausted in its turn. But there is also 'intensive'
agriculture, which is already worked, and will be more and more
so, by machinery. Its object is to cultivate a limited space well, to
manure, to improve, to concentrate work, and to obtain the largest
crop possible. This kind of culture spreads every year, and whereas
agriculturists in the south of France and on the fertile plains of
Western America are content with an average crop of 11 to 15
bushels per acre by extensive culture, they reap regularly 39, even
55, and sometimes 60 bushels per acre in the north of France.
The annual consumption of a man is thus obtained from less than
a quarter of an acre.

And the more intense the culture is, the less work is expended
to obtain a bushel of wheat. Machinery replaces man at the prelimi-
nary work and for the improvements needed by the land – such
as draining, clearing of stones – which will double the crops in
future, once and for ever. Sometimes nothing but keeping the soil
free of weeds, without manuring, allows an average soil to yield
excellent crops from year to year. It has been done for forty years
in succession at Rothamstead, in Hertfordshire.

However, let us not write an agricultural romance, but be satisfied
with a crop of 44 bushels per acre. That needs no exceptional
soil, but merely a rational culture; and let us see what it means.

The 3,600,000 individuals who inhabit the two departments of
Seine and Seine-et-Oise consume yearly for their food a little less
than 22 million bushels of cereals, chiefly wheat; and in our
hypothesis they would have to cultivate, in order to obtain this
crop, 494,200 acres out of the 1,507,300 acres which they possess.
It is evident they would not cultivate them with spades. That would
need too much time – 96 work-days of 5 hours per acre. It would
be preferable to improve the soil once for all – to drain what

needed draining, to level what needed levelling, to clear the soil of stones, were it even necessary to spend 5 million days of 5 hours in this preparatory work – an average of 10 work-days to each acre.

Then they would plough with the steamdigger, which would take one and three-fifths of a day per acre, and they would give another one and three-fifths of a day for working with the double plough. Seeds would be sorted by steam instead of taken haphazard, and they would be carefully sown in rows instead of being thrown to the four winds. Now all this work would not take 10 days of 5 hours per acre if the work were done under good conditions. But if 10 million work-days are given to good culture during three or four years, the result will be that later on crops of 44 to 55 bushels per acre will be obtained by only working half the time.

Fifteen million work-days will thus have been spent to give bread to a population of 3,600,000 inhabitants. And the work would be such that everyone could do it without having muscles of steel, or without having even worked the ground before. The initiative and the general distribution of work would come from those who know the soil. As to the work itself, there is no townsman of either sex so enfeebled as to be incapable of looking after machines and of contributing his share to agrarian work after a few hours' apprenticeship.

Well, when we consider that in the present chaos, in a city like Paris, without counting the unemployed of the upper classes, there are always about 100,000 workmen out of work in their several trades, we see that the power lost in our present organization would alone suffice to give, with a rational culture, all the bread that is necessary for the 3 or 4 million inhabitants of the two departments.

We repeat, this is no fancy dream, and we have not yet spoken of the truly intensive agriculture. We have not depended upon the wheat (obtained in three years by Mr Hallett) of which one grain, replanted, produced 5,000 or 6,000, and occasionally 10,000 grains, which would give the wheat necessary for a family of five individuals on an area of 120 square yards. On the contrary, we have only mentioned what is being already achieved by numerous farmers in France, England, Belgium, etc., and what might be done tomorrow with the experience and knowledge acquired already by practice on a large scale.

But without a revolution, neither tomorrow, nor after tomorrow will see it done, because it is not to the interest of landowners and capitalists; and because peasants who would find their profit in it have neither the knowledge nor the money, nor the time to obtain what is necessary to go ahead.

The society of today has not yet reached this stage. But let Parisians proclaim an anarchist commune, and they will of necessity come to it, because they will not be foolish enough to continue making luxurious toys (which Vienna, Warsaw and Berlin make as well already), and to run the risk of being left without bread.

Moreover, agricultural work, by the help of machinery, would soon become the most attractive and the most joyful of all occupations.

'We have had enough jewellery and enough dolls' clothes', they would say; 'it is high time for the workers to recruit their strength in agriculture, to go in search of vigour, of impressions of nature, of the joy of life, that they have forgotten in the dark factories of the suburbs.'

In the Middle Ages it was Alpine pasture lands, rather than guns, which allowed the Swiss to shake off lords and kings. Modern agriculture will allow a city in revolt to free itself from the combined bourgeois forces.

III

We have seen how the $3\frac{1}{2}$ million inhabitants of the two departments round Paris could find ample bread by cultivating only a third of their territory. Let us now pass on to cattle.

Englishmen, who eat much meat, consume on an average a little less than 220 lb. a year per adult. Supposing all meats consumed were oxen, that makes a little less than the third of an ox. An ox a year for five individuals (including children) is already a sufficient ration. For $3\frac{1}{2}$ million inhabitants this would make an annual consumption of 700,000 head of cattle.

Today, with the pasture system, we need at least 5 million acres to nourish 660,000 head of cattle. This makes 9 acres per each head of horned cattle. Nevertheless, with prairies moderately watered by spring water (as recently done on thousands of acres in the southwest of France), $1\frac{1}{4}$ million acres already suffice. But if intensive culture is practised, and beet-root is grown for fodder, you only need a quarter of that area, that is to say, about 310,000 acres. And if we have recourse to maize and practise ensilage (the compression of fodder while green) like Arabs, we obtain fodder on an area of 217,500 acres.

In the environs of Milan, where sewer water is used to irrigate the fields, fodder for two to three horned cattle per each acre is obtained on an area of 22,000 acres; and on a few favoured fields, up to 177 tons of hay to the 10 acres have been cropped, the yearly provender of 36 milch cows. Nearly nine acres per head of cattle are needed under the pasture system, and only 2½ acres for nine oxen or cows under the new system. These are the opposite extremes in modern agriculture.

In Guernsey, on a total of 9,884 acres utilized, nearly half (4,695 acres) are covered with cereals and kitchen-gardens; only 5,189 acres remain as meadows. On these 5,189 acres, 1,480 horses, 7,260 head of cattle, 900 sheep and 4,200 pigs are fed, which makes more than three head of cattle per 2 acres, without reckoning the sheep or the pigs. It is needless to add that the fertility of the soil is made by seaweed and chemical manures.

Returning to our 3½ million inhabitants belonging to Paris and its environs, we see that the land necessary for the rearing of cattle comes down from 5 million acres to 197,000. Well, then, let us not stop at the lowest figures, let us take those of ordinary intensive culture; let us liberally add to the land necessary for smaller cattle which must replace some of the horned beasts and allow 395,000 acres for the rearing of cattle – 494,000 if you like, on the 1,013,000 acres remaining after bread has been provided for the people.

Let us be generous and give 5 million work-days to put this land into a productive state.

After having therefore employed in the course of a year 20 million work-days, half of which are for permanent improvements, we shall have bread and meat assured to us, without including all the extra meat obtainable in the shape of fowls, pigs, rabbits, etc.; without taking into consideration that a population provided with excellent vegetables and fruit consumes less meat than Englishmen, who supplement their poor supply of vegetables by animal food. Now, how much do 20 million work-days of 5 hours make per inhabitant? Very little indeed. A population of 3½ millions must have at least 1,200,000 adult men, and as many women capable of work. Well, then, to give bread and meat to all, it would need only 17 half-days of work a year per man. Add 3 million work-days, or double that number if you like, in order to obtain milk. That will make 25 work-days of 5 hours in all – nothing more than a little pleasurable country exercise – to obtain the three principal products: bread, meat and milk. The three products which, after housing, cause daily anxiety to nine-tenths of mankind.

And yet – let us not tire of repeating – these are not fancy dreams. We have only told what is, what has been, obtained by experience on a large scale. Agriculture could be reorganized in this way tomorrow if property laws and general ignorance did not offer opposition.

The day Paris has understood that to know what you eat and how it is produced, is a question of public interest; the day when everybody will have understood that this question is infinitely more important than all the parliamentary debates of the present times – on that day the revolution will be an accomplished fact. Paris will take possession of the two departments and cultivate them. And then the Parisian worker, after having laboured a third of his existence in order to buy bad and insufficient food, will produce it himself, under his walls, within the enclosure of his forts (if they still exist), in a few hours of healthy and attractive work.

And now we pass on to fruit and vegetables. Let us go outside Paris and visit the establishment of a market-gardener who accomplishes wonders (ignored by learned economists) at a few miles from the academies.

Let us visit, suppose, M. Ponce, the author of a work on market-gardening, who makes no secret of what the earth yields him, and who has published it all along.

M. Ponce, and especially his workmen, work like niggers. It takes eight men to cultivate a plot a little less than three acres (2.7). They work 12, and even 15 hours a day, that is to say, three times more than is needed. Twenty-four of them would not be too many. To which M. Ponce will probably answer that as he pays the terrible sum of £100 rent a year for his 2.7 acres of land, and £100 for manure bought in the barracks, he is obliged to exploit. He would no doubt answer, 'Being exploited, I exploit in my turn.' His installation has also cost him £1,200, of which certainly more than half went as tribute to the idle barons of industry. In reality, this establishment represents at most 3,000 work-days, probably much less.

But let us examine his crops: nearly 10 tons of carrots, nearly 10 tons of onions, radishes, and small vegetables, 6,000 heads of cabbage, 3,000 heads of cauliflower, 5,000 baskets of tomatoes, 5,000 dozen of choice fruit, 154,000 salads; in short, a total of 123 tons of vegetables and fruit to 2.7 acres – 120 yards long by 109 yards broad, which makes more than 44 tons of vegetables to the acre.

But a man does not eat more than 660 lb. of vegetables and fruit a year, and 2½ acres of a market-garden yield enough vegetables and fruit to richly supply the table of 350 adults during the year. Thus 24 persons, employed a whole year in cultivating 2.7 acres of land, and only working 5 hours a day, would produce sufficient vegetables and fruit for 350 adults, which is equivalent at least to 500 individuals.

To put it in another way: in cultivating like M. Ponce – and his results have already been surpassed – 350 adults should each give a little more than a hundred hours a year (103) to produce vegetables and fruit necessary for 500 people.

Let us mention that such a production is not the exception. It takes place, under the walls of Paris, on an area of 2,220 acres, by 5,000 market-gardeners. Only these market-gardeners are reduced nowadays to a state of beasts of burden, in order to pay an average rent of £32 per acre.

But do not these facts, which can be verified by everyone, prove that 17,300 acres (of the 519,000 remaining to us) would suffice to give all necessary vegetables, as well as a liberal amount of fruit to the 3½ million inhabitants of our two departments?

As to the quantity of work necessary to produce these fruits and vegetables, it would amount to 50 million work-days of 5 hours (50 days per adult male), if we measure by the market-gardeners' standard of work. But we could reduce this quantity if we had recourse to the process in vogue in Jersey and Guernsey. We must also remember that the Paris market-gardener is forced to work so hard because he mostly produces early season fruits, the high prices of which have to pay for fabulous rents, and that this system of culture entails more work than is necessary for growing the ordinary staple vegetables and fruit. Besides, the market-gardeners of Paris, not having the means to make a great outlay on their gardens, and being obliged to pay heavily for glass, wood, iron and coal, obtain their artificial heat out of manure, while it can be had at much less cost in hothouses.

IV

The market-gardeners, we say, are forced to become machines and to renounce all joys of life in order to obtain their marvellous crops. But these hard grinders have rendered a great service to humanity in teaching us that the soil can be 'made'. They *make* it with old hot-beds of manure, which have already served to give the necessary warmth to young plants and to early fruit; and they make it in such great quantity that they are compelled to sell it in part, otherwise it would raise the level of their gardens by one inch every year. They do it so well (so Barral teaches us, in his *Dictionary of Agriculture*, in an article on market-gardeners) that in recent contracts, the market-gardener stipulates that he will carry away his soil with him when he leaves the bit of ground he is cultivating. Loam carried away on carts, with furniture and glass frames – that is the answer of practical cultivators to the learned treatises of a Ricardo, who represented rent as a means of equalizing the natural advantages of the soil. 'The soil is worth what the man is worth,' that is the gardeners' motto.

And yet the market-gardeners of Paris and Rouen labour three times as hard to obtain the same results as their fellow workers in Guernsey or in England. Applying industry to agriculture, these last make their climate in addition to their soil, by means of the greenhouse.

Fifty years ago the greenhouse was the luxury of the rich. It was kept to grow exotic plants for pleasure. But nowadays its use begins to be generalized. A tremendous industry has grown up lately in Guernsey and Jersey, where hundreds of acres are already covered with glass – to say nothing of the countless small greenhouses kept in every little farm garden. Acres and acres of greenhouses have lately been built also at Worthing (103 acres in 1912), in the suburbs of London, and in several other parts of England and Scotland.

They are built of all qualities, beginning with those which have granite walls, down to those which represent mere shelters made in planks and glass frames, which cost, even now, with all the tribute paid to capitalists and middlemen, less than 3*s*. 6*d*. per square yard under glass. Most of them are heated for at least three or four months every year; but even the cool greenhouses, which are not heated at all, give excellent results – of course, not for growing grapes and tropical plants, but for potatoes, carrots, peas, tomatoes, and so on.

In this way man emancipates himself from climate, and at the same time he avoids also the heavy work with the hot-beds, and he saves both in buying much less manure and in work. Three men to the acre, each of them working less than sixty hours a week, produce on very small spaces what formerly required acres and acres of land.

The result of all these recent conquests of culture is, that if one-half only of the adults of a city gave each about fifty half-days for the culture of the finest fruit and vegetables *out of season*, they would have all the year round an unlimited supply of that sort of fruit and vegetables for the whole population.

But there is a still more important fact to notice. The greenhouse has nowadays a tendency to become a mere *kitchen garden under glass*. And when it is used to such a purpose, the simplest plank-and-glass unheated shelters already give fabulous crops – such as, for instance, 500 bushels of potatoes per acre as a first crop, ready by the end of April; after which a second and a third crop are obtained in the extremely high temperature which prevails in the summer under glass.

I gave in my *Fields, Factories, and Workshops* most striking facts in this direction. Sufficient to say here, that at Jersey, 34 men, with one trained gardener only, cultivate 13 acres under glass, from which they obtain 143 tons of fruit and early vegetables, using for this extraordinary culture less than 1,000 tons of coal.

And this is done now in Guernsey and Jersey on a very large scale, quite a number of steamers constantly plying between Guernsey and London, only to export the crops of the greenhouses.

Nowadays, in order to obtain that same crop of 500 bushels of potatoes, we must plough every year a surface of 4 acres, plant it, cultivate it, weed it, and so on; whereas with the glass, even if we shall have to give perhaps, to start with, half a day's work per square yard in order to build the greenhouse – we shall save afterwards at least one-half, and probably three-quarters of the yearly labour required formerly.

These are *facts*, results which everyone can verify himself. And these facts are already a hint as to what man could obtain from the earth if he treated it with intelligence.

V

In all the above we have reasoned upon what already withstood the test of experience. Intensive culture of the fields, irrigated meadows, the hothouse, and finally the kitchen garden under glass are realities. Moreover, the tendency is to extend and to generalize these methods of culture, because they allow of obtaining more produce with less work and with more certainty.

In fact, after having studied the most simple glass shelters of Guernsey, we affirm that, taking all in all, far less work is expended for obtaining potatoes under glass in April, than in growing them in the open air, which requires digging a space four times as large, watering it, weeding it, etc. Work is likewise economized in employing a perfected tool or machine, even when an initial expense had to be incurred to buy the tool.

Complete figures concerning the culture of common vegetables under glass are still wanting. This culture is of recent origin, and is only carried out on small areas. But we have already figures concerning the fifty-year-old culture of early season grapes, and these figures are conclusive.

In the north of England, on the Scotch frontier, where coal only costs 3s. a ton at the pit's mouth, they have long since taken to growing hothouse grapes. Thirty years ago these grapes, ripe in January, were sold by the grower at 20s. per lb. and resold at 40s. per lb. for Napoleon III's table. Today the same grower sells them at only 2s. 6d. per lb. He tells us so himself in a horticultural journal. The fall in the prices is caused by the tons and tons of grapes arriving in January to London and Paris.

Thanks to the cheapness of coal and an intelligent culture, grapes from the north travel now southwards, in a contrary direction to ordinary fruit. They cost so little that in May, English and Jersey grapes are sold at 1*s*. 8*d*. per lb. by the gardeners, and yet this price, like that of 40*s*. thirty years ago, is only kept up by slack production.

In March, Belgian grapes are sold at from 6*d*. to 8*d*., while in October, grapes cultivated in immense quantities – under glass, and with a little artificial heating in the environs of London – are sold at the same price as grapes bought by the pound in the vineyards of Switzerland and the Rhine, that is to say, for a few halfpence. Yet they still cost two-thirds too much, by reason of the excessive rent of the soil and the cost of installation and heating, on which the gardener pays a formidable tribute to the manufacturer and middleman. This being understood, we may say that it costs 'next to nothing' to have delicious grapes under the latitude of, and in our misty London in autumn. In one of the suburbs, for instance, a wretched glass and plaster shelter, 9 ft. 10 in. long by 6½ ft. wide, resting against our cottage, gave us about fifty pounds of grapes of an exquisite flavour in October, for nine consecutive years. The crop came from a Hamburg vine-stalk, six years old. And the shelter was so bad that the rain came through. At night the temperature was always that of outside. It was evidently not heated, for it would have been as useless as heating the street! And the care which was given was: pruning the vine, half an hour every year; and bringing a wheelbarrowful of manure, which was thrown over the stalk of the vine, planted in red clay outside the shelter.

On the other hand, if we estimate the amount of care given to the vine on the borders of the Rhine or Lake Leman, the terraces constructed stone upon stone on the slopes of the hills, the transport of manure and also of earth to a height of two or three hundred feet, we come to the conclusion that on the whole the expenditure of work necessary to cultivate vines is more considerable in Switzerland or on the banks of the Rhine than it is under glass in London suburbs.

This may seem paradoxical, because it is generally believed that vines grow of themselves in the south of Europe, and that the vine-grower's work costs nothing. But gardeners and horticulturists, far from contradicting us, confirm our assertions. 'The most advantageous culture in England is vine culture,' wrote a practical gardener, editor of the *English Journal of Horticulture*, in the *Nineteenth Century*. Prices speak eloquently for themselves, as we know.

Translating these facts into communist language, we may assert that the man or woman who takes twenty hours a year from his leisure time to give some little care – very pleasant in the main – to two or three vine-stalks sheltered by simple glass under any European climate, will gather as many grapes as their family and friends can eat. And that applies not only to vines, but to all fruit trees.

The commune that will put the processes of intensive culture into practice on a large scale will have all possible vegetables, indigenous or exotic, and all desirable fruits, without employing more than about ten hours a year per inhabitant.

In fact, nothing would be easier than to verify the above statements by direct experiment. Suppose 100 acres of a light loam (such as we have at Worthing) are transformed into a number of market-gardens, each one with its glass houses for the rearing of the seedlings and young plants. Suppose also that 50 more acres are covered with glass houses, and the organization of the whole is left to practical experienced French *maraîchers*, and Guernsey or Worthing greenhouse gardeners.

In basing the maintenance of these 150 acres on the Jersey average, requiring the work of three men per acre under glass – which makes less than 8,600 hours of work a year – it would need about 1,300,000 hours for the 150 acres. Fifty competent gardeners could give 5 hours a day to this work, and the rest would be simply done by people who, without being gardeners by profession, would soon learn how to use a spade, and to handle the plants. But this work would yield at least – we have seen it in a preceding chapter – all necessaries and articles of luxury in the way of fruit and vegetables for at least 40,000 or 50,000 people. Let us admit that among this number there are 13,500 adults, willing to work at the kitchen garden; then, each one would have to give 100 hours a year distributed over the whole year. These hours of work would become hours of recreation spent among friends and children in beautiful gardens, more beautiful probably than those of the legendary Semiramis.

This is the balance sheet of the labour to be spent in order to be able to eat to satiety fruit which we are deprived of today, and to have vegetables in abundance, now so scrupulously rationed out by the housewife, when she has to reckon each halfpenny which must go to enrich capitalists and landowners.[2]

If only humanity had the consciousness of what it *can*, and if that consciousness only gave it the power to *will*!

If it only knew that cowardice of the spirit is the rock on which all revolutions have stranded until now.

VI

We can easily perceive the new horizons opening before the social revolution.

Each time we speak of revolution, the face of the worker who has seen children wanting food darkens and he asks – 'What of bread? Will there be sufficient, if everyone eats according to his appetite? What if the peasants, ignorant tools of reaction, starve our towns as the black bands did in France in 1793 – what shall we do?'

Let them do their worst! The large cities will have to do without them.

At what, then, should the hundreds of thousands of workers, who are asphyxiated today in small workshops and factories, be employed on the day they regain their liberty? Will they continue to shut themselves up in factories after the revolution? Will they continue to make luxurious toys for export when they see their stock of corn getting exhausted, meat becoming scarce, and vegetables disappearing without being replaced?

Evidently not! They will leave the town and go into the fields! Aided by a machinery which will enable the weakest of us to put a shoulder to the wheel, they will carry revolution into previously enslaved culture as they will have carried it into institutions and ideas.

Hundreds of acres will be covered with glass, and men, and women with delicate fingers, will foster the growth of young plants. Hundreds of other acres will be ploughed by steam, improved by manures, or enriched by artificial soil obtained by the pulverization of rocks. Happy crowds of occasional labourers will cover these acres with crops, guided in the work and experiments partly by those who know agriculture, but especially by the great and practical spirit of a people roused from long slumber and illumined by that bright beacon – the happiness of all.

And in two or three months the early crops will relieve the most pressing wants, and provide food for a people who, after so many centuries of expectation, will at last be able to appease their hunger and eat according to their appetite.

In the meanwhile, popular genius, the genius of a nation which revolts and knows its wants, will work at experimenting with new processes of culture that we already catch a glimpse of, and that only need the baptism of experience to become universal. Light will be experimented with – that unknown agent of culture which makes barley ripen in 45 days under the latitude of Yakutsk; light, concentrated or artificial, will rival heat in hastening the growth of plants. A Mouchot of the future will invent a machine to guide the rays of the sun and make them work, so that we shall no longer seek sun-heat stored in coal in the depths of the earth. They will experiment the watering of the soil with cultures of micro-organisms – a rational idea, conceived but yesterday, which will permit us to give to the soil those little living beings, necessary to feed the rootlets, to decompose and assimilate the component parts of the soil.

They will experiment . . . But let us stop here, or we shall enter into the realm of fancy. Let us remain in the reality of acquired facts. With the processes of culture in use, applied on a large scale, and already victorious in the struggle against industrial competition, we can give ourselves ease and luxury in return for agreeable work. The near future will show what is practical in the processes that recent scientific discoveries give us a glimpse of. Let us limit ourselves at present to opening up the new path that consists in *the study of the needs of man, and the means of satisfying them.*

The only thing that may be wanting to the revolution is the boldness of initiative.

With our minds already narrowed in our youth and enslaved by the past in our mature age, we hardly dare to think. If a new idea is mentioned – before venturing on an opinion of our own, we consult musty books a hundred years old, to know what ancient masters thought on the subject.

It is not food that will fail, if boldness of thought and initiative are not wanting to the revolution.

Of all the great days of the French Revolution, the most beautiful, the greatest, was the one on which delegates who had come from all parts of France to Paris, worked all with the spade to plant the ground of the Champ de Mars, preparing it for the fête of the Federation.

That day France was united: animated by the new spirit, she had a vision of the future in the working in common of the soil.

And it will again be by the working in common of the soil that the enfranchized societies will find their unity and will obliterate the hatred and oppression which has hitherto divided them.

Henceforth, able to conceive solidarity – that immense power which increases man's energy and creative forces a hundredfold – the new society will march to the conquest of the future with all the vigour of youth.

Ceasing to produce for unknown buyers, and looking in its midst for needs and tastes to be satisfied, society will liberally assure the life and ease of each of its members, as well as that moral satisfaction which work gives when freely chosen and freely accomplished, and the joy of living without encroaching on the life of others.

Inspired by a new daring – born of the feeling of solidarity – all will march together to the conquest of the high joys of knowledge and artistic creation.

A society thus inspired will fear neither dissensions within nor enemies without. To the coalitions of the past it will oppose a new harmony, the initiative of each and all, the daring which springs from the awakening of a people's genius.

Before such an irresistible force 'conspiring kings' will be powerless. Nothing will remain for them but to bow before it, and to harness themselves to the chariot of humanity, rolling towards new horizons opened up by the social revolution.

Notes

1 Consult *La Répartition métrique des impôts*, by A. Toubeau, 2 vols., published by Guillaumin in 1880. (We do not in the least agree with Toubeau's conclusions, but it is a real encyclopaedia,

indicating the sources which prove what can be obtained from the soil.) *La Culture maraîchere*, by M. Ponce, Paris, 1869. *Le Potager Gressent*, Paris, 1885, an excellent practical work. *Physiologie et culture du blé*, by Risler, Paris, 1881. *Le Blé, sa culture intensive et extensive*, by Lecouteux, Paris, 1883. *La Cité chinoise*, by Eugène Simon. *Le Dictionnaire d'agriculture*, by Barral (Hachette, editor). *The Rothamstead Experiments*, by Wm Fream, London, 1888 – culture without manure, etc. (the *Field* office, editor). *Fields, Factories, and Workshops*, by the author, Thomas Nelson and Sons.

2 Summing up the figures given on agriculture, figures proving that the inhabitants of the two departments of Seine and Seine-et-Oise can live perfectly well on their own territory by employing very little time annually to obtain food, we have:

Departments of Seine and Seine-et-Oise

Number of inhabitants in 1889	3,900,000
Area in acres	1,507,300
Average number of inhabitants per acre	2.6

Areas to be cultivated to feed the inhabitants (in acres):

Corn and cereals	494,000
Natural and artificial meadows	494,000
Vegetables and fruit	from 17,300 to
	25,000
Leaving a balance for houses, roads, parks, forests	494,000

Quantity of annual work necessary to improve and cultivate the above surfaces in five-hour work-days:

Cereals (culture and crop)	15,000,000
Meadows, milk, rearing of cattle	10,000,000
Market-gardening culture, high-class fruit	33,000,000
Extras	12,000,000
Total	70,000,000

If we suppose that only half of the able-bodied adults (men and women) are willing to work at agriculture, we see that 70 million work-days must be divided among 1,200,000 individuals, which gives us 58 work-days of 5 hours for each of these workers. With that the population of the two departments would have all necessary bread, meat, milk, vegetables, and fruit, both for ordinary and even luxurious consumption. Today a workman spends for the necessary food of his family (generally less than what is necessary) at least one-third of his 300 work-days a year, about 1,000 hours be it, instead of 290. That is, he thus gives about 700 hours too much to fatten the idle and the would-be administrators, because he does not produce his own food, but buys it of middlemen, who in their turn buy it of peasants who exhaust themselves by working with bad tools, because, being robbed by the landowners and the state, they cannot procure better ones.

Other writings

'Western Europe', from *Memoirs of a Revolutionist*

Kropotkin's autobiography, *Memoirs of a Revolutionist*, was first serialized in the American magazine *Atlantic Monthly* in 1898–9 and appeared in book form in 1899. Kropotkin composed both Russian and English versions of the memoirs, which differed somewhat from each other, and never completed the Russian text. Some passages contained in the Russian version, however, were omitted from the 1899 publication, including an entire chapter entitled 'Western Europe'. This chapter, which Kropotkin left unfinished, recounts his activities in the Jura Federation in Switzerland in the late 1870s. (The book as published treats the subject briefly and in different form in Part Six, also entitled 'Western Europe'.) It is illuminating in regard both to his anarchism and to his personality. On the one hand, it details his strong objections to Marxism and Social Democracy, and on the other it paints a series of characteristically warm-hearted portraits of his fellow anarchists.

The Russian text, first published in 1924, is from the seventh Russian edition of *Memoirs of a Revolutionist* (*Zapiski revoliutsionera*), edited by N. K. Lebedev (Moscow: Politkatorzhan, 1929), II, 235–66. It has been translated and annotated for this volume by Marshall Shatz.

In 1876, it must have been in November, I made it to Switzerland, to the Jura, and renewed my acquaintance with Guillaume, Schwitzguébel, and the other Jurassians.[1]

---

[1] James Guillaume, a close associate of Bakunin, was a central figure in the anarchist movement and the author of an important chronicle of the First International. He

I had written to James Guillaume as soon as I landed in England in the summer of 1876, and since then we had corresponded frequently. Guillaume was overjoyed at my escape and invited me to Switzerland. From time to time I would send him notices on Russia or on English affairs and strikes for the *Bulletin de la Fédération Jurassienne*,[2] and we kept up a correspondence.

Although I thought a good deal about moving to Switzerland and working in the Jura Federation, I had to remain in England. There I had some income writing geographical notes and articles for the journal *Nature*, whose editor was John Keltie (subsequently secretary of the London Geographical Society), a very kind and decent man. The work paid little, but my needs were modest. A pound a week was quite sufficient.

I soon moved from Edinburgh to London. Nowhere is the life of an émigré as hard as it is in London. Once a man begins to feel at home, becomes acclimatized, and finds steady work, he comes to love London for its independent style of life, absence of police harassment, and freedom of activity. Now, when a good many émigré workers of all nations live in London, it is much easier for a new arrival. He can settle in a neighbourhood where other émigrés like himself live.

Nevertheless, even today many émigrés have a terribly hard time in their first years in London. Back in those days, when there were just a few émigré communards,[3] and the English socialist movement did not yet exist, it was extremely difficult for an émigré, especially a Russian.

London is a dreadful city, a monster grown to enormous proportions. The cost of living is high – high, that is, for a man to whom the sum of sixpence represents a day's, or sometimes two days' sustenance. If work, or simply fate, has cast him to one end of the city, and his acquaintances or comrades live at the other end, he must go whole weeks and months without seeing anyone close to him. Even those of us who have got used to London do

and Adhémar Schwitzguébel were among the leaders of the Jura Federation, the bastion of anarchism within the First International. Kropotkin had met them both on his visit to Switzerland in 1872.
[2] The Jura Federation's *Bulletin*, edited by Guillaume, was published from 1872 to 1878.
[3] The 'communards' were participants in the Paris Commune of 1871.

not see each other for months at a time, because it takes half a day to visit a friend and costs a couple of shillings.

Once I had settled in London, I wanted some more vital activity than journalism and literary work. Right from the start, therefore, I tried to get acquainted with workers. My landlord, who was a worker, introduced me to some of his comrades, and I initiated conversations with them on socialist issues. But at that time (1876) English workers did not want to hear about socialism. They had not progressed beyond trade-unionism and co-operatives.

I do not know what more I might have done in London if my Jura friends had not shortly found me steady work in Switzerland. A publishing firm was planning to put out a big Geographical Dictionary and it was proposed that I write the articles dealing with Russia and Sweden. It was rather a lot of work, to be sure, and the pay was killing – eight shillings a column. But, given my needs, I could exist even on such remuneration, and I decided to move to Switzerland. By January (1877) I had arrived there, and now I began my anarchist activity in the Jura Federation.

Bakunin had died in Berne on 1 July 1876, and within a month after his death preparations began for a congress of the International, also in Berne. At his graveside it was decided to attempt a reconciliation between the Marxists and the Bakuninists, to take place publicly at the congress of the International to be held that autumn.[4]

Guillaume wrote me about it, but I foresaw that nothing would come of this reconciliation. I read the Social Democratic newspapers, I saw their disgusting attitude towards anything that bore even the slightest revolutionary character, and I realized that there could be no reconciliation between a revolutionary party and a party trying to earn a reputation for 'moderation' in the eyes of the government and the bourgeoisie.

Guillaume, who always 'leaned towards the centre', stood for reconciliation. (Incidentally, in Zurich, when a number of Russians lived there, someone put out a series of quite well-done but

---

[4] At the Hague Congress of 1872, Bakunin and his adherents had been expelled from the International by Marx and his adherents. This action effectively destroyed the International and created a breach between the two groups that never healed.
   The Eighth Congress of the International was held in Berne at the end of October, 1876.

inoffensive caricatures. In one of them, Guillaume was represented as learning to ride horseback at a riding school. In the middle stood Bakunin, crying, 'Guillaume, you're always leaning towards the centre!')

Guillaume sincerely wanted reconciliation and sincerely wanted to extend his hand. A partial reconciliation was arranged. It was resolved that each country should be free to give its socialist activity whatever orientation it found necessary. If parliamentary Social Democratic activity was most suitable for Germany, then so be it. The anarchists would not attack the Germans for it, but in return the Germans would let Italy, Spain, French Switzerland and Belgium follow their own path, neither attacking the Bakuninists nor resorting to such vile accusations as, for example, the one the Marxists made in the 1850s that Bakunin was a spy for the Russian government. Liebknecht and Bebel, who came to the Berne Congress, vouched for this in the name of their party.[5]

Then suddenly, amid these effusions of reconciliation, Becker's thunderous and poisonous article against the Bakuninists came out in Geneva.[6]

This article rekindled passions that had died down for a time, and hostility once again erupted between the Marxists and the Bakuninists. 'It would be interesting to know', Peter Lavrov,[7] a friend of Marx and Engels, said to me, 'how this article was written: against Marx's wishes or by his order?'

His remark so took me aback that I have always remembered it.

Now it is fully clear to me that it was not Marx's doing but Engels'. Engels could not approve of Liebknecht's conciliatory tone. He did not want reconciliation – he recognized only the *subordination* of everyone to the secret committees of Social Democracy, and, of course, with his characteristic personal hatred of Bakunin and the Bakuninists, he poured fat on the fire. Evidently Marx, as

---

[5] Karl Liebknecht and August Bebel were two of the foremost leaders of the German Social Democratic Party.

[6] Johann-Philipp Becker, a friend of Marx, was a German veteran of the 1848 revolution and a member of the Geneva section of the International. The article Kropotkin refers to, signed by Becker and others, appeared in the Social Democratic paper *Tagwacht* on 17 and 21 October 1876.

[7] The Russian philosopher Peter Lavrov, one of the inspirers of Populism, had left Russia in 1870. Unlike Bakunin, who sought an immediate popular insurrection, Lavrov favoured a long-term programme of educating the peasants to socialism.

always, submitted to Engels, who was his party's leader. It is even said (I heard it myself from Hyndman)[8] that Marx's dependence on Engels weighed heavily on him throughout his life. But he believed in the greatness of his work, he wanted passionately to continue it, of course, and it was Engels who provided his subsistence. Marx, similar to Engels in character and in his hatred of Herzen[9] and Bakunin, readily submitted to his influence.

Marx profoundly hated Bakunin and Herzen, and not only slandered Bakunin, accusing him of swindling, but was not even ashamed to call Herzen, in the German and Russian editions of *Capital*, a proponent of autocracy! In the French edition he did not dare to retain this comment and omitted it.

'Reconciliation' at the Berne Congress, therefore, led to nothing. On the contrary, from then on the two parties inevitably began to diverge more and more: one of them became more definitely the party of *popular revolution*, the other the party of semi-bourgeois – that is, radical but not socialist – peaceful progress, in other words, a reformist party.

After the attempts at reconciliation at the Berne Congress, the anarchist party was even more isolated in the socialist movement than before.

German Social Democracy, led principally by Engels – in essence, by a secret organization of which Engels was the main leader, along with Marx and his sons-in-law Lafargue and Longuet,[10] as well as Liebknecht and Bebel – became more than ever a party of peaceful parliamentary agitation, quasi-republican, quasi-socialist, but most of all a party of the German Reichstag.

More and more they moved away from a pure labour movement, in the sense of a direct struggle against the capitalists by means

---

[8] Henry Mayers Hyndman was the leading British Marxist before the First World War and the founder of the Social Democratic movement in Britain.

[9] Alexander Herzen was one of the foremost Russian radicals of the nineteenth century and one of the ideological creators of Russian Populism. Although not an anarchist, he was a longtime friend and sometime collaborator of Michael Bakunin, with whom he shared an antipathy to Marx.

[10] Paul Lafargue was married to Marx's daughter Laura. In 1871 he went to Spain as an agent of the Marxists to challenge the predominance of the Bakuninists there, and he played a role in Bakunin's expulsion from the International in 1872. Charles Longuet, who played a prominent role in the Paris Commune, married Marx's daughter Jenny.

of strikes, unions, and so forth. Strikes repelled them because they diverted the workers' forces from parliamentary agitation. They viewed labour unions with hostility because, again, these were organizations which in and of themselves diverted forces from electoral agitation. They set themselves the goal of capturing as many seats in parliament as possible (and in local parliaments, too, but that came much later). Even if their deputies were not quite socialists, what did it matter, as long as they adhered to the party and accepted the obligation to support the programme drawn up for a given election and to vote in concert with the party? The main thing, obviously, was not so much to foster the dissemination of purely socialist views among the workers, but to gather as many votes as possible for their own candidates. The leaders, of course, thought that as long as the workers stood under the banner of Social Democracy at election time, socialist views would little by little take possession of them when they went to meetings and read Social Democratic newspapers. Having grown used to the *word* socialism, the workers would little by little grow used to the *idea*. That, at least, is what socialist leaders like Bebel and Liebknecht must have thought. Apparently, they had all decided that since God only knew when the social revolution would come, they would at least create a *political* force which under certain conditions might play a prominent role in the state.

They could not get by without illusions, of course. Seeing that the number of representatives in the Reichstag grew with each election – first two deputies were elected, then seven, then nine, and so on – even the most intelligent of them began to calculate that at some point the Social Democrats would have a majority in the chamber. Even as sensible a man as Lavrov made calculations of this sort for my benefit, failing to understand that there are electoral districts where it is relatively easy for a Social Democratic candidate to succeed, but once those districts are filled, others have to be won where the majority is not sympathetic to socialism. A Social Democratic candidate will not be elected there, but a candidate who is merely a radical rather than a socialist (although for the sake of the election he may nominally join the Social Democratic Party) – a Rittinghausen, for example, or the factory-owner Singer [11] – will succeed, though with difficulty and not right away.

The anarchists, on the other hand, rejecting a narrowly political struggle, inevitably became a more and more revolutionary party both in theory and in practice. Anarchism began to spread, especially in Spain, Italy and France.

In Italy and Spain the state of affairs at the time was such as to keep the people in a revolutionary mood, just as they are now.[12] The monarchy installed in Spain after 1873 was very precarious, and at any moment a republican revolution could be expected to dethrone the 'boy', that is, Alfonso,[13] and then without doubt popular revolutionary movements would break out in various parts of the country. Several times in those years, 1876–81, a revolution was ready to break out in Spain. If it had done, a popular, peasant uprising would doubtless have occurred in Andalusia, an area of large landed properties, among the farmers who lived in purely Irish conditions, and in the industrial centres of Catalonia, where labour unions had attained a high degree of development. In Catalonia in the 1880s organized workers numbered more than 100,000, almost every one of them belonging, as before – even more strongly than before – to the International. The Spanish, great formalists in this respect, are people of duty, and every year they punctiliously paid to their national council the dues required of members of the International. I myself (in 1878) saw these dues.[14] They came from 80,000 individuals. An entire army. And not even all the *organized* labour unions had joined. This army, it should be noted, was ready not only for strikes (the construction workers in Barcelona had already won an eight-hour work-day for themselves by means of strikes), but even for an insurrection in the name of collectivism, had there been any hope that the army would refrain from opposing them.

[11] Moritz Rittinghausen was a leader of the moderate wing of the Social Democratic Party. Paul Singer was a wealthy Berlin clothing manufacturer. Both served as Social Democratic deputies to the Reichstag.
[12] Kropotkin was writing in 1898.
[13] After the downfall of a short-lived republic, the Spanish monarchy was restored in 1875 in the person of 18-year-old Alfonso XII.
[14] Kropotkin spent several weeks in Spain in 1878.

In Italy there were no such professional organizations. The labour unions in northern Italy, especially in Milan, developed much later. But the Italian people were in general so burdened by state taxes that disturbances, peasant or urban, occurred all the time. In the towns, and in some parts of central and southern Italy in the villages, too, the people were always ready to support an insurrection, again if there had been any hope that the troops, uncertain whom to obey, would not close ranks against them.

The mood was revolutionary in France, too. The wealthy classes were conducting a large-scale campaign of intimidation and bribery to restore the monarchy, and to prevent a restoration the radicals were working feverishly throughout France to organize armed resistance to the pro-monarchist *coup d'état* being prepared from above. The whole of France was covered with groups, secret societies of republicans who were stockpiling arms and preparing to confront a *coup d'état* with weapons in hand.

When I arrived in Montpellier in the summer of 1878 on my way to Spain, with letters of recommendation from Paul Brousse,[15] I found a fully organized republican committee which had stockpiled weapons and was ready for armed resistance in the event of a monarchist movement. A Russian student from the Caucasus was even supposed to be its leader. In Besançon, many workers belonged to similar committees in this industrial town of small workshops, where the workers are on the whole more developed and more revolutionary than in the factory centres. Committees of the same sort were scattered throughout the French Jura, dating from the time of the Commune, when the Jurassians, Bakunin's friends, had made preparations to set out from Switzerland, incite the French Jura, and go to the assistance of the Commune.

The soul of the republican organization, or, more accurately, of the radical republican organization, at that time was Clemenceau,[16] who held much more extreme views then than he does now. The possibility of a second attack by the Germans was very great, and, of course, it was being discussed in the republican committees. I have it from a thoroughly reliable individual that Clemenceau said

[15] Paul Brousse, one of the most militant anarchists in the Jura Federation in the 1870s, later became the leader of a reformist wing of French socialism.

[16] Georges Clemenceau was a radical republican and leader of the anti-monarchist forces in the 1870s. He would later serve as prime minister of France.

that in the event of a German invasion it would be necessary to raise a popular insurrection in the name of expropriation of the land. Rumours of this even reached the peasants, especially in the Jura, and, of course, the peasants wished for nothing better.

In the towns, where there were groups of more or less conscious revolutionaries, people everywhere were talking about a commune. And if MacMahon[17] had decided on a *coup d'état* at that moment, communes would have been proclaimed in a great many places, especially in southeastern France.

In a word, the mood in France too was revolutionary. We all understood, of course, that a revolution called forth by an attempt to restore the monarchy would have been a political revolution. Revolutions are not made to order, like a suit at the tailor's. They begin regardless of the will of individuals and have to be taken as they come. But we all knew, too, that however the revolution began, it would not stop with a mere change of government. The very fact of proclaiming communes would inevitably lead to a re-examination of the whole state organization of France, and in each separate town the movement would scarcely have begun than attempts at expropriation would have been initiated as well. Where a revolution that began in such circumstances would go, no one in the world could predict. It would all depend on the duration of the period of movement, on how long the country succeeded in living without a strong, cohesive central government, which, like any government, would begin to suppress the popular movement and restore 'order'.

That a revolution has not yet erupted does not mean, of course, that we were mistaken. Thanks to the existence of such a revolutionary mood in Spain, Italy and France, and of a party ready to make use of the first barricades or of a popular uprising to begin implementing the ideals of communism or a general socialist expropriation – thanks to that, the reaction that was beginning to overspread the whole of Europe after the Franco-Prussian War was not allowed to pursue its designs as far as it would have wished.

There seems no need to demonstrate that it was precisely the fear of popular uprisings, whose consequences no one can predict

---

[17] In 1873, the monarchist majority of the National Assembly elected Marshal Edmé MacMahon president of the Third Republic for a seven-year term. He resigned in 1879.

Other writings

beforehand, that prevented the reactionaries from implementing
their schemes and forcing the workers to knuckle under.

In France it was nothing but the fear of serious uprisings in
the cities that prevented the proclamation of a monarchy during
MacMahon's seven-year term, when even the horses and the fleur-
de-lis coats of arms on the carriages had already been prepared
for the triumphal entry of Henry V.[18] Of course, the rebuff was
prepared and the committees organized by Gambetta,[19] that is, by
the Opportunists and the Radicals[20] headed by Clemenceau. But
if the initiative for the committees belonged to the radical bourgeoisie, it was the workers who constituted their strength: they did
not forget the traditions of the International and did not give up
on revolutionary socialism, as the Germans wanted, but continued
to await the moment when it could be proclaimed in the streets.
I have no intention of exaggerating the significance of the Jura in
supporting this spirit. But if anything was done to support it, it
was done only by the Jura, on the one hand, and by the Blanquists[21]
on the other. Some of the Blanquists, having understood at last
that the Social Democrats, whom they had supported at the Hague
Congress, were not their allies at all, decided that it was better to
deal with the anarchists, who recognized neither the state nor
pyramidal organizations but were revolutionaries, than with the
Marxists, who recognized the state and pyramidal methods of organization based on strict discipline and stifled the revolutionary spirit
of the rank-and-file workers.

In Spain it is even more obvious that fear of a popular revolution
prevented the reaction from going to extremes. Several times during
those years the bourgeois republicans in Spain were about to initiate
a revolutionary movement against the monarchy. Each time the
most extreme of them alerted the anarchists: 'Be ready.' The
anarchists were ready, but nothing came of it. On the one hand,
the more moderate bourgeois republicans were terrified of an
inevitable *popular* uprising. On a couple of occasions I read frank

[18] The Comte de Chambord was the Bourbon pretender to the French throne under
the name of Henry V.
[19] The republican lawyer Léon Gambetta was a central figure in the establishment
of the Third Republic in 1871 and served as prime minister in 1881–2.
[20] These were the moderate and left wings of the republican forces.
[21] The Blanquists were followers of the French socialist Auguste Blanqui, who
advocated the establishment of a revolutionary dictatorship on behalf of the workers.

212

articles in the republican newspapers in the following vein: 'We are not initiating a republican uprising because we know that you anarchists will take advantage of it to put your theories into practice.' And, of course, in some places in Spain – at the first shots in the streets of Barcelona and Madrid, if the bourgeois republicans had not succeeded *immediately* in organizing a strong government with the army firmly in their hands – that would have been the case.

It is not to be doubted, however, that the threat of such an uprising prevented a clerical–aristocratic or even a bourgeois–clerical reaction from developing as it sought to develop – and without fail would have developed if not for that threat, and if that threat had not been a *reality* and not a myth.

If Europe in those years – after the triumph of the German Empire over France and of Bismarck's policies in Europe in general – did not experience an incomparably more bitter reaction than it did, and if the reaction in France lasted only until 1878, Europe owes it, I am now deeply convinced, to the fact that the insurrectionary spirit of the International maintained itself fully intact in Spain, in Italy, in Belgium, in the Jura, and even in France itself. The Jura had practically no contact with western France, but it had active dealings with northeastern, and especially eastern and southeastern France – the part that in 1789–93 was the real centre of the revolution, the only one aside from Paris. And those contacts emanated both from the leaders and from the rank-and-file workers, both from the Blanquists and Jacobins who had found refuge in Switzerland and from the Internationalists of the Jura Federation.

It is curious that when the first glimmers of a workers' socialist and revolutionary movement appeared in Paris in 1878, they were initiated by those half-dozen workers who had maintained ties with the Jura anarchists, and by Jules Guesde,[22] who at the time (1876) was still writing protests in concert with the Jurassians against the Marxist General Council of the International and was an avowed enemy of parliamentary agitation.

The Social Democrats understood nothing of this. For them, any talk of revolution was merely an obstacle to their parliamentary

[22] Jules Guesde, a French journalist, was a Bakuninist in the 1870s and in the 1880s became the leading French Marxist.

agitation. Their position in Germany, of course, was unenviable. Bismarck merely tolerated them from time to time. Their continual declarations in the Reichstag that they had nothing in common with revolutionaries were in vain: no one believed them. Windthorst[23] once very appropriately replied to them: 'Why go on about your peaceable inclinations? During a revolution extreme parties gain the upper hand, and should a revolution occur you will be *compelled* to adopt a revolutionary course!'

But while the Social Democrats tried to assume a very modest air in Germany in order to avoid persecution, they had no desire to confine themselves to the modest role of a party compelled by circumstances to act modestly in their own country. They wanted to squeeze the *whole* European movement into the same narrow confines within which they had to operate in Germany. They did not want to be a party forced by the political life of their country to limit itself to the role of a moderate–socialist party, but wanted to hold sway over the whole socialist movement and force it everywhere to become just as modest and quiet as it was in Germany. Liebknecht wrote that Social Democrats could have nothing in common with wild men like the Russian terrorists or the Italian revolutionaries. Therefore they sought to demonstrate that Social Democrats nowhere did anything different from what they did in Germany, *nor should they.*

Once they began to diverge from a revolutionary path out of tactical considerations, they truly came to hate revolutionaries. They listened more and more to the voices of those within their party who wholeheartedly hated revolution – the people out in the streets, the noise of the crowd, the violation of historical custom, and so forth. They began to hate the revolutionaries who disturbed their calculations much more than they hated the bourgeoisie, whom they made up to and whose approval they tried to win with their modesty. Little by little their entire doctrine took on an antirevolutionary character. 'Economic materialism', which Marx and Engels had never even developed in detail into a rigorous system, began to be passed off as a rigorously scientific theory according to which revolution will come *of itself* through the development of productive forces, and all efforts to bring it about are therefore

[23] Ludwig Windthorst was the leader of the Centre Party in Germany.

useless. They began trying to prove that social change can be achieved *only* by a parliamentary path, that a revolution in the streets is nonsense and can be accomplished only in parliament after a certain number of years (and Engels was determining the year), when it will have a socialist majority. They began to foam at the mouth when speaking of anyone who tried to sustain or arouse the spirit of revolution. Moreover, they began to reject any criticism of the state: they represented the state the way it was represented in olden times, as the main and then the sole impetus to progress. They even began to propagandize not the kind of state that might be termed the highest type among those existing today, namely, the *federated* state, but the Roman type, unitary, indivisible and centralized in the Roman manner.

Against this Germanic spirit, therefore, the Latin peoples had to defend the very right to revolutionary agitation. They had to wage a difficult struggle against their governments and against the socialists of the German school.

Any revolutionary agitation exacts enormous sacrifices, not so much in terms of prison sentences and years of incarceration – which have been raining down by the hundreds of years annually – as in terms of the manifold personal sacrifices sustained by those who commit themselves to revolutionary agitation. If anyone were to publish a martyrology of anarchism for those years in Italy, Spain or France, comparable to what has been done for the Russian movement in the *Calendar of the People's Will* or by Burtsev in his book *A Century of Political Life in Russia (1800–1896)*,[24] it would prove more horrifying than anything that can be imagined, even knowing the number of sacrifices in Russia.

But all this is nothing compared to what has to be endured by thousands and thousands of individuals and workers' families in their daily lives. If things are painful at times for us intellectuals, for the worker they are incomparably, endlessly more difficult. For

---

[24] The *Calendar of the People's Will for 1883*, published in Geneva, was a collection of documents on the People's Will Party, which had assassinated Alexander II in 1881. It included a 'martyrology' of those revolutionaries who had been subjected to repression by the government.

Vladimir Burtsev was a Russian journalist and revolutionary who specialized in exposing police agents within the revolutionary organizations. His book was a collection of materials on the Russian revolutionary movement and was published in London in 1897.

the worker a house search and a two-day arrest mean the loss of his job, months of unemployment, and, consequently, hunger, literally hunger, for his family. The intellectual moves often from one city to another without any difficulty; for the worker, having to leave a city nearly always means becoming an itinerant and going whole months without a piece of bread and frequently even without shelter. What the families go through is impossible to recount. When we were arrested in Lyons,[25] we were fed in jail. The wives of my worker comrades, however, were forced to seek work in the midst of an industrial crisis (the movement itself had been born of the crisis) and were lucky if they found a job as a silk-winder at 1 franc and 30 centimes a day. Try living on 6 or 8 francs a week, sometimes with one or two children! The workers help each other more than is generally thought, but no such help will bring relief in these circumstances. That is why it used to be said even in those years – and now it is deemed an axiom in France – that if you were going to join the anarchists, be sure you were a first-class worker whom your employer would value and retain even if the police came every two or three days to interrogate him and warn him that such and such a worker of his was an anarchist. Otherwise you would not survive.

A difficult struggle had to be waged against the government and the bourgeoisie. Meanwhile, the very right to be a revolutionary had to be defended against the German Social Democrats. And they would stop at nothing, even actual denunciations – Jacobinism permits everything. 'See that man', a Social Democratic leader once said at a public meeting – that is, in the presence of the police – in Leipzig, pointing at Reinsdorf,[26] who was carrying out anarchist propaganda in that city, 'that man in black who is writing in his notebook, that is not so-and-so but the anarchist Reinsdorf.' After that, of course, Reinsdorf had only one recourse – to slip out of Leipzig.

---

[25] Kropotkin was arrested at the end of 1882, and in January of 1883 he and other anarchists were put on trial in Lyons. He was convicted of belonging to the International, which had been outlawed in France, and served three years in a French prison.

[26] August Reinsdorf was a German practitioner of 'propaganda by deed'. In 1885 he was beheaded for an assassination attempt against the German Emperor William I and other officials at Niederwald in 1883.

'And that Werner', Liebknecht wrote in *Vorwärts*, 'who was arrested with a typeset anarchist manifesto in Berlin, that is the same Werner whom Hödel went to consult before he shot at the German emperor.'[27] I read that myself. Liebknecht knew perfectly well that Werner, a very kindly soul, earnestly advised Hödel *not* to shoot the old man! . . .

A whole system of ridicule, caustic abuse, and lies was organized by this party in order to set the Germans against anything in the Latin countries that bore a revolutionary character. And the organization was exemplary. To begin with, each of the party's newspapers received a subsidy from the central administration and was threatened with withdrawal of the subsidy if the editor did not precisely follow the spirit of the party, that is, of its secret committee. For running an anarchist article, for example, or even a 'correction' sent in by an anarchist which was accepted by the majority of bourgeois newspapers, the editor would be given a scolding and threatened with deprivation of his post or his subsidy. The central committee of the party published a lithographed sheet containing *its* version of all the foreign news, with *its* discussion, and distributed it to all the party's provincial newspapers. They had only to reprint it. 'You don't understand such things! You're no match for the people who draw up this sheet: Engels and his equals! They know everything there is to know!'

Thus, at a time when the revolutionary spirit surviving from the International was the sole bulwark against the reaction that raised its head everywhere after the triumph of imperialism and Bismarckism in Germany, the Jura Federation had to serve as the main bulwark of this revolutionary orientation, defending it against the attacks, distortions and intimidations of the governments, on the one hand, and against the attacks, lies and distortions, both factual and theoretical, of German Social Democracy.

[27] Emil Werner, a German compositor, was arrested in Berlin in 1879 with the plates for a clandestine anarchist newspaper, *Der Kampf*. He later worked with Kropotkin on *Le Révolté*.

Max Hödel, a former Social Democrat and then an anarchist, was executed for an assassination attempt on William I in 1878. After a second attempt in the same year by another anarchist, Karl Nobiling, Bismarck succeeded in passing an anti-socialist law aimed at suppression of the Social Democratic Party, although the latter had not been involved in these incidents.

Vorwärts was the chief newspaper of the German Social Democratic Party.

If Vera Zasulich shot Trepov, or the Russians' patience was
finally exhausted and the students and a few workers staged a
demonstration on Kazan Square,[28] or the workers in some small
town of Italy or Spain burned the customs booths or rioted against
the salt tax; if peasants in Andalusia chopped down the landowners'
forests or destroyed the lords' tree-plantings, or a solitary worker
settled accounts with his boss, or a strike took place in which
hungry workers beat up a manager or simply marched through the
streets with a red flag and staged a demonstration; if a revolutionary
prank was played somewhere – hanging a red flag from a bell-tower
on the night of 18 March,[29] for example – on every occasion,
Vorwärts would spew out all its venom and its entire vocabulary of
authentic German invective, whether on Zasulich, on the workers,
on the Kazan demonstration, or on the peasants who had dared
give vent to their rebellious spirit in a demonstration, a strike, or
a rebuff to their master. *'Putschmachers'* ('insurrectionists'), *Vorwärts*
would write contemptuously, and would extol *its* tactics, by virtue
of which no one would dare reply in kind even to the rudeness
of a policeman, but would save all his energy for the day when
he would have to run round to the workers and persuade them to
vote in an election for some Social Democrat or other.

The newspaper of the Jura Federation had to defend the demonstration, the prank, the strike and Vera Zasulich's shot alike, so as
to reveal to its readers the meaning of these events, their causes,
their origin and their significance for sustaining and developing
the revolutionary mood among the workers. The once respected
occupation of revolutionary was now represented as a useless relic,
a kind of buffoonery or provocation. A revolutionary who in any
way expressed his attitude was made out to be either a fool or an
agent provocateur. This is what the Social Democratic papers actually
said and wrote. The rebelling masses, accordingly, were called the

[28] Vera Zasulich achieved fame in 1878 when she shot and wounded General Fyodor
Trepov, the Governor of St Petersburg, to avenge the flogging of an imprisoned
student. She later became one of the founders of the Russian Social Democratic
Party.
   The Kazan Square demonstration in St Petersburg, a display of Populist sentiment, took place in December 1876. The student Zasulich was defending in 1878
had been arrested in connection with this incident.
[29] March 18 marked the anniversary of the start of the Paris Commune of 1871
and was commemorated annually by socialists.

same dirty names as the *provocateurs*: asses, ignoramuses, lumpen-proletariat, ragamuffins, *la canaille*. How much bile was poured out on those unfortunate ragamuffins whenever they dared proclaim that they intended to consider themselves men, and not brutes!

In Spain and in Italy former members of the International maintained their earlier revolutionary viewpoint. The Spanish and Italian newspapers – the former supported by a robust labour organization, the latter popping up here and there, disappearing as a result of persecution or hopelessness after five or six issues, then springing up again in another city – carried out vigorous revolutionary propaganda. The manifestos of the International's Spanish federations – which maintained their existence as clandestine but solid organizations and regularly convened secret provincial and national congresses – were sometimes superb, magnificent in the full sense of the word not only as expressions of steadfast energy but especially as principled expositions of anarchism. But the Spanish and Italian languages are little known in Europe, and the publications themselves rarely went beyond the borders of their own countries. France, weighed down by reaction, did not raise its voice. It was impossible not merely to start a newspaper but even to sing the 'Marseillaise' in the street without the risk of winding up in jail. Thus, the French newspaper of the Jura Federation, which Guillaume had edited since 1872, became the sole popular paper of a revolutionary bent in Europe, to which Paul Brousse, with Werner and Rinke, soon added the German anarchist newspaper *Arbeiter-Zeitung*.[30] Also from the Jura, and often from Geneva, where former communist-Blanquists congregated, there was an active correspondence with the revolutionaries in France, Italy and Spain. Subsequently, Henri Rochefort settled in Geneva and from there would send *Les Droits de l'Homme*[31] his caustic attacks, which always hit their mark, on the reactionary party that had triumphed in France and on the Opportunists who had adopted Gambetta's slogan

[30] The *Arbeiter-Zeitung* was a Swiss German anarchist newspaper published in Berne from 1876 to 1877. The Frenchman Paul Brousse (see note 15), along with Emil Werner (see note 27) and Otto Rinke, both German-born, were among the leaders of the anarchist movement in Switzerland in the 1870s.

[31] Henri Rochefort, a French journalist and politician, had been a critic of the Second Empire and a sympathizer of the Commune. From Geneva in the 1870s he published in radical Paris newspapers such as *Les Droits de l'Homme* unsigned but readily identifiable articles critical of the French government.

'Enrich yourselves!' The latter, sticking their greedy paws into every commercial and state enterprise, prepared the ground for all kinds of reaction and for all the scandals that broke out subsequently: the prison scandals (embezzlement of prison funds), and the Wilson, Panama and Dreyfus scandals.[32]

But it was not just in sustaining the spirit of revolution that the Jura Federation played a prominent role. It was also the centre of the theoretical development of *anarchy*.

In 1869 Marx published his *Capital*. In the theoretical part of this enormous revolutionary pamphlet the author used the basic principles of bourgeois political economy to attack its own conclusions in favour of capitalism. In the second part he used examples from English history to present the origins of capitalism in the most subversive fashion, and the exposures of the English parliamentary commission on the situation of the workers in the 1840s to present the consequences of capitalism in the most terrible light. The book was greeted sympathetically by everyone as a powerful weapon with which to strike at the contemporary bourgeois organization of society.

To be sure, even then Bakunin foresaw that 'Marxism', which in fact was trying to seize the workers' movement and govern it, would inevitably try to give itself the sanction derived from the halo of scientific infallibility. But not enough attention was paid to this. Everyone saw in Karl Marx's *Capital* a powerful means of arousing socialist thought and resolved not to attack it.

I read this book while I was still in Petersburg, where it appeared in 1872 in German Lopatin's translation.[33] Even then I very much disliked the pretentiousness of the book as well as its unscientific character – the theory of value, for example, is not demonstrated scientifically but has to be taken on faith – and its indulgence in scientific jargon. Marx's excursions into the realm of numerical expressions and algebraic formulae were comical: they demonstrate his utter inability to think concretely, in quantitative terms, and

---

[32] The Wilson and Panama scandals of the 1880s involved official corruption and financial manipulation. The anti-Semitic Dreyfus Affair, in which a Jewish army officer was wrongfully accused of treason, broke out in 1898.

[33] German Lopatin was active in the Russian revolutionary movement in the 1870s and 1880s. He and another Populist co-translated *Das Kapital* into Russian, the first foreign translation of the work.

Nicholas Tsinger (an astronomer)[34] and I had a good laugh over his 'formulae', which he sets out so pretentiously without even suspecting how amusing they are to a mathematician accustomed to the idea of units of measurement. Highly comical as well is his penchant for expressing himself in formulae where formulae express nothing. In 1876, when I met German Lopatin in London, we spoke a bit about Marx's book, which as its translator he knew thoroughly, and I remarked that Marx's theory is both old (it derives from Adam Smith) and untrue. In contemporary society goods are not exchanged in proportion to the amount of socially necessary labour (as Adam Smith had already remarked); but to the extent that this is *desirable* in the future society – another question which Marx never even touches on – he was still more or less a communist. To my astonishment, Lopatin replied that the theory of value was not important. Marx's main task was *to establish the historical origins of capital.* But Lopatin was obviously expressing the opinion of their circle.

In this last respect, as a superbly illustrated commentary on Proudhon's 'Property is theft', and one that created the impression of being scientific, Marx's book, of course, deserved to play a prominent role. In essence, this is the only part of it that is familiar to thousands of Marxists; but the erroneous division between the *primary* accumulation of capital and its present-day formation seemed to us then not to merit serious criticism. 'Let the description of the brutality of capitalism and its brutal origins ignite the spark of socialism', we thought. 'Then the socialists themselves will sort things out.' We did not realize at the time what a harmful practical application this minimizing of the role of the contemporary state in the process of capital accumulation might receive.

Besides, in all previous revolutions so much attention had been paid to the political form of the state and so little to the economic forms of life. Socialists had to struggle so much against the enthusiasm for political overturns played out on a grand stage, effective according to circumstances and celebrated by all bourgeois historians, that we rejoiced over this new ally who placed the struggle on its true foundations, which many individuals, and especially Proudhon, had identified back in 1848 – *economic* foundations. In

[34] Nicholas Tsinger was a Russian astronomer and geodesist.

view of that, we passed over the scientifically incorrect posing of the question; the minimizing of the role of the contemporary state and its system of robbery of the people by means of taxes; and Marx's disregard of the significance of the period of the formation of centralized states in the sixteenth century. We passed over all the defects in his theory in view of the fact that he turned his principal attention to the economic forms of life, which are always forgotten by revolutionaries who come from the bourgeoisie and generally have a bourgeois education.

What grated on me also was Marx's belief in the fatalism of capitalism's self-negation and the ease with which its expropriation could supposedly be achieved once all capital was concentrated in a few hands. In the 1840s many socialists thought in these terms: generalizing from the actual concentration of certain industries, especially textiles and iron, which had been carried out before their eyes, they hastened to draw the conclusion of a universal concentration of capital and prophesied that the time was coming when the task of revolution would become so simplified as to consist of the expropriation of a few Rothschilds. Marx merely repeated, quite unthinkingly, propositions that were generally accepted at the time.

But what really interested us was not a critique of the Marxist Bible but a critique of the Marxist ideal and the development of the principles of anarchism.

It was Bakunin who initiated both the critique of Marxism and the political development of anarchism, partly in his published works but most of all in the enormous letters which he wrote to the workers of Spain and Italy. Even *God and the State*, published after his death, began as one of those letters. His *Statism and Anarchy* is filled with the most remarkable general principles, as are his *Letters to a Frenchman on the Present Crisis*, written at the time of the war of 1870, *The Knouto-Germanic Empire*, written immediately after the war, and the shorter works on specific events – *Mazzini, The Bears of Berne*, and so forth – all of them filled with brilliant general principles of a historical and philosophical nature.[35]

---

[35] Bakunin's *God and the State* was first published in 1882. It was actually part of a larger work, *The Knouto-Germanic Empire and the Social Revolution*, which he wrote in 1870–1. *Statism and Anarchy* was published in 1873. *The Political Theology of Mazzini and the International*, published in 1871, was a response to an attack by Giuseppe Mazzini on the International, while *The Bears of Berne and the Bear of St Petersburg* of 1870 was a defence of the Russian revolutionary Sergei Nechaev.

Subsequently the Jura Federation published Guillaume's *Ideas on Social Organization* and the history course for the people which he initiated,[36] and the Russian Bakuninists published *Anarchy according to Proudhon*, Bakunin's *Statism and Anarchy*, and his *Historical Development of the International*.[37]

Guillaume's *Ideas on Social Organization* contained an exposition of the anarchist political ideal as it was then being worked out in the Jura Federation. An association of artisans' unions, without a state, entering into direct agreement for the exchange of the goods they produced, was the response to the ideal of the centralized state to which all the communists of the statist school, and thus the Social Democrats, then adhered.

When I joined the Jura Federation, all my time was taken up with the everyday concerns of local propaganda. Even then I saw how much needed to be done to ground the anarchist point of view in scientific, philosophical principles. I devoted myself to this task on a regular basis only later, in 1879, when I began to edit *Le Révolté*.[38] The concerns of everyday propaganda absorbed all my time in those first years. Once I arrived in the Jura, I of course consulted with Guillaume and his comrades as to what I should do. They advised me to settle in La Chaux-de-Fonds and help our two friends, Pindy and Spichiger,[39] who lived there, 'win over' to our views the population of watchmakers in that city; they had not hitherto submitted to anarchist propaganda, perhaps because – so our comrades thought – Pindy and Spichiger did not get along particularly well. The fiery Pindy was a Frenchman to the marrow of his bones, though a northerner, and got on badly with the slow,

[36] James Guillaume's popular history survey, entitled *Historical Sketches*, was published in two parts in 1874 and 1875. His pamphlet *Ideas on Social Organization* was published in 1876.

[37] In 1873, a group of Bakunin's Russian followers established a press in Zurich which succeeded in publishing several Russian-language volumes. *Anarchism according to Proudhon* was written by Guillaume, while the *Historical Development of the International* was a collection of articles to which Bakunin contributed.

[38] Kropotkin founded and for a time largely wrote *Le Révolté* in 1879. The paper moved from Geneva to Paris in 1885 and in 1887 changed its name to *La Révolte*. It was succeeded in 1895 by *Les Temps Nouveaux*, which was published until 1914.

[39] The Frenchman Jean-Louis Pindy, a veteran of the Paris Commune, and the Swiss Auguste Spichiger were two of the militants of the Jura Federation, which Spichiger had helped to found.

philosophizing Swiss. Always deep in thought, weighing every step and every word, Spichiger continually got mired in difficulty and scarcely managed to get anything done; even when Pindy succeeded in persuading him, he would set to work with a purely English doggedness. Both of them worked all day, however, and were free only in the evening. Pindy had learned the assayer's trade and spent the whole day in incredible heat next to his red-hot assay furnace, with his miniature wheelbarrows of gold and silver samples received from the watchmakers, analysing the little ingots formed of grains of gold and silver swept out from under the grated floors of the engraving shops or smelted from burnt-up floor-mats. For this he received 150 francs a month. With a wife and three or four children, he really had to struggle fiercely.

Spichiger, on the other hand, sat importantly at his engraver's bench in a small co-operative workshop set up with funds provided by the Bakuninists – a workshop which subsequently, as it happened, fell into the hands of a certain shark to whom it ran into debt during the industrial crisis. In the workshop everyone shared the profits equally, although a master engraver at his machine could earn (on piecework) 10 or 15 francs a day, while an engraver of average skill earned scarcely half that. But this winter a crisis in the watch industry had struck the 'mountains'. There were no orders, or very few; the only work was *'patraque'*, that is, rubbish, which paid very badly, and by the end of the winter even that was not available.

The poverty of the watchmakers was so terrible that the municipal authorities of La Chaux-de-Fonds had to open a low-cost lunchroom for the workers. The winter was a very severe one, too. Piles of snow shovelled from the sidewalks lay along the streets, just like Moscow. Things got very bad for poor Spichiger. Master engravers still managed to find some sort of work, but the co-operative workshop, even though Spichiger was considered one of the best engravers, had only intermittent work or none at all. To get work in such a crisis is a real art: the art of grovelling, of entertaining in restaurants, and of selling one's vote to one party or another – the Freemasons, the Catholics, the conservatives or the radicals. The anarchist and atheist Spichiger, who never cast a vote and did not belong to any church, did not sin by practising this art – and things went badly for the co-operative and for our

friend. By the end of the winter, to earn a few francs, he often
had to *carder le crin*, that is, to comb out old horse-hair mattresses
for a fellow Frenchman who was an upholsterer. At home his wife
and two children went hungry.

Besides Pindy and Spichiger, there belonged to our family
Ferré,[40] a Blanquist, the brother of the Ferré who had been shot
almost a year after the destruction of the Commune; Bertrand, an
upholsterer; old Jeallot,[41] also a Blanquist, with a broken hand,
who had miraculously escaped the wholesale massacre of the federalists, that is, of the workers who participated in the Commune,
at the end of May; Albagès, or Albarracín, a Spanish student who
had fled Spain after the commune that had been proclaimed in
Alcoy following a strike in the building trades;[42] and a few Swiss:
Nicou and two or three young men whose names I forget. I lived
under the name of Levashev.

In a small town or village everyone knows everything about
everyone else, and I can say that we all enjoyed indubitable respect
in the town.

All of us, with the exception of the Swiss, were fugitives who
had been saved from death by a miracle.

When the Versaillists,[43] who finally burst into Paris on 21 May
1871, were slaughtering all the communards who fell into their
hands and shooting prisoners by the hundreds, salvation was not
easy. The Freemasons, themselves bourgeois, saved many people;
there were even priests who saved their acquaintances among the
communards. Pindy was saved by a girl, a seamstress who later
became his wife.

Pindy was commandant of the Tuileries during the Commune.[44]
A young carpenter who had risen in the International during the
strikes, he was elected commander of his battalion of the National

---

[40] Hippolyte Ferré was the brother of Théophile Ferré, who played a prominent
role in the Paris Commune.

[41] Pierre Jeallot (sometimes spelled Jallot), a house-painter and printing-shop worker,
was one of the activists in La Chaux-de-Fonds.

[42] The uprising at Alcoy, a small town that was a centre of the International's activities
in Spain, took place in 1873. Severino Albarracín (who used the pseudonym Gabriel
Albagès) took refuge in Switzerland after the uprising and died in Spain in 1878.

[43] Versailles was the seat of the government forces which suppressed the Commune.

[44] Pindy was actually governor of the Hôtel de Ville, which he ordered to be set on
fire, not of the Tuileries.

Guard – the Belleville one, I believe, but in any case a predominantly working-class battalion. He became commandant of the Tuileries, which was considered a main stronghold when the street-fighting with the Versaillists began, and where the shoemaker Gaillard[45] therefore built the strongest barricades – very pretty, but completely useless. I saw photographs of them in Geneva at Gaillard's.

Gaillard[46] was a shoemaker, but not an ordinary one. He had devised a special kind of 'hygienic' boot, and, of course, attributed no small share in France's defeat to the fact that the soldiers were not wearing them.

'Boots, that's the most important thing for a soldier', he said more than once. 'How could the French soldiers have fought well when half the army lacked boots, and when the new ones it received turned out to have paper soles?'

Thus, the Tuileries was defended by enormous barricades. But there was no one to defend the barricades. When the Versaillists entered Paris and began to massacre the workers, shooting prisoners indiscriminately, in heaps, with machine-guns to speed the process, the workers withdrew to their home ground of Belleville and Montmartre, to the Père-Lachaise cemetery. There they desperately defended their improvised barricades, giving the army of the rich a last desperate battle. Meanwhile, the city of the rich was consigned to the flames. The Tuileries was abandoned, and when commandant Pindy went out in the morning there were just a dozen defenders in the former palace. Pindy divided the money at his disposal among them equally – each one got about 300 francs – and they dispersed. Before they did so, they set fire to the former imperial palace, having stockpiled combustible materials beforehand. 'Let the imperial palace, this shame of France, perish in flames, and never again rise from the ashes.'

Only half their dream was destined to come true. There have not been any new imperial palaces in France, nor will there be, but the Tuileries was rebuilt. What a pity! In 1878 its ruins, which were already becoming overgrown with new vegetation, were the most beautiful monument in Paris. Even aside from the historical

[45] Napoléon Gaillard was Director of Barricades in the Commune.
[46] The text says Pindy, but clearly Gaillard was meant.

significance of these ruins – how fine it is that in at least one city of Europe the dwelling-place of emperors should be a scenic ruin – they were actually extraordinarily picturesque. The window-holes affording glimpses of the sky in a framework of greenery were highly artistic. As the young plant life increasingly took possession of the cracked walls, they would have become more and more artistically resplendent.

Pindy found his way to the home of a young seamstress with whom he had become acquainted during the Commune and stayed with her. In the streets all the communards were being seized; in the next few days several men were shot in the belief that they were Pindy. They died without disabusing their executioners: we all have to die sooner or later, and meanwhile Pindy may get away.

Denunciations poured forth from all sides, not by the hundreds and not by the thousands but by the tens of thousands: 200,000 denunciations in some two weeks. If a petty shopkeeper had something against someone, he hastened to inform the police that so-and-so had fought for the Commune and was now hiding in such-and-such a place. Bourgeois women of all ranks were distinguished by a particular ferocity: they knew that anyone arrested as a result of their denunciations would be shot. But there is nothing more ferocious and more merciless than a coward. The Commune made them tremble for their wallets. They, and they especially, took revenge with their denunciations.

Pindy, too, was denounced. Someone recognized him and provided information that he was hiding in such-and-such a house. The house was surrounded, and soldiers began searching the apartments. The only recourse was audacity. When the search began, Pindy was in the courtyard, filling buckets of water from the pump. It was impossible to leave the house. There was nothing to be done but to fill the buckets and carry them up to his apartment on the fifth floor – the apartment of the seamstress. So he did, setting the buckets on the landing of the staircase while the soldiers searched the apartment. The seamstress did not lose heart or get flustered but chatted with the soldiers, who by now had probably grown sick of carrying out executions, checking to see who was alive and who was dead, heaping the bodies into a pit, and pouring quicklime over them. They had already adopted a slipshod attitude towards their duties and responded half-ashamed to the seamstress's questions: 'We're fed up with it!' The seamstress, with seeming unconcern, brought them a glass of wine. Pindy was introduced as her brother and stood among them, remaining calm. And so the soldiers left. For a whole year Pindy lived with this seamstress, who loved him all the more for having saved him. In La Chaux-de-Fonds they lived very well, bringing up their children and adding hot water to their soup when they had no money for vegetables.

Old Jeallot had been saved by quite a different sort of miracle. A fervent Blanquist, he fought on the barricades for several days. When the last barricade had been taken, he went to a certain comrade who lived near the 'ramparts' of Paris, that is, near the outer walls surrounding the city, with the intention of hiding there.

Night fell, Paris was burning, in the ditches around the walls prisoners were being shot. He planned to move elsewhere in the morning, but during the night a search-party of soldiers appeared unexpectedly. He made a dash for the stairs, knocked someone over, flew down head over heels, and started running. There was a railroad track not far away, and he collapsed exhausted on the embankment. He lay there until dawn. In falling down the stairs he had broken his hand. It hurt terribly, but where could he go during the night? There were patrols everywhere, and he would surely be caught. By morning his situation had become intolerable: his hand hurt unbearably, and he was half delirious. With the first rays of dawn, summoning the last of his strength, he began crawling, with no idea where he should go. Finally, he decided at random to go to an acquaintance of his who had not taken part in the Commune: perhaps with a broken hand he would not be driven away. His acquaintance, a semi-worker, semi-bourgeois, did in fact take him in and called a doctor who would not give him away, and for a month Jeallot lay with his hand in a splint. Then he was packed off to Switzerland. The hand healed, and the old man learned how to paint with his left hand and worked in La Chaux-de-Fonds as a house-painter, sometimes suspended on a plank four storeys high. But his right arm would not bend, and he himself would laugh when in the heat of conversation he wanted to raise his hand to smooth his beard or scratch his nose, and the hand would stop a foot from his face.

Ferré was saved only because he happened to have a nervous ailment. He was placed in an asylum and in a year or two, when he recovered, he was released. He moved to Switzerland, married a Swiss German woman, and lived very amicably with his wife, who idolized him and looked after him lovingly. He was very handsome and elegant, with an unusually noble bearing, a true gentleman in manners, dress, and behaviour. He was simply crazy about his child.

Bertrand was a true French street urchin. As a street urchin he had taken part in the Commune, probably bringing dinner to the older workers on the barricades, and, as a street urchin, extricated himself without particular adventures.

Albarracín, or Albagès, as he was called in Switzerland, was a very interesting man. He was a student, carried out propaganda in the International, and happened to be in Alcoy in 1872 when a general strike of construction workers broke out. The mayor and the town officials, to gain time, made a show of taking the workers' side and promised to force the employers to grant concessions. It was an impassioned time, however, and the employers would not grant any concessions. The Commune had just been proclaimed in Cartagena, which gave in only after being bombarded by two German warships, and the Commune was also proclaimed in Alcoy. A white horse was brought to Albarracín, he was mounted on it – he had never ridden a horse in his life and was more afraid of the horse than he was of enemy bullets – and was ordered to lead a crowd to the mayor's office, where the mayor and some of the councillors and police had barricaded themselves.

After a brief exchange of fire the mayoralty was taken and the Commune was proclaimed, which lasted three days. Then it was learned that the mayor had summoned military force, that infantry and cavalry equipped with artillery were on their way to Alcoy, and the crowd ordered Albarracín to carry out executions – that is, the crowd shot the mayor and councillors, and Albarracín, on his white horse, was left to take the blame. He took some initiative of his own, however. Going on foot this time, he imposed a heavy indemnity on the rich bourgeoisie to aid the starving workers, put the homeless into empty houses, and in general dealt with what was most needed – feeding the hungry.

In two or three days the city was surrounded by troops. But Spanish generals know their people, and they realized that taking the city by storm would exact massive casualties. They entered into negotiations with the Commune and promised that all transgressions would be forgotten if the government of the Commune were handed over. Albarracín instructed his comrades to claim that he, Albarracín, was the sole instigator of the whole affair and would be turned in. The generals agreed; meanwhile, Albarracín hid. The troops entered the city and kept their word. There were no persecutions: it was not the time to initiate them.

The following day Albarracín, in disguise, boarded a train for France.

'But imagine my horror', he said. 'I was dressed as a gentleman and went into first class. I entered the car, sat down in a corner – it was evening – and suddenly I saw opposite me a certain bourgeois, one of those from whom I had extracted a healthy indemnity. Well, I thought, he will certainly denounce me at the next station. We came to the station – he left the car. Well, I thought, he has surely gone for the police. But no! He walked up and down the platform, traded a few words with one person or another, and returned to the car. We reached the French border, and as he left he said to me: "Have a good trip, Mr Albarracín!"'

In an honest fight he might have killed Albarracín, but it is not the Spanish custom to assist the police. In Spain an educated man hates the police, and denunciation is a base act to which he will not resort.

So Albarracín was living now in La Chaux-de-Fonds, expecting from one day to the next that a revolution would break out in Spain and he would be called home. Several times he received messages to get ready. What he would have done in a revolution, I have no idea. He was a very good-natured soul, from whom no one ever heard anything but a kind word. Handsome, delicate, with elegant manners, he looked more like a pretty girl than a revolutionary. But if it came to a popular revolution he, like the Spaniards in general, would have stopped at nothing to achieve its triumph. He would not have joined a purely political revolution, though.

Meanwhile, he painted signs. In La Chaux-de-Fonds they are painted not on sheets of metal but directly on the walls of houses. So he too hung suspended on a plank and with his unsteady, feminine hands painted in fanciful letters between rows of windows the names of watchmakers, shop owners, and tavern-keepers. Sometimes in La Chaux-de-Fonds such a fierce wind would blow that it would freeze the blood in your veins even if you were on the move, while poor Albarracín, in his thin clothes, swayed on his plank and traced his fanciful black letters on the grey or pink stucco. He never complained, but it was obvious that he pined deeply for his warm, bountiful country, for the sun, and perhaps for a lady love.

In the following year, the desired moment finally came. In Catalonia a revolution was ready to break out, arms were being stockpiled, and a movement was anticipated from day to day. Albarracín was summoned by telegraph. We got him a passport and some money, and he immediately set out for Spain, unconcerned that the scaffold lay in store for him if he were recognized.

The republicans again compromised with the monarchists, having taken fright at the anarchist movement, and things settled down once more. But Albarracín had frozen enough in La Chaux-de-Fonds and stayed in Spain. He became the superintendent of a school, quite a large and good one, which the anarchists maintained in one of the towns around Barcelona, and there, within a year, he died of the tuberculosis he had contracted up on his planks in the cold Jura. He died raving about a white horse.

This was the milieu in which I spent the winter and summer of 1877, trying to improve our propaganda in La Chaux-de-Fonds and neighbouring Le Locle. I will not say that the enterprise was very successful. A terrible crisis had hit the watchmaking industry. Machine-made American watches were reducing the market for cheap Swiss watches, which had sold in huge numbers previously, especially in America. The best workers barely found work a few days a week, the majority sold or pawned whatever they could, and many did not even have the wherewithal to buy cheap soup in the municipal lunchroom. In the workers' boarding-house where I took my meals for a fabulously low price (1 franc and 40 centimes a day for morning coffee, dinner and a cold supper), the workers, if they took a bottle of cheap red wine, tried to make it last for four or five days, and many took no bottle at all. Destitution hung over the city, indeed over the region as a whole.

Under such conditions, socialist propaganda always goes very badly. Everyone is afraid of losing even the little work that comes his way. Moreover, every meeting costs something, if only 12 centimes for a glass of beer or wine, and most of the workers lacked even that. We organized meetings, and one of the younger men and I would distribute our little posters in the taverns and workshops, but we never succeeded in gathering more than forty or fifty men, and if a few young fellows did rally around us more closely, the great majority remained indifferent.

From time to time I travelled to Neuchâtel for heart-to-heart talks with Guillaume. Or I went to Sonvilliers to see Schwitzguébel and the young men grouped around him and around the consumers' co-operative set up by the anarchists and largely supported by them. It was a means of uniting the workers as well as a small source of support for the *Bulletin*. When the co-operative's affairs went well, its members, at the suggestion of the anarchists, would decide from time to time to spare a few hundred francs for our newspaper . . .

'Anarchism', from *The Encyclopaedia Britannica*

The article 'Anarchism' was written for the eleventh edition of *The Encyclopaedia Britannica*, 1910. It is an outstanding example of Kropotkin's ability to communicate with a broad, non-anarchist audience. While it reflects Kropotkin's own commitment to anarchist communism, it is comprehensive in nature and stands as a classic summary of the ideological foundations of anarchism.

ANARCHISM (from the Gr. ἀν, and ἀϱχή, contrary to authority), the name given to a principle or theory of life and conduct under which society is conceived without government – harmony in such a society being obtained, not by submission to law, or by obedience to any authority, but by free agreements concluded between the various groups, territorial and professional, freely constituted for the sake of production and consumption, as also for the satisfaction of the infinite variety of needs and aspirations of a civilized being. In a society developed on these lines, the voluntary associations which already now begin to cover all the fields of human activity would take a still greater extension so as to substitute themselves for the state in all its functions. They would represent an interwoven network, composed of an infinite variety of groups and federations of all sizes and degrees, local, regional, national and international – temporary or more or less permanent – for all possible purposes: production, consumption and exchange, communications, sanitary arrangements, education, mutual protection, defence of the territory, and so on; and, on the other side, for the satisfaction of an

233

ever-increasing number of scientific, artistic, literary and sociable needs. Moreover, such a society would represent nothing immutable. On the contrary – as is seen in organic life at large – harmony would (it is contended) result from an ever-changing adjustment and readjustment of equilibrium between the multitudes of forces and influences, and this adjustment would be the easier to obtain as none of the forces would enjoy a special protection from the state.

If, it is contended, society were organized on these principles, man would not be limited in the free exercise of his powers in productive work by a capitalist monopoly, maintained by the state; nor would he be limited in the exercise of his will by a fear of punishment, or by obedience towards individuals or metaphysical entities, which both lead to depression of initiative and servility of mind. He would be guided in his actions by his own understanding, which necessarily would bear the impression of a free action and reaction between his own self and the ethical conceptions of his surroundings. Man would thus be enabled to obtain the full development of all his faculties, intellectual, artistic and moral, without being hampered by overwork for the monopolists, or by the servility and inertia of mind of the great number. He would thus be able to reach full *individualization*, which is not possible either under the present system of *individualism*, or under any system of state socialism in the so-called *Volkstaat* (popular state).

The anarchist writers consider, moreover, that their conception is not a utopia, constructed on the *a priori* method, after a few desiderata have been taken as postulates. It is derived, they maintain, from an *analysis of tendencies* that are at work already, even though state socialism may find a temporary favour with the reformers. The progress of modern technics, which wonderfully simplifies the production of all the necessaries of life; the growing spirit of independence, and the rapid spread of free initiative and free understanding in all branches of activity – including those which formerly were considered as the proper attribution of church and state – are steadily reinforcing the no-government tendency.

As to their economical conceptions, the anarchists, in common with all socialists, of whom they constitute the left wing, maintain that the now prevailing system of private ownership in land, and our capitalist production for the sake of profits, represent a monopoly which runs against both the principles of justice and the dictates of utility. They are the main obstacle which prevents the successes of modern technics from being brought into the service of all, so as to produce general well-being. The anarchists consider the wage-system and capitalist production altogether as an obstacle to progress. But they point out also that the state was, and continues to be, the chief instrument for permitting the few to monopolize the land, and the capitalists to appropriate for themselves a quite disproportionate share of the yearly accumulated surplus of production. Consequently, while combating the present monopolization of land, and capitalism altogether, the anarchists combat with the same energy the state, as the main support of that system. Not this or that special form, but the state altogether, whether it be a monarchy or even a republic governed by means of the *referendum*.

The state organization, having always been, both in ancient and modern history (Macedonian Empire, Roman Empire, modern European states grown up on the ruins of the autonomous cities), the instrument for establishing monopolies in favour of the ruling minorities, cannot be made to work for the destruction of these monopolies. The anarchists consider, therefore, that to hand over to the state all the main sources of economical life – the land, the mines, the railways, banking, insurance, and so on – as also the management of all the main branches of industry, in addition to all the functions already accumulated in its hands (education, state-supported religions, defence of the territory, etc.), would mean to create a new instrument of tyranny. State capitalism would only increase the powers of bureaucracy and capitalism. True progress lies in the direction of decentralization, both *territorial* and *functional*, in the development of the spirit of local and personal initiative, and of free federation from the simple to the compound, *in lieu* of the present hierarchy from the centre to the periphery.

In common with most socialists, the anarchists recognize that, like all evolution in nature, the slow evolution of society is followed from time to time by periods of accelerated evolution which are called revolutions; and they think that the era of revolutions is not yet closed. Periods of rapid changes will follow the periods of slow evolution, and these periods must be taken advantage of – not for increasing and widening the powers of the state, but for reducing them, through the organization in every township or commune of the local groups of producers and consumers, as also the regional, and eventually the international, federations of these groups.

In virtue of the above principles the anarchists refuse to be party to the present state organization and to support it by infusing fresh blood into it. They do not seek to constitute, and invite the working men not to constitute, political parties in the parliaments. Accordingly, since the foundation of the International Working Men's Association in 1864–1866, they have endeavoured to promote their ideas directly amongst the labour organizations and to induce those unions to a direct struggle against capital, without placing their faith in parliamentary legislation.

The historical development of anarchism

The conception of society just sketched, and the tendency which is its dynamic expression, have always existed in mankind, in opposition to the governing hierarchic conception and tendency – now the one and now the other taking the upper hand at different periods of history. To the former tendency we owe the evolution, by the masses themselves, of those institutions – the clan, the village community, the guild, the free medieval city – by means of which the masses resisted the encroachments of the conquerors and the power-seeking minorities. The same tendency asserted itself with great energy in the great religious movements of medieval times, especially in the early movements of the reform and its forerunners. At the same time it evidently found its expression in the writings of some thinkers, since the times of Lao-tsze, although, owing to its non-scholastic and popular origin, it obviously found less sympathy among the scholars than the opposed tendency.

As has been pointed out by Prof. Adler in his *Geschichte des Sozialismus und Kommunismus*, Aristippus (b. *c.* 430 BC), one of the founders of the Cyrenaic school, already taught that the wise must not give up their liberty to the state, and in reply to a question by Socrates he said that he did not desire to belong either to the governing or the governed class. Such an attitude, however, seems to have been dictated merely by an Epicurean attitude towards the life of the masses.

The best exponent of anarchist philosophy in ancient Greece was Zeno (342–267 or 270 BC), from Crete, the founder of the

Stoic philosophy, who distinctly opposed his conception of a free community without government to the state-utopia of Plato. He repudiated the omnipotence of the state, its intervention and regimentation, and proclaimed the sovereignty of the moral law of the individual – remarking already that, while the necessary instinct of self-preservation leads man to egotism, nature has supplied a corrective to it by providing man with another instinct – that of sociability. When men are reasonable enough to follow their natural instincts, they will unite across the frontiers and constitute the cosmos. They will have no need of law-courts or police, will have no temples and no public worship, and use no money – free gifts taking the place of the exchanges. Unfortunately, the writings of Zeno have not reached us and are only known through fragmentary quotations. However, the fact that his very wording is similar to the wording now in use, shows how deeply is laid the tendency of human nature of which he was the mouthpiece.

In medieval times we find the same views on the state expressed by the illustrious bishop of Alba, Marco Girolamo Vida, in his first dialogue *De dignitate reipublicae* (Ferd. Cavalli, in *Mem. dell'Istituto Veneto*, xiii.; Dr E. Nys, *Researches in the History of Economics*). But it is especially in several early Christian movements, beginning with the ninth century in Armenia, and in the preachings of the early Hussites, particularly Chojecki, and the early Anabaptists, especially Hans Denk (cf. Keller, *Ein Apostel der Wiedertäufer*), that one finds the same ideas forcibly expressed – special stress being laid of course on their moral aspects.

Rabelais and Fénelon, in their utopias, have also expressed similar ideas, and they were also current in the eighteenth century amongst the French Encyclopaedists, as may be concluded from separate expressions occasionally met with in the writings of Rousseau, from Diderot's *Preface* to the *Voyage* of Bougainville, and so on. However, in all probability such ideas could not be developed then, owing to the rigorous censorship of the Roman Catholic Church.

These ideas found their expression later during the great French Revolution. While the Jacobins did all in their power to centralize everything in the hands of the government, it appears now, from recently published documents, that the masses of the people, in their municipalities and 'sections', accomplished a considerable constructive work. They appropriated for themselves the election of the judges, the organization of supplies and equipment for the army, as also for the large cities, work for the unemployed, the management of charities, and so on. They even tried to establish a direct correspondence between the 36,000 communes of France through the intermediary of a special board, outside the National Assembly (cf. Sigismund Lacroix, *Actes de la commune de Paris*).

It was Godwin, in his *Enquiry concerning Political Justice* (2 vols., 1793), who was the first to formulate the political and economical conceptions of anarchism, even though he did not give that name to the ideas developed in his remarkable work. Laws, he wrote, are not a product of the wisdom of our ancestors: they are the product of their passions, their timidity, their jealousies and their ambition. The remedy they offer is worse than the evils they pretend to cure. If and only if all laws and courts were abolished, and the decisions in the arising contests were left to reasonable men chosen for that purpose, real justice would gradually be evolved. As to the state, Godwin frankly claimed its abolition. A society, he wrote, can perfectly well exist without any government: only the communities should be small and perfectly autonomous. Speaking of property, he stated that the rights of every one 'to every substance capable of contributing to the benefit of a human being' must be regulated by justice alone: the substance must go 'to him who most wants it'. His conclusion was communism. Godwin, however, had not the courage to maintain his opinions. He entirely rewrote later on his chapter on property and mitigated his communist views in the second edition of *Political Justice* (8vo, 1796).

Proudhon was the first to use, in 1840 (*Qu'est-ce que la propriété?* first memoir), the name of anarchy with application to the no-government state of society. The name of 'anarchists' had been freely applied during the French Revolution by the Girondists to those revolutionaries who did not consider that the task of the Revolution was accomplished with the overthrow of Louis XVI, and insisted upon a series of economical measures being taken (the abolition of feudal rights without redemption, the return to the village communities of the communal lands enclosed since 1669, the limitation of landed property to 120 acres, progressive income-tax, the national organization of exchanges on a just value basis, which already received a beginning of practical realization, and so on).

Now Proudhon advocated a society without government, and used the word anarchy to describe it. Proudhon repudiated, as is known, all schemes of communism, according to which mankind would be driven into communistic monasteries or barracks, as also all the schemes of state or state-aided socialism which were advocated by Louis Blanc and the collectivists. When he proclaimed in his first memoir on property that 'Property is theft', he meant only property in its present, Roman-law, sense of 'right of use and abuse'; in property-rights, on the other hand, understood in the limited sense of *possession*, he saw the best protection against the encroachments of the state. At the same time he did not want violently to dispossess the present owners of land, dwelling-houses, mines, factories and so on. He preferred to attain the same end by rendering capital incapable of earning interest; and this he proposed to obtain by means of a national bank, based on the mutual confidence of all those who are engaged in production, who would agree to exchange among themselves their produces at cost-value, by means of labour cheques representing the hours of labour required to produce every given commodity. Under such a system, which Proudhon described as 'Mutuellisme', all the exchanges of services would be strictly equivalent. Besides, such a bank would be enabled to lend money without interest, levying only something like 1 per cent, or even less, for covering the cost of administration. Everyone being thus enabled to borrow the money that would be required to buy a house, nobody would agree to pay any more a yearly rent for the use of it. A general 'social liquidation' would thus be rendered easy, without violent expropriation. The same applied to mines, railways, factories and so on.

In a society of this type the state would be useless. The chief relations between citizens would be based on free agreement and regulated by mere account keeping. The contests might be settled by arbitration. A penetrating criticism of the state and all possible forms of government, and a deep insight into all economic problems, were well-known characteristics of Proudhon's work.

It is worth noticing that French mutualism had its precursor in England, in William Thompson, who began by mutualism before he became a communist, and in his followers John Gray (*A Lecture on Human Happiness*, 1825; *The Social System*, 1831) and J. F. Bray (*Labour's Wrongs and Labour's Remedy*, 1839). It had also its precursor in America. Josiah Warren, who was born in 1798 (cf. W. Bailie, *Josiah Warren, the First American Anarchist*, Boston, 1900), and belonged to Owen's 'New Harmony', considered that the failure of this enterprise was chiefly due to the suppression of individuality and the lack of initiative and responsibility. These defects, he taught, were inherent to every scheme based upon authority and the community of goods. He advocated, therefore, complete individual liberty. In 1827 he opened in Cincinnati a little country store which was the first 'equity store', and which the people called 'time store', because it was based on labour being exchanged hour for hour in all sorts of produce. 'Cost – the limit of price', and consequently 'no interest', was the motto of his store, and later on of his 'equity village', near New York, which was still in existence in 1865. Mr Keith's 'House of Equity' at Boston, founded in 1855, is also worthy of notice.

While the economical, and especially the mutual-banking, ideas of Proudhon found supporters and even a practical application in the United States, his political conception of anarchy found but little echo in France, where the Christian socialism of Lamennais and the Fourierists, and the state socialism of Louis Blanc and the followers of Saint-Simon, were dominating. These ideas found, however, some temporary support among the left-wing Hegelians in Germany, Moses Hess in 1843, and Karl Grün in 1845, who advocated anarchism. Besides, the authoritarian communism of Wilhelm Weitling having given origin to opposition amongst the Swiss working men, Wilhelm Marr gave expression to it in the 1840s.

On the other side, individualist anarchism found, also in Germany, its fullest expression in Max Stirner (Kaspar Schmidt), whose remarkable works (*Der Einzige und sein Eigenthum* and articles contributed to the *Rheinische Zeitung*) remained quite overlooked until they were brought into prominence by John Henry Mackay.

Prof. V. Basch, in a very able introduction to his interesting book, *L'Individualisme anarchiste: Max Stirner* (1904), has shown how the development of the German philosophy from Kant to Hegel, and 'the absolute' of Schelling and the *Geist* of Hegel, necessarily provoked, when the anti-Hegelian revolt began, the preaching of the same 'absolute' in the camp of the rebels. This was done by Stirner, who advocated, not only a complete revolt against the state and against the servitude which authoritarian communism would impose upon men, but also the full liberation of the individual from all social and moral bonds – the rehabilitation of the 'I', the supremacy of the individual, complete 'amoralism', and the 'association of the egotists'. The final conclusion of that sort of individual anarchism has been indicated by Prof. Basch. It maintains that the aim of all superior civilization is, not to permit *all* members of the community to develop in a normal way, but to permit certain better endowed individuals 'fully to develop', even at the cost of the happiness and the very existence of the mass of mankind. It is thus a return towards the most common individualism, advocated by all the would-be superior minorities, to which indeed man owes in his history precisely the state and the rest, which these individualists combat. Their individualism goes so far as to end in a negation of their own starting-point – to say nothing of the impossibility for the individual to attain a really full development in the conditions of oppression of the masses by the 'beautiful aristocracies'. His development would remain unilateral. This is why this direction of thought, notwithstanding its undoubtedly correct and useful advocacy of the full development of each individuality, finds a hearing only in limited artistic and literary circles.

Anarchism in the International Working Men's Association

A general depression in the propaganda of all fractions of socialism followed, as is known, after the defeat of the uprising of the Paris working men in June 1848 and the fall of the Republic. All the socialist press was gagged during the reaction period, which lasted fully twenty years. Nevertheless, even anarchist thought began to make some progress, namely in the writings of Bellegarrique (*Cœurderoy*), and especially Joseph Déjacque (*Les Lazaréennes, L'Humanisphère*, an anarchist-communist utopia, lately discovered and reprinted). The socialist movement revived only after 1864, when some French working men, all 'mutualists', meeting in London during the Universal Exhibition with English followers of Robert Owen, founded the International Working Men's Association. This association developed very rapidly and adopted a policy of direct economical struggle against capitalism, without interfering in the political parliamentary agitation, and this policy was followed until 1871. However, after the Franco-German War, when the International Association was prohibited in France after the uprising of the Commune, the German working men, who had received manhood suffrage for elections to the newly constituted imperial parliament, insisted upon modifying the tactics of the International, and began to build up a Social Democratic political party. This soon led to a division in the Working Men's Association, and the Latin federations, Spanish, Italian, Belgian and Jurassic (France could not be represented), constituted among themselves a Federal union which broke entirely with the Marxist general council of the International. Within these federations developed now what may be described as *modern anarchism*. After the names of 'Federalists' and 'Anti-authoritarians' had been used for some time by these federations the name of 'anarchists', which their adversaries insisted upon applying to them, prevailed, and finally it was revindicated.

Bakunin (*q.v.*) soon became the leading spirit among these Latin federations for the development of the principles of anarchism, which he did in a number of writings, pamphlets and letters. He demanded the complete abolition of the state, which – he wrote – is a product of religion, belongs to a lower state of civilization, represents the negation of liberty, and spoils even that which it undertakes to do for the sake of general well-being. The state was an historically necessary evil, but its complete extinction will be, sooner or later, equally necessary. Repudiating all legislation, even when issuing from universal suffrage, Bakunin claimed for each nation, each region and each commune, full autonomy, so long as it is not a menace to its neighbours, and full independence for the individual, adding that one becomes really free only when, and in proportion as, all others are free. Free federations of the communes would constitute free nations.

As to his economical conceptions, Bakunin described himself, in common with his Federalist comrades of the International (César De Paepe, James Guillaume, Schwitzguébel), a 'collectivist anarchist' – not in the sense of Vidal and Pecqueur in the 1840s, or of their modern Social Democratic followers, but to express a state of things in which all necessaries for production are owned in common by the labour groups and the free communes, while the ways of retribution of labour, communist or otherwise, would be settled by each group for itself. Social revolution, the near approach of which was foretold at that time by all socialists, would be the means of bringing into life the new conditions.

The Jurassic, the Spanish and the Italian federations and sections of the International Working Men's Association, as also the French, the German and the American anarchist groups, were for the next years the chief centres of anarchist thought and propaganda. They refrained from any participation in parliamentary politics, and always kept in close contact with the labour organizations. However, in the second half of the 'eighties and the early 'nineties of the nineteenth century, when the influence of the anarchists began to be felt in strikes, in the 1st of May demonstrations, where they promoted the idea of a general strike for an eight hours' day, and in the anti-militarist propaganda in the army, violent prosecutions were directed against them, especially in the Latin countries (including physical torture in the Barcelona Castle) and the United States (the execution of five Chicago anarchists in 1887). Against these prosecutions the anarchists retaliated by acts of violence which in their turn were followed by more executions from above, and new acts of revenge from below. This created in the general public the impression that violence is the substance of anarchism, a view repudiated by its supporters, who hold that in reality violence is resorted to by all parties in proportion as their open action is obstructed by repression, and exceptional laws render them outlaws. (Cf. *Anarchism and Outrage*, by C. M. Wilson, and *Report of the Spanish Atrocities Committee*, in 'Freedom Pamphlets'; *A Concise History of the Great Trial of the Chicago Anarchists*, by Dyer Lum (New York, 1886); *The Chicago Martyrs: Speeches*, etc.).

Anarchism continued to develop, partly in the direction of Proudhonian 'mutuellisme', but chiefly as communist-anarchism, to which a third direction, Christian-anarchism, was added by Leo Tolstoy, and a fourth, which might be ascribed as literary-anarchism, began amongst some prominent modern writers.

The ideas of Proudhon, especially as regards mutual banking, corresponding with those of Josiah Warren, found a considerable following in the United States, creating quite a school, of which the main writers are Stephen Pearl Andrews, William Grene, Lysander Spooner (who began to write in 1850, and whose unfinished work,

Natural Law, was full of promise), and several others, whose names will be found in Dr Nettlau's *Bibliographie de l'anarchie*.

A prominent position among the individualist anarchists in America has been occupied by Benjamin R. Tucker, whose journal *Liberty* was started in 1881 and whose conceptions are a combination of those of Proudhon with those of Herbert Spencer. Starting from the statement that anarchists are egotists, strictly speaking, and that every group of individuals, be it a secret league of a few persons, or the Congress of the United States, has the right to oppress all mankind, provided it has the power to do so, that equal liberty for all and absolute equality ought to be the law, and 'mind every one your own business' is the unique moral law of anarchism, Tucker goes on to prove that a general and thorough application of these principles would be beneficial and would offer no danger, because the powers of every individual would be limited by the exercise of the equal rights of all others. He further indicated (following H. Spencer) the difference which exists between the encroachment on somebody's rights and resistance to such an encroachment; between domination and defence: the former being equally condemnable, whether it be encroachment of a criminal upon an individual, or the encroachment of one upon all others, or of all others upon one; while resistance to encroachment is defensible and necessary. For their self-defence, both the citizen and the group have the right to any violence, including capital punishment. Violence is also justified for enforcing the duty of keeping an agreement. Tucker thus follows Spencer, and, like him, opens (in the present writer's opinion) the way for reconstituting under the heading of 'defence' all the functions of the state. His criticism of the present state is very searching, and his defence of the rights of the individual very powerful. As regards his economical views B. R. Tucker follows Proudhon.

The individualist anarchism of the American Proudhonians finds, however, but little sympathy amongst the working masses. Those who profess it – they are chiefly 'intellectuals' – soon realize that the *individualization* they so highly praise is not attainable by individual efforts, and either abandon the ranks of the anarchists, and are driven into the liberal individualism of the classical economists, or they retire into a sort of Epicurean amoralism, or superman-theory, similar to that of Stirner and Nietzsche. The great bulk of the anarchist working men prefer the anarchist-communist ideas which have gradually evolved out of the anarchist collectivism of the International Working Men's Association. To this direction belong – to name only the better known exponents of anarchism – Elisée Reclus, Jean Grave, Sebastien Faure, Emile Pouget in France; Errico Malatesta and Covelli in Italy; R. Mella, A. Lorenzo, and the mostly unknown authors of many excellent manifestos in Spain; John Most amongst the Germans; Spies, Parsons and their followers in the United States, and so on; while Domela Nieuwenhuis occupies an intermediate position in Holland. The chief anarchist papers which have been published since 1880 also belong to that direction; while a number of anarchists of this direction have joined the so-called syndicalist movement – the French name for the non-political labour movement, devoted to direct struggle with capitalism, which has lately become so prominent in Europe.

As one of the anarchist-communist direction, the present writer for many years endeavoured to develop the following ideas: to show the intimate, logical connection which exists between the modern philosophy of natural sciences and anarchism; to put anarchism on a scientific basis by the study of the tendencies that are apparent now in society and may indicate its further evolution; and to work out the basis of anarchist ethics. As regards the substance of anarchism itself, it was Kropotkin's aim to prove that communism – at least partial – has more chances of being established than collectivism, especially in communes taking the lead, and that free, or anarchist-communism is the only form of communism that has any chance of being accepted in civilized societies; communism and anarchy are therefore two terms of evolution which complete each other, the one rendering the other possible and acceptable. He has tried, moreover, to indicate how, during a revolutionary period, a large city – if its inhabitants have accepted the idea – could organize itself on the lines of free communism; the city guaranteeing to every inhabitant dwelling, food and clothing to an extent corresponding to the comfort now available to the middle classes only, in exchange for a half-day's, or five-hours' work; and how all those things which would be considered as luxuries might be obtained by everyone if he joins for the other half of the day all sorts of free associations pursuing all possible aims – educational, literary, scientific, artistic, sports and so on. In order to prove the first of these assertions he has analysed the possibilities of agriculture and industrial work, both being combined with brain work. And in order to elucidate the main factors of human evolution, he has analysed the part played in history by the popular constructive agencies of mutual aid and the historical role of the state.

Without naming himself an anarchist, Leo Tolstoy, like his predecessors in the popular religious movements of the fifteenth and sixteenth centuries, Chojecki, Denk and many others, took the anarchist position as regards the state and property rights, deducing his conclusions from the general spirit of the teachings of the Christ and from the necessary dictates of reason. With all the might of his talent he made (especially in *The Kingdom of God in Yourselves*) a powerful criticism of the church, the state and law altogether, and especially of the present property laws. He describes the state as the domination of the wicked ones, supported by brutal force. Robbers, he says, are far less dangerous than a well-organized government. He makes a searching criticism of the prejudices which are current now concerning the benefits conferred upon men by the church, the state and the existing distribution of property, and from the teachings of the Christ he deduces the rule of non-resistance and the absolute condemnation of all wars. His religious arguments are, however, so well combined with arguments borrowed from a dispassionate observation of the present evils, that the anarchist portions of his works appeal to the religious and the non-religious reader alike.

It would be impossible to represent here, in a short sketch, the penetration, on the one hand, of anarchist ideas into modern literature, and the influence, on the other hand, which the libertarian ideas of the best contemporary writers have exercised upon the development of anarchism. One ought to consult the ten big volumes of the *Supplément Littéraire* to the paper *La Révolte* and later the *Temps Nouveaux*, which contain reproductions from the works of hundreds of modern authors expressing anarchist ideas, in order to realize how closely anarchism is connected with all the intellectual movement of our own times. J. S. Mill's *Liberty*, Spencer's *Individual versus the State*, Marc Guyau's *Morality without Obligation or Sanction*, and Fouillée's *La Morale, l'art et la religion*, the works of Multatuli (E. Douwes Dekker), Richard Wagner's *Art and Revolution*, the works of Nietzsche, Emerson, W. Lloyd Garrison, Thoreau, Alexander Herzen, Edward Carpenter and so on; and in the domain of fiction, the dramas of Ibsen, the poetry of Walt Whitman, Tolstoy's *War and Peace*, Zola's *Paris* and *Le Travail*, the latest works of Merezhkovsky, and an infinity of works of less known authors, are full of ideas which show how closely anarchism is interwoven with the work that is going on in modern thought in the same direction of enfranchisement of man from the bonds of the state as well as from those of capitalism.

Kropotkin on the Russian Revolution

'Message to the Workers of the Western World', 10 June 1920
Two letters to Lenin, 4 March 1920 and 21 December 1920
'What Is to Be Done?' 23 November 1920

Kropotkin's return to Russia in 1917 after four decades in emigration was bittersweet. No longer able to play an active political role, he could only bear witness as the long-anticipated revolution gave way to the one-party rule of the Bolsheviks. A sampling of his brief pronouncements in his last years shows him trying to come to terms with a phenomenon that aroused both his brightest hopes and his worst fears.

'Message to the Workers of the Western World' was given to the members of a British Labour Delegation that came to visit him on 10 June 1920. It is reprinted from *The Labour Leader* of 22 July 1920. The two letters to Lenin are reprinted from Martin A. Miller, ed., *Selected Writings on Anarchism and Revolution: P. A. Kropotkin* (Cambridge, Mass., and London: MIT Press, 1970), pp. 335–39. 'What Is to Be Done?', dated 23 November 1920, was published in Berlin in 1923. Reprinted here is the somewhat abridged translation which appears under the title 'What to Do?' in Roger N. Baldwin, ed., *Kropotkin's Revolutionary Pamphlets* (New York and London: Benjamin Blom, 1927; reissued 1968), pp. 256–59.

Message to the Workers of the Western World

Dmitrov, 10 June 1920

I have been asked whether I have not some message to send to the working men of the Western world? Surely, there is much to say about the current events in Russia, and much to learn from them. The message might be long. But I shall indicate only some main points.

First of all, the working men of the civilized world and their friends in the other classes ought to induce their governments entirely to abandon the idea of an armed intervention in the affairs of Russia – whether open or disguised, whether military or in the shape of subventions to different nations.

Russia is now living through a revolution of the same depth and the same importance as the British nation underwent in 1639–48, and France in 1789–94; and every nation should refuse to play the shameful part that Great Britain, Prussia, Austria and Russia played during the French Revolution.

Moreover, it must be kept in view that the Russian Revolution – while it is trying to build up a society where the whole produce of the joint efforts of labour, technical skill and scientific knowledge, should go entirely to the commonwealth itself – is not a mere accident in the struggle of different parties. It is something that has been prepared by nearly a century of communist and socialist propaganda, since the times of Robert Owen, Saint Simon and Fourier; and although the attempt at introducing the new society by means of the dictatorship of one party is apparently doomed to be a failure, it nevertheless must be recognized that the Revolution has already introduced into our everyday life new conceptions about the rights of labour, its true position in society, and the duties of every citizen, which have come to stay.

Altogether, not only the working men, but all the progressive elements of the civilized nations ought to put a stop to the support hitherto given to the opponents of the Revolution. Not that there should be nothing to oppose in the methods of the Bolshevist government! Far from that! But because every armed intervention of a foreign power necessarily results in the reinforcement of the dictatorial tendencies of the rulers, and paralyses the efforts of those Russians who are ready to aid Russia, independently of the government, in the reconstruction of its life on new lines.

The evils naturally inherent in party dictatorships have thus been increased by the war conditions under which this Party maintained itself. The state of war has been an excuse for strengthening the dictatorial methods of the Party, as well as its tendency to centralize every detail of life in the hands of the government – with the result that immense branches of the usual activities of the nation have been brought to a standstill. The natural evils of state communism are thus increased tenfold under the excuse that all misfortunes of our life are due to the intervention of foreigners.

Besides, I must also mention that a military intervention of the Allies, if it is continued, will certainly develop in Russia a bitter feeling against the Western nations, and this will someday be utilized by their enemies in possible future conflicts. Such a bitterness is already developing.

In short, it is high time that the West European nations should enter into direct relations with the Russian nation. And in this direction you – the working classes and the advanced portions of all nations – ought to have your say.

One word more about the general question. A renewal of relations between the European and American nations and Russia certainly must not mean the admission of a supremacy of the Russian nation over those nationalities, of which the empire of the Russian tsars was composed. Imperial Russia is dead, and will not return to life. The future of the various provinces, of which the empire was composed, lies in the direction of a great federation. The natural territories of the different parts of that federation are quite distinct, for those of us who are acquainted with the history of Russia, its ethnography and its economic life; and all attempts to bring the constituent parts of the Russian Empire, Finland, the Baltic Provinces, Lithuania, the Ukraine, Georgia, Armenia, Siberia, and so on, under one central rule, are surely doomed to failure. The future of what was the Russian Empire is in the direction of a federation of independent units. It would, therefore, be in the interest of all that the Western nations should declare beforehand that they are recognizing the right of self-government for every portion of what was once the Russian Empire.

As to my own views on the subject, they go still further. I see the coming, in a near future, of a time when every portion of that federation will itself be a federation of free rural communes and free cities; and I believe still that portions of Western Europe will soon take the lead in that direction.

Now, as regards our present economical and political situation – the Russian Revolution being a continuation of the two great Revolutions in England and in France – Russia is trying now to make a step in advance of where France stopped, when it came to realize in life what was described then as *real equality (egalité de fait)*, that is, economic equality.

Unfortunately, the attempt to make that step has been undertaken in Russia under the strongly centralized *dictatorship of one party* – the Social Democratic Maximalists; and the attempt was made on the lines taken in the utterly centralist and Jacobinist conspiracy of Babeuf. About this attempt I am bound frankly to tell you that, in my opinion, the attempt to build up a communist republic on the lines of strongly centralized state communism under the iron rule of the dictatorship of a Party is ending in a failure. We learn in Russia *how communism cannot be introduced*, even though the populations, sick of the old regime, opposed no active resistance to the experiment made by the new rulers.

The idea of soviets, that is, of labour and peasant councils, first promoted during the attempted revolution of 1905 and immediately realized by the Revolution of February, 1917, as soon as the Tsar's regime broke down – the idea of such councils controlling the political and the economic life of the country is a grand idea. The more so as it leads necessarily to the idea of these councils being composed of all those who take a *real part* in the production of national wealth by their own personal effort.

But so long as a country is governed by the dictatorship of a party, the labour and peasant councils evidently lose all their significance. They are reduced to the passive role played in times past by 'general states' and parliaments, when they were convoked by the king and had to oppose an all-powerful king's council.

A labour council ceases to be a free and valuable adviser when there is no free press in the country, and we have been in this position for nearly two years, the excuse for such conditions being the state of war. More than that, the peasant and labour councils lose all their significance when no free electoral agitation precedes the elections, and the elections are made under the pressure of party dictatorship. Of course, the usual excuse is that a dictatorial rule was unavoidable as a means of combating the old regime. But such a rule evidently becomes a formidable drawback as soon as the Revolution proceeds towards the building up of a new society on a new economic basis. It becomes a death sentence on the new construction.

The ways to be followed for overthrowing an already weakened government and taking its place are well known from history, old and modern. But when it comes to build up quite new forms of life – especially new forms of production and exchange – without having any examples to imitate; when everything has to be worked out by men on the spot, then an all-powerful centralized government which undertakes to supply every inhabitant with every lamp-glass and every match to light the lamp proves absolutely incapable of doing that through its functionaries – no matter how countless they may be: it becomes a nuisance. It develops such a formidable bureaucracy that the French bureaucratic system which requires the intervention of forty functionaries to sell a tree felled by a storm on a public road becomes a trifle in comparison. This is what we now learn in Russia. And this is what you, the working men of the West, can and must avoid by all means, since you care for the success of a social reconstruction, and sent here your delegates to see how a social revolution works in real life.

The immense constructive work that is required from a social revolution cannot be accomplished by a central government, even if it had to guide it in its work something more substantial than a few socialist and anarchist booklets. It requires the knowledge, the brains, and the willing collaboration of a mass of local and specialized forces, which alone can cope with the diversity of economical problems in their local aspects. To sweep away that collaboration, and to trust to the genius of party dictators is to destroy all the independent *nuclei*, such as trade unions (called in Russia 'professional unions'), and the local distributive co-operative organizations – turning them into bureaucratic organs of the Party, as is being done now. But this is the way *not* to accomplish the Revolution; the way to render its realization impossible. And this is why I consider it my duty earnestly to warn you from taking such a line of action.

Imperialist conquerors of all nationalities may desire that the populations of the ex-empire of Russia should remain in miserable economic conditions as long as possible, and thus be doomed to supply Western and Middle Europe with raw stuffs, while the Western manufacturers, producing manufactured goods, should cash all the benefits that the population of Russia might otherwise obtain from their work. But the working classes of Europe and America, and the intellectual *nuclei* of these countries surely understand that only by the force of conquest could they keep Russia in that subordinate condition. At the same time, the sympathies with which our Revolution was met all over Europe and America show that you were happy to greet in Russia a new member of the international comradeship of nations. And you surely soon see that it is in the interest of the workers of all the world that Russia should issue as soon as possible from the conditions that paralyse now her development.

A few words more. The last war has inaugurated new conditions of life in the civilized world. Socialism is sure to make considerable progress, and new forms of a more independent life surely will be soon worked out on the lines of local political independence and free scope in social reconstruction, either in a pacific way, or by revolutionary means if the intelligent portions of the civilized nations do not join in the task of an unavoidable reconstruction.

But the success of this reconstruction will depend to a great extent upon the possibility of a close co-operation of the different nations. For this co-operation the labouring classes of all nations must be closely united, and for that purpose the idea of a great International of all working men of the world must be renewed; not in the shape of a union directed by one single party, as was the case in the Second International, and is again in the Third. Such unions have, of course, full reason to exist, but besides them and uniting them all there must be a union of all the trade unions of the world – of all those who produce the wealth of the world –

united, in order to free the production of the world from its present enslavement to capital.

Two letters to Lenin

Dmitrov, 4 March 1920

Esteemed Vladimir Ilich,

Several employees of the postal-telegraph department have come to me with the request that I bring to your attention information about their truly desperate situation. As this problem concerns not only the commissariat of mail and telegraphs alone, but the general condition of everyday life in Russia, I hasten to fulfil their request.

You know, of course, that to live in the Dmitrov district on the salary received by these employees is *absolutely impossible*. It is impossible even to buy a bushel of potatoes with this [salary]; I know this from personal experience. In exchange they ask for soap and salt, of which there is none. Since [the price] of flour has gone up – if you manage to get any – it is impossible to buy eight pounds of grain and five pounds of wheat. In short, without receiving provisions, the employees are doomed to a very real famine.

Meanwhile, along with such prices, the meagre provisions which the postal and telegraph employees received from the Moscow postal and telegraph supply centre (according to the decree of 15 August 1918: eight pounds of wheat to an employee or to employees, and five pounds of wheat to incapacitated members of a family) *have not been delivered for two months already*. The local supply centres cannot distribute their provisions, and the appeal of the employees (125 persons in the Dmitrov area) to Moscow remains unanswered. A month ago one of the employees wrote you personally, but he has received no answer thus far.

I consider it a duty to testify that the situation of these employees is truly desperate. The majority are *literally starving*. This is obvious from their faces. Many are preparing to leave home without knowing where to go. And in the meantime, I will say openly that they carry out their work conscientiously; they have familiarized themselves with [their jobs] and to lose such workers would not be in the interests of local life in any way.

I will add only that whole categories of other Soviet employees can be found in the same desperate condition.

In concluding, I cannot avoid mentioning something about the general situation to you. Living in a great centre – in Moscow – it is impossible to know the true condition of the country. To know the truth about current experiences, one must live in the provinces, in close contact with daily life, with its needs and misfortunes, with the starving – adults and children – with running back and forth to offices in order to get permission to buy a cheap kerosene lamp, and so forth.

There is now one way out of these trials for us. It is necessary to hasten the transition to more normal conditions of life. We will not continue like this for long, and we are moving towards a bloody catastrophe. The locomotives of the Allies, the export of Russian grain, hemp, flax, hides, and other things that are so indispensable to us will not help the population.

One thing is indisputable. Even if the dictatorship of the party were an appropriate means to bring about a blow to the capitalist system (which I strongly doubt), *it is nevertheless harmful for the creation of a new socialist system.* What are necessary and needed are local institutions, local forces; but there are none, anywhere. Instead of this, wherever one turns there are people who have never known anything of real life, who are committing the gravest errors which have been paid for with thousands of lives and the ravaging of entire districts.

Consider the supply of firewood, or that of last season's spring seed . . .

Without the participation of local forces, without an organization from below of the peasants and workers themselves, it is impossible to build a new life.

It would seem that the soviets should have served precisely this function of creating an organization from below. But Russia has already become a Soviet Republic only in name. The influx and taking over of the people by the 'party', that is, predominantly the newcomers (the ideological communists are more in the urban centres), has already destroyed the influence and constructive energy of this promising institution – the soviets. At present, it is the party committees, not the soviets, who rule in Russia. And their organization suffers from the defects of bureaucratic organization.

To move away from the current disorder, Russia must return to the creative genius of local forces which, as I see it, can be a factor in the creation of a new life. And the sooner that the necessity of this way is understood, the better. People will then be all the more likely to accept [new] social forms of life. If the present situation continues, the very word 'socialism' will turn into a curse. This is what happened to the conception of 'equality' in France for forty years after the rule of the Jacobins.

With comradely greetings,
P. Kropotkin

Dmitrov (Moscow province)
21 December 1920

Respected Vladimir Ilich,

An announcement has been placed in *Izvestiia* and in *Pravda* which makes known the decision of the Soviet government to seize as hostages SRs [Social Revolutionary party members] from the Savinkov and Chernov groups, White Guards of the nationalist and tactical centre, and Wrangel officers; and, in case of an [assassination] attempt on the leaders of the soviets, to 'mercilessly exterminate' these hostages.

Is there really no one around you to remind your comrades and to persuade them that such measures represent a return to the worst period of the Middle Ages and religious wars, and are undeserving of people who have taken it upon themselves to create a future society on communist principles? Whoever holds dear the future of communism cannot embark upon such measures.

Is it possible that no one has explained what a hostage really is? A hostage is imprisoned not as punishment for some crime. He is held in order to blackmail the enemy with his death. 'If you kill one of ours, we will kill one of yours.' But is this not the same thing as leading a man to the scaffold each morning and taking him back, saying: 'Wait awhile, not today ...'?

And don't your comrades understand that this is tantamount to a *restoration of torture* for the hostages and their families?

I hope no one will tell me that people in power also do not lead easy lives. Nowadays even among kings there are those who regard the possibility of assassination as an 'occupational hazard'.

And revolutionaries assume the responsibility of defending themselves before a court which threatens their lives. Louise Michel chose this way. Or they refuse to be persecuted, as did Malatesta and Voltairine de Cleyre.

Even kings and popes have rejected such barbaric means of self-defence as the taking of hostages. How can apostles of a new life and architects of a new social order have recourse to such means of defence against enemies?

Won't this be regarded as a sign that you consider your communist experiment unsuccessful, and [that] you are not saving the system that is so dear to you but only [saving] yourselves?

Don't your comrades realize that you, communists (despite the errors you have committed), are *working for the future?* And that therefore you must in no case stain your work by acts so close to primitive terror? [You must know] that precisely these acts performed by revolutionaries in the past make the new communist endeavours so difficult.

I believe that for the best of you, the future of communism is more precious than your own lives. And thoughts about this future must compel you to renounce such measures.

With all of its serious deficiencies (and I, as you know, see them well), the October Revolution brought about enormous progress. It has demonstrated that social revolution is not impossible, as people in Western Europe had begun to think. And, for all its defects, it is bringing about progress in the direction of *equality*, which will not be corroded by attempts to return to the past.

Why, then, push the revolution on a path leading to its destruction, primarily because of defects which are not at all inherent in socialism or communism, but represent the survival of the old order and old disturbances, of an unlimited, omnivorous authority?

P. Kropotkin

What is to be done?

Dmitrov, 23 November 1920

The revolution we have gone through is the sum total, not of the efforts of separate individuals, *but a natural phenomenon, independent of the human will*, a natural phenomenon similar to a typhoon such as rises suddenly on the coasts of eastern Asia.

Thousands of causes, in which the work of separate individuals and even of parties has been only a grain of sand, one of the minute local whirlwinds, have contributed to form the great natural phenomenon, the great catastrophe which shall either renew or destroy; or perhaps both destroy and renew.

All of us prepared this great inevitable change. But it was also prepared by all the previous revolutions of 1793, 1848–71; by all the writings of the Jacobins, socialists; by all the achievements of science, industry, art and so on. In a word, millions of natural causes have contributed just in the same way as millions of movements of particles of air or water cause the sudden storm which sinks hundreds of ships or destroys thousands of houses – as the trembling of the earth in an earthquake is caused by thousands of small tremors and by the preparatory movements of separate particles.

In general, people do not see events concretely, solidly. They think more in words than in clearly imagined pictures, and they have absolutely no idea what a revolution is – of those many millions of causes which have gone to give it its present form – and they are therefore inclined to exaggerate the importance in the progress of the revolution of their personality and of that attitude which they, their friends and co-thinkers will take up in this enormous upheaval. And of course they are absolutely incapable of understanding how powerless is any individual, whatever his intelligence and experience, in this whirlpool of hundreds of thousands of forces which have been put into motion by the upheaval.

They do not understand that once such a great natural phenomenon has begun, such as an earthquake, or, rather, such as a typhoon, separate individuals are powerless to exercise any kind of influence on the course of events. A party perhaps can do something – far less than is usually thought – and on the surface of the oncoming waves, its influence may, perhaps, be very slightly noticeable. But separate small aggregations not forming a fairly large mass are undoubtedly powerless – their powers are certainly *nil* . . .

It is in this position that I, an anarchist, find myself. But even parties of far greater numbers in Russia at the present moment are in a very similar position.

I will even go farther; the governing party itself is in the same position. It no longer governs, it is being carried along by the current which it helped to create but which is now already a thousand times stronger than the party itself . . .

What is then to be done?

We are experiencing a revolution which has advanced not at all along those ways which we had prepared for it, but which we had no time to prepare sufficiently. What is to be done now?

To prevent the revolution? Absurd!

Too late. The revolution will advance in its own way, in the direction of the least resistance, without paying the least attention to our efforts.

At the present moment the Russian Revolution is in the following position. It is perpetrating horrors. It is ruining the whole country. In its mad fury it is annihilating human lives. That is why it is a revolution and not a peaceful progress, because it is destroying without regarding what it destroys and whither it goes.

And we are powerless for the present to direct it into another channel, until such time as it will have played itself out. It must wear itself out.

And then? *Then – inevitably will come a reaction.* Such is the law of history, and it is easy to understand why this cannot be otherwise. People imagine that we can change the form of development of a revolution. That is a childish illusion. A revolution is such a force that its growth cannot be changed. *And a reaction is absolutely inevitable,* just as a hollow in the water is inevitable after every wave, as weakness is inevitable in a human being after a period of feverish activity.

Therefore the only thing we can do is to use our energy to lessen the fury and force of the oncoming reaction.

But of what can our efforts consist?

To modify the passions – on one as on the other side? Who is likely to listen to us? Even if there exist such diplomats as can do anything in this role, the time for their *début* has not yet come; neither the one nor the other side is as yet disposed to listen to them. I see one thing; we must gather together people *who will be capable of undertaking constructive work in each and every party after the revolution has worn itself out.* [Italics Kropotkin's.]

Index

261

Index

Hyndman, Henry, 207

International Working Men's
Association, xi, xiv, xvi, 6, 203–32,
passim, 241–3, 245; Berne
Congress, 1876, 205–7; founding
of, 8, 236; Hague Congress, 1872,
xi, 205n; in Spain, 207 n. 10, 209,
219; see also Jura Federation

Jacobins, xxi, 28, 52, 60, 61, 66, 69,
123, 213, 237, 251, 256, 258
Jacquard, Joseph-Marie, xxxii, 179
Jeallot, Pierre, 225, 228
Joule, James, xxxiii, 101
Jura Federation, xi, xiii, 203–32,
passim; Bulletin of, 204, 219, 232

Keltie, John, 204
Kropotkin, Alexander, viii
Kropotkin, Peter, writings: 'An Appeal
to the Young', xix; The Conquest of
Bread, xv–xvii, 3; Ethics, xviii, xxi;
Fields, Factories, and Workshops, xvi,
169n, 182, 191; The Great French
Revolution, xv, xviii; Memoirs of a
Revolutionist, viii, xiii, xv, xix, 203;
Modern Science and Anarchism, xviii;
'Must We Occupy Ourselves with
an Examination of the Ideal of a
Future System?', xii–xiii; Mutual
Aid, xv, xviii; In Russian and French
Prisons, 142n; The Terror in Russia,
xxi; 'What Is to Be Done?', xxii–
xxiii
Kropotkin, Sofia, xiv

labour-cheques, labour-notes, 136,
145–7, 152, 155, 156, 239
La Bruyère, Jean de, xxxiii, 180
Lafargue, Paul, 207
Lamarck, Jean-Baptiste, xxxiii, 177
Laplace, Pierre-Simon, xxxiii, 177
Lavoisier, Antoine-Laurent, xxxiii, 177
Lavrov, Peter, 206, 208
Lenin, V. I., xxi, xxii, 254–7
Leverdays, Emile, xxxiii, 39
Liebig, Justus, xxxiii, 181
Liebknecht, Karl, 206, 207, 208, 214,
217
Lifeboat Association, English, 122–5
Littré, M., xxxiii, 99–100

Longuet, Charles, 207
Lopatin, German, 220–1
Lyell, Charles, xxxiii, 101

Malatesta, Errico, 245, 257
Marx, Karl, 8, 32, 58, 89, 146, 149,
158, 205; Capital, 207, 220–2;
'economic materialism' of, 214
Marxism, 212, 242; and 'dictatorship
of the proletariat', xv; and science,
xviii, 214, 220–1; and state
socialism, xvi, xxi, 9, 35, 68
Maury, Matthew, xxxiii, 155
Mayer, Julius von, xxxiv, 15
Mendeleeff (Mendeleyev), Dmitry,
xxxiii, 101
Michel, Louise, 256–7
Michelet, Jules, xxxiii, 72
Mignet, François-Auguste-Marie,
xxxiii, 59
Morris, William, xxxiii, 105
Mouchot, A., xxxiii, 196

Nobiling, Karl, 217n

Owen, Robert, 6, 8, 10, 145, 240,
241, 249

Paris Commune, 1871, xxxiv, 8, 26,
28, 54, 76, 151, 204, 210, 225–9;
anniversary of, 218 n. 28
peasant communes, 59–60; in Russia,
xii, 83, 131
phalansterians, phalansteries, xxxiii, 7,
9, 35, 109, 110; see also Fourier,
Charles
Pindy, Jean-Louis, 223–8
Playfair, Lyon, xxxiii, 101n
Ponce, M., 188–9
Populism, Russian, xii, xiv, 206 n. 7,
207 n. 9, 218 n. 28
'propaganda by deed', xvii, 216 n. 26
Proudhon, Pierre-Joseph, vii, x, xii–
xiii, xxxiv, 56, 157, 221, 238–9,
244; mutualism of, 6, 8, 145, 239,
241, 243

Red Cross, 125–7
Reinsdorf, August, 216
Le Révolté (La Révolte, Les Temps
Nouveaux), xiii, xiv, xv, xxii, 217n,
223, 246

Index

Revolution, English, 4, 66, 249, 251
Revolutions, French
  1789: xxi, 4, 5, 28, 50, 52–4, 55,
    85, 237–8, 249, 251, 258;
    Michelet on, 73; Mignet on, 59;
    peasants in, 66, 69, 130, 151
  1830: 6
  1848: 4, 7–8, 26, 28, 54, 66–7,
    241; national workshops in, 29,
    55–6
Revolutions, Russian
  1905: xx–xxi, 67n, 251
  1917: xx–xxii, 248–54, 257–9
Rinke, Otto, 219 n. 30
Rittinghausen, Moritz, 208
Robespierre, Maximilien, 28, 59
Rochefort, Henri, 219
Rodbertus, Johann, xxxiv, 89
Ruskin, John, xxxiv, 105

Saint-Simon, Claude-Henri de, 6, 10,
  240, 249
Say, J. B., xxxiv, 166
Schwitzguébel, Adhémar, 203, 232,
  242
Second International, xx, 253
Séguin, Marc, xxxiv, 15

Singer, Paul, 209
Sismondi, Jean de, xxxiv, 166
Social Democrats, 59, 205, 223, 242;
  German, xx, 206–9, 213–19;
  Russian, 218 n. 28, 251
Spichiger, Auguste, 223–5
Stephenson, George, xxxiv, 141, 179
Stirner, Max, 240–1, 244

Thiers, Adolph, 26
Third International, 253
Thomas, Clément, xxxiv, 26
Tolstoy, Leo, vii, 243, 246, 247
Tsinger, Nicholas, 221
Tucker, Benjamin, 244

Vorwärts, 217, 218

Warren, Josiah, 240, 243
Watrin, xxxiv, 26
Watt, James, xxxiv, 15, 179
Werner, Emil, 217, 219 n. 30
Windthorst, Ludwig, 214

Young Icaria (Icaria), xxxiv, 110n

Zasulich, Vera, 218

Cambridge Texts in the History of Political Thought

Titles published in the series thus far

Aristotle *The Politics* (edited by Stephen Everson)

Arnold *Culture and Anarchy and Other Writings* (edited by Stefan Collini)

Bakunin *Statism and Anarchy* (edited by Marshall Shatz)

Baxter *A Holy Commonwealth* (edited by William Lamont)

Bentham *A Fragment on Government* (introduction by Ross Harrison)

Bernstein *The Preconditions of Socialism* (edited by Henry Tudor)

Bodin *On Sovereignty* (edited by Julian H. Franklin)

Bossuet *Politics Drawn from the Very Words of Holy Scripture* (edited by Patrick Riley)

Burke *Pre-Revolutionary Writings* (edited by Ian Harris)

Christine de Pizan *The Book of Body Politic* (edited by Kate Langdon Forhan)

Cicero *On Duties* (edited by M. T. Griffin and E. M. Atkins)

Constant *Political Writings* (edited by Biancamaria Fontana)

Diderot *Political Writings* (edited by John Hope Mason and Robert Wokler)

The Dutch Revolt (edited by Martin van Gelderen)

Filmer *Patriarcha and Other Writings* (edited by Johann P. Sommerville)

Gramsci *Pre-Prison Writings* (edited by Richard Bellamy)

Guicciardini *Dialogue on the Government of Florence* (edited by Alison Brown)

Harrington *A Commonwealth of Oceana* and *A System of Politics* (edited by J. G. A. Pocock)

Hegel *Elements of the Philosophy of Right* (edited by Allen W. Wood and H. B. Nisbet)

Hobbes *Leviathan* (edited by Richard Tuck)

Hobhouse *Liberalism and Other Writings* (edited by James Meadowcroft)

Hooker *Of the Laws of Ecclesiastical Polity* (edited by A. S. McGrade)

Hume *Political Essays* (edited by Knud Haakonssen)

John of Salisbury *Policraticus* (edited by Cary Nederman)

Kant *Political Writings* (edited by H. S. Reiss and H. B. Nisbet)

King James VI and I *Political Writings* (edited by Johann P. Sommerville)

Knox *On Rebellion* (edited by Roger A. Mason)

Kropotkin *The Conquest of Bread and Other Anarchist Writings* (edited by Marshall Shatz)

Lawson *Politica sacra et civilis* (edited by Conal Condren)

Leibniz *Political Writings* (edited by Patrick Riley)

Locke *Two Treatises of Government* (edited by Peter Laslett)

Loyseau *A Treatise of Orders and Plain Dignities* (edited by Howell A. Lloyd)

Luther and Calvin on Secular Authority (edited by Harro Höpfl)

图书在版编目（CIP）数据

"面包的征服"及其他著作/（俄罗斯）彼得·克鲁泡特金著.—北京：
中国政法大学出版社,2003.5
剑桥政治思想史原著系列（影印本）
ISBN 7－5620－2388－3

Ⅰ.面...　Ⅱ.彼...　Ⅲ.政治思想史—俄罗斯—近代—英文
Ⅳ.D095.124

中国版本图书馆 CIP 数据核字（2003）第 037298 号

＊ ＊ ＊ ＊ ＊ ＊ ＊ ＊ ＊ ＊ ＊ ＊

书　　名	《〈面包的征服〉及其他著作》
出 版 人	李传敢
经　　销	全国各地新华书店
出版发行	中国政法大学出版社
承　　印	清华大学印刷厂
开　　本	880×1230mm　1/32
印　　张	9.625
版　　本	2003 年 5 月第 1 版　　2003 年 5 月第 1 次印刷
书　　号	ISBN 7－5620－2388－3/D·2348
印　　数	0 001－2 000
定　　价	21.00 元
社　　址	北京市海淀区西土城路 25 号　　邮政编码　100088
电　　话	（010）62229563　（010）62229278　（010）62229803
电子信箱	zf5620@263.net
网　　址	http://www.cup1.edu.cn/cbs/index.htm